THE RISE OF THE THIRD REICH

BOOKS BY ROBERT LYMAN

Slim, Master of War

First Victory

Iraq, 1941

The Generals

Tobruk

Japan's Last Bid for Victory

Kohima, 1944

Operation Suicide

Into the Jaws of Death

Bill Slim

The Jail Busters

The Real X-Men

Among the Headhunters

THE RISE OF THE THIRD REICH

THE TAKEOVER OF THE CONTINENT IN THE WORDS OF OBSERVERS

ROBERT LYMAN

AMBERLEY

First published 2018

Amberley Publishing
The Hill, Stroud
Gloucestershire, GL5 4EP

www.amberley-books.com

British Library Cataloguing in Publication Data.
A catalogue record for this book is available from the British
Library.

ISBN 978 1 4456 8726 1 (hardback)
ISBN 978 1 4456 8727 8 (ebook)

Interior design by Maria Fernandez.
Printed in the UK.

This book is dedicated to those American men and women who took up the fight against fascism in Europe between September 1939 and December 1941, before their country was formally at war, especially those who paid the ultimate sacrifice for their commitment to the cause of political liberty and personal freedom under the law.

"It is not enough for those who love peace to talk peace. A lover of peace must understand war—its causes and its course. It is not enough to hope. We must also work desperately on practical measures that sometimes seem far short of our dreams."

—John G. Winant,
US ambassador to Britain,
1941–1946

Si vis pacem, para bellum

—*Plato*

CONTENTS

PREFACE

As a soldier, I once lived with my young family at Lager Bergen-Hohne, the old Wehrmacht barracks complex that sits next door to the site of the notorious transit camp of Bergen-Belsen, where the Dutch teenager, Anne Frank, lost her life. Scores of thousands of *Untermenschen*, the human detritus of a Nazified Europe, died of neglect in the human garbage dump that once lay hidden amidst the towering silver birches of these remote forests in Lower Saxony. Standing at the entrance to the Bergen-Belsen memorial today is a sobering experience, the bleak surroundings bringing a rush of melancholia triggered by the thought of so many lives wasting to death on the cold, gray sod amidst the terror of starvation, disease, loneliness, and deliberate, criminal neglect. The shadow that invariably passes over my soul on these occasions is made worse by the realization that this horror came about as the result of human design and political purpose. Men—some men—wanted this to happen, and many men, and women, allowed it to be so. Horror did not take place of its own accord but was the result of action by some—a few perhaps—and inaction by many. Bergen-Belsen today stands mute but terrible testimony to human evil and the failure of people to recognize malevolence for what it was, and to act, in a timely manner, against it. Both in Germany during the 1930s, and in the wider world of the democracies, political liberalism failed catastrophically to assert, and protect, its primary virtue, namely liberty under the law. Bergen-Belsen—one small place among many—was the product of deliberate calculation, in which in the space of a single generation an entire nation was persuaded to hate. The real travesty is that most of what happened among these bleak birch forests was foreseen. From the moment Hitler took power the world began to know and understand—albeit through a glass darkly—what the Nazi Party was attempting to do. It was clear to many observers that the Nazi plan was to mobilize an entire society in a program of racial and national aggrandizement that would overturn many hundreds of years of Judeo-Christian civilization, not to mention the culture of Bach, Beethoven, Goethe, and Schiller. It would do so at the expense of her neighbors, as well as those—inside Germany and out—considered by the Nazis not to reach the physical and moral standard set by nature for the Teuton, the Aryan master race destined to rule the world. The *Untermenschen* were people unworthy of life, or at least worthy only of being ruled—as slaves—by Germans. John Winant, the United States ambassador to Britain between March 1941 and April 1946, and one of the great libertarian heroes of this story, concluded that the Nazis "not only knew, they planned, with cold premeditation, the slaughter of a race, and all others who opposed their will. Long before war came at all the indifference of an appeasement-minded world allowed these enemies of humanity, bereft of charity, an open field to sow and reap their nightmare harvests."

It was far less easy at the time in the West to see what was happening in the Soviet Union and the horrors of Stalinization, as this happened behind a carefully constructed curtain, designed to prevent outsiders seeing the truth within, but this could not be said for Germany. For an entire decade before Hitler in a pique calamitously (for Germany) declared war on America on December 11, 1941, considerable numbers of North Americans—travelers, academics, journalists, diplomats, housewives, businessmen, among others—possessed a window into the darkening soul of this ancient, declining culture, and made their findings known, often in clear and unequivocal terms, to the folks back home. Some of these warnings strike the modern reader to be remarkably prescient. But was anyone listening? Some, a courageous few, decided to take the fight to the Nazis by direct action well before America found itself committed to war. It is to them that this book is dedicated.

Some people argue today that the Second World War could not have been foreseen. I disagree. When Abbott ("A.J.") Liebling of the *New Yorker* asked long-retired General Pershing in 1940 whether he argued against reductions in American military power after the Great War because he feared the consequences of the rise of totalitarianism in Europe, the grizzled veteran snarled back, "Who the hell could have foreseen this?" Well, many, actually. Some limply, and wrongly, like the Nazis themselves, blame Versailles. It is historically fraudulent to argue such a thing as causal inevitability, or historic determinism with respect to the start of the Second World War, suggesting for instance that the peace agreement in 1919 *caused* the next war. It was the Nazis who brought about this war, aided and abetted by incontinent Western politicians who failed to understand the impact of their own pacific inactivity with respect to the looming threats facing them. Could the Nazis have been stopped? Yes, if free nations had done more to stand up for the political cultures they led and in which they purported to believe. The problem with arguing that nothing could have been done to prevent an out-of-control Nazi dictator thrusting his country into destructive war based on a repulsive ideology is that it denies the power of human contingency. All men and women have the power to act to prevent the encroachment of evil. The first challenge is to recognize malevolence for what it is (a good place to start is to accept that humans are capable of extraordinary depravity); the second to act in a timely way against it. Unfortunately, the only ones who acted precipitately during the 1930s were the dictators.

Appeasement—allowing Nazi Germany to achieve its political goals at the expense of the precious sovereignty of others, simply to avert the threat of war against themselves—ironically enabled totalitarianism to flourish, and led to calamitous war. The failure of appeasement was at two levels. First, many appeasers assumed that national decision makers on the opposing side of international arguments were rational actors and wanted the same thing for their people as they did themselves. This view was morally naive. But the second level was far more profound in its moral declension. Many of those who pursued a policy of compromise (by accepting that Hitler and Mussolini, for example, did not want the same thing as the liberal democracies, namely peace, personal liberty, and the pursuit of happiness) knew only too well that the consequence of this approach was that the dictators would simply continue their policies of territorial and racial aggrandizement: they hoped (wrongly, as it turned out) that appeasement would have no negative consequences for themselves, and their own countries, even though it spelled doom for the victims of the dictators. The moral disaster at the heart of appeasement was that too many politicians accepted that in attempting to contain the dictators, bad things would happen to others and (hopefully) not to themselves. It was a policy of acceptable harm. Winston Churchill described an appeaser as someone "who feeds a crocodile, hoping it will eat him last."

The great failure of the 1930s was that both Europe and the United States refused to acknowledge the rise of fascism for what it was—a threat to the sanctity of personal liberty, democracy, and the rule of law within independent sovereign states—and do anything practical about preventing its unchecked growth. The rise of totalitarian politics based on perverse social and racial ideologies (either communist, fascist, or nationalistic) was nowhere adequately confronted and denied, and was allowed to march unchecked for fear that positive action might lead again to war. Thus were the impulses of appeasement bred. Indeed, such was the topsy-turvy world of domestic French and British politics during this period that significant minorities became noisy advocates for both fascism and communism, creeds most only vaguely understood, supporting their favorite cheerleaders (Stalin and Hitler) like opposing teams in a baseball game. However, few passionate supporters of either ideology in France or Britain at the time had any real comprehension of the bloody reality these political regimes had on their countries of origin. These political supporters' groups, when combined with the wave of postwar pacifism, emasculated the efforts of those who advocated taking the threat to peace and security seriously by pushing back against German and Italian belligerence, and adequately preparing for war. It was fear of war that perversely allowed war and violence to flourish. Germany's political trajectory was repeatedly excused and the consequences of Nazi ideology denied or ignored.

The fundamental problem with appeasement was that France and Britain did not think that defending the basic principles of liberal democracy, including the rule of law and the sovereignty of independent states, was as important as preserving the flawed status quo. At its heart the policy of appeasement was an exchange between the aggressor and the appeaser, in which it was agreed that the price for not doing a bad thing (let's say, for example, invading Czechoslovakia) was allowing the aggressor to do another, albeit slightly less bad, thing (such as being allowed to absorb the territory of a neighbor without resorting to bloodshed). The exchange at Munich was that Europe was promised a wider peace in exchange for the enslavement of Czechoslovakia. It was a chimera. The tragedy of 1938 was that the price of the exchange was not paid for by those making the agreement (Britain and France on the one hand, and Germany on the other) but by Czechoslovakia itself, the victim. The agreement, dressed up by Chamberlain as delivering "peace in our time," was fundamentally deceitful, because it was written on a check from a bank in which London and Paris did not even have an account. It is extraordinary to modern observers that this dishonesty was ever allowed, either by democratic states or by what constituted at that time the "international community."

How did they get away with it? The answer was that there was no functioning "community" in the international sphere worth talking about following the collapse of the benighted League of Nations, and that there was overwhelming fear in the liberal democracies at the time of another devastating war close on the heels of the "war to end all wars." In attempting to preserve the uncertain peace that had existed since 1918, British and French politicians did not have the honesty or the moral courage to accept that peace required them to make every effort short of actual war—including the threat of war—to defend it. The great weakness of liberalism in its interwar context was its inability to see threats to itself for what they were, and to defend against them. The raw truth, which appeasers seemed conveniently to forget, was that the essentials of liberalism were not attractive to all: communist and fascist ideologies alike saw liberal liberties as a threat to their own exercise of power. In the mid-to-late 1930s the vast bulk of political opinion in France and Britain considered that any price was preferable to the unbearable consequences of another war. Unfortunately, in this equation, the autocracies (Italy, Germany, and the Soviet Union) did not have the same qualms. Just as many in France and Britain were prepared to trade the freedoms of Czechs for a wider peace, kowtowing to the war drums beating from Berlin, the weight of American public opinion at the time was likewise strongly for nonintervention in another European imbroglio. Americans might have wanted the British and French to win in the fight against Germany (85 percent, in fact, in March 1940), but few saw this as a war that required their direct involvement. Widespread pacifism, industrial interests, and significant ethnic groups (German-Americans, Italian-Americans, and Irish-Americans especially) rejected any American military commitment in favor of defending the European democracies who were threatened by Germany.

—⁂—

The best history is sourced from the memories of those who were there, who watched and made it happen. This book begins and ends with the premise that the views of a wide range of different people—students, housewives, soldiers, diplomats, engineers, journalists, civil servants, businessmen, scientists, and many others—looking at history as it is made, though from differing perspectives and prejudices, offer in their accumulation an interpretation of events as valuable as the political and military memoirs of those intimately involved in political affairs, and of the specialist historical accounts written retrospective to the events they recount. For the most part people carrying out their ordinary lives see other things, too, that are more often missed—or ignored—in what might be considered more rarefied, analytical accounts of events. The rise of Nazi Germany during the 1920s and 1930s was closely observed by many North Americans, who, like the children opening the wardrobe door into Narnia, found themselves entering a world dramatically different from their own, and one which they could not entirely comprehend. As they—Dorothy Thompson, Leland Stowe, Bill Shirer, Matthew Halton, Sigrid Schultz, Janet Flanner, Edgar Mowrer, and many others—began to report their findings back home, they encountered something they did not expect. On the one hand, many of their listeners and readers seemed resistant to the story they were telling, and reluctant to accept its veracity. On the other, many people simply expressed disinterest. The accusation of exaggeration, bias, and even warmongering became common. One was understandable—people often need to see and touch, like doubting Thomas, before they believe—but the other reaction surprised them. As the years went by, and the true nature of Nazism was increasingly revealed to American observers in Europe, the implications for deeply entrenched personal, societal, economic, and religious freedoms, in the United States, Canada, and other European democracies, became starkly apparent. How was it that their own countrymen and women could not comprehend the scale of the threat facing liberal democracy emanating from the new Nazi regime in Germany? How, then, to deal with a member of the community of nations whose values—in respect of human liberty—were now so dramatically different from the others'? How to do so, especially when the type of political repression represented by Nazism was sold to both internal and external audiences as an antidote to bolshevism? How to sound the alarm without appearing to beat the war drum?

In respect to the war in Europe, generally regarded to have begun on September 3, 1939 (although the Czechs and Poles would suggest earlier dates and many, then and now, argue that this date was simply the end of the armed truce that had lasted since November 11, 1918), what has rarely been heard are the voices of those living in Europe at the time but who were not from, or of, this troubled continent. Many North Americans living in London, Paris, and Berlin experienced in full the march to war and the violent Nazi tidal wave that swept across Europe between 1939 and 1941, smashing the Versailles settlement on the jagged rocks of total war. The world had never seen war like it before, either in its ideological fury or its disciplined, machinelike execution, its ruthless, exterminatory xenophobia, or its extraordinary scale and the extent of the misery and suffering it engendered. Scores of thousands of non-Europeans were caught up in the conflagration, reporting back home in letters, diaries, newspaper articles, radio broadcasts, and in their published accounts the full spectrum of their experiences. Importantly, it was the experiences of a vast cohort of American expatriates in the war's swirling tides that were transmitted to families and audiences back home, and which intimately wove America into the destiny of Europe, despite the overwhelming imperative across America in 1939 to remain aloof from the world and let the troubled continent of Europe settle its own problems.

This book does not pretend to be a history of Europe during this period, or a history of Nazism and German expansionism. That has been done far better, by others. Rather, it is a synthesis of the memories, remembrances, attitudes, and experiences of a handful of North American expatriates who lived through this period in Europe, and who wrote, and spoke of what they saw at the time, especially during the two years of war when America remained neutral. It was hard for many who could see and experience what was going on in Germany to comprehend the argument for maintaining neutrality in the face of the Nazi destruction of European civilization. "Who is neutral when the house is burning down?" asked the author Jimmy Sheean in rhetorical exasperation at the isolationist policies of his homeland. He, and many others, worked tirelessly from 1933 to warn America that the fire engine was required, that this was no mere war of national interest in which Americans could make anything other than a full commitment to the anti-Nazi cause. Germany under Hitler and his henchmen constituted an existential threat to American liberty in a way that the Great War did not. The powerful impulses towards isolationism, some of which were built on fears that America had been hoodwinked into joining the fighting in Europe in 1917, needed to be reversed to persuade

American popular opinion that wholehearted intervention in Europe was again required.

My greatest challenge has been to determine what stories and testimonies to include, given the wide choice available from the bright panoply of stars who illuminated this dark night sky between 1939 and 1941. Wherever possible, these characters have been allowed to speak for themselves, and to speak vicariously for the many thousands who shared their views at the time and who have left no diaries, memoirs, or published accounts of their experiences. The truth is that I ran out of space to include the widest array of characters I had first hoped, and with some heartbreak have been forced to exclude some extraordinary people—such as Varian Fry, Charles Sweeny, Johnney Dodge, Sigrid Schultz, Betty Watson, Helen Kirkpatrick, Margaret Bourke-White, Mildred Harnack, and Billy Fiske, for instance—whom I have left to other commentators. My intention is to allow the multitude of voices that remain—this cloud of witnesses, even—together to tell the story of the onset of terror, as the storm clouds burst over Europe and grew rapidly closer to American shores in the years and months before the United States found itself embroiled, for the second time that century, with war in Europe. The difference now was that this war was a life-and-death struggle, a war for the very soul and heart of humanity. Those who realized this became the evangelists of freedom and did all they could to sound the alarm amidst a fog of competing narratives, confusion, propaganda, and misinformation. The world continues to owe them, many decades on, the greatest of debts.

DRAMATIS PERSONAE

Josephine Baker: A Missouri-born dancer and singer who became a French citizen in 1937 after first travelling to Paris in 1925. She gained fame in France as a chanteuse. She was recruited by the French Secret Service in 1939, and after the German invasion in 1940 she worked assiduously for Charles de Gaulle and the Free French movement.

Sylvia Beach: Owner of the famous bookshop Shakespeare and Company at 12, rue de l'Odéon, and publisher of James Joyce.

Edward W. Beattie: Correspondent for United Press, who, fluent in German, arrived in Berlin in 1932 and immediately began to warn of Hitler's megalomania. He was in Warsaw when the Germans invaded Poland in 1939. Thereafter he covered the Blitz from London.

Clare Boothe: Writer and playwright Clare Boothe Luce (Luce was her married name) toured Britain, Belgium, the Netherlands, Italy, and France for *Life* magazine as the curtain fell in 1940, when she wrote *Europe in the Spring*.

Dr. Charles F. Bove: Chief surgeon at the American Hospital at Neuilly-sur-Seine, Paris, and colleague of Dr. Sumner Jackson. He wrote *Surgeon's Story* in 1956.

William Bullitt: US ambassador to France from October 1936. He disobeyed the president's instructions to leave Paris when the Germans entered the city, incurring Roosevelt's wrath.

Henry "Chips" Channon: Illinois-born British Member of Parliament, an outrageous diarist and homosexual, who came to reject his American heritage. His diaries give a fascinating insight into the London of the early war years.

Virginia Cowles: A noted pro-intervention American journalist, biographer, and travel writer. She worked in Europe from the mid-1930s, covering the Spanish Civil War and the onset of war from Berlin, Paris, and London.

Pauline Avery Crawford: Living in Paris from 1926 until her death in 1952, Crawford reported on the Paris scene for *Vogue* and the *International Herald Tribune*.

Wallace R. Deuel: Born in 1905, Wallace Deuel joined the *Chicago Daily News* in 1929. From 1934 to 1941 he was chief of the *Chicago Daily News* bureau in Berlin.

Arthur Donahue: Minnesota-born Arthur "Art" Donahue pretended to be a Canadian to join the RAF at the outset of the war. He was one of eleven American pilots who flew with RAF Fighter Command between July 10 and October 31, 1940, during the Battle of Britain, flying a Spitfire. He wrote *Tally-Ho! Yankee in a Spitfire*, and was killed in action over the English Channel in 1942.

Janet Flanner: Paris-based American reporter for the *New Yorker* from the inception of the magazine in 1925.

Martha Gellhorn: Novelist, travel writer, and journalist Gellhorn, who was briefly married to Hemingway, reported on events in Europe from 1937, including Spain and Czechoslovakia.

Matthew Halton: Canadian journalist who travelled across Germany extensively in the early to mid-1930s and became one of those arguing vociferously in print for the Western democracies to stand up to Hitler and contain his hegemonic ambitions.

Josephine ("Josie") Herbst: Left-wing writer who spent several months in Berlin in 1935, writing for the *New York Post*.

Stewart Herman: Ordained into the United Lutheran Church in America, he was minister of the American Church in Berlin from 1936 to the point at which Americans were interned, December 1941.

Roscoe Hillenkoetter: Naval attaché in Paris at the time of the German invasion. Hillenkoetter was a member of the Office of Naval Intelligence and in 1947 became head of the Central Intelligence Agency (CIA).

Ralph Ingersoll: Writer, editor, and publisher, who founded *PM*, an advertisement-free left-wing daily newspaper, in 1940.

Dr. Sumner Jackson: A well-known surgeon based at the American Hospital in Paris. He died in the final days of the war, a prisoner of the Nazis in Germany.

George Keenan: A diplomat and expert on the Soviet Union, Keenan worked in several US embassies across Europe from 1929. He joined the US legation in Prague in September 1938. He moved to Berlin in September 1939.

Walter B. Kerr: Correspondent for the *New York Herald Tribune*, Kerr was in Prague during the German occupation in 1938, and Paris in 1940.

Joseph Kennedy: Best known today perhaps as the father of JFK, Joseph Kennedy was the US ambassador to London between March 1938 and November 1940.

Leonard Kenworthy : Kenworthy served as the director of the International Quaker Center in Berlin from 1940 to 1941 under the auspices of the American Friends Service Committee and a steering committee of German Quakers.

Virginia D'Albert Lake : The American wife of a French soldier, and later a member of the French Resistance. She left a vivid diary of the early days of the war. Captured by the Germans, she survived Ravensbrück.

Raymond Lee: Brigadier General Raymond Lee was reappointed US military attaché to Britain in 1940 by General Marshall, following a long period in that role between 1935 and 1939. He was a firsthand observer of Britain's fight for survival in 1940 and 1941.

Abbott Liebling: Writer for the *New Yorker,* who covered the war in Europe from October 1939, leaving Paris on June 10, 1940. His articles are collected in *The Road Back to Paris,* published in 1944.

Louis Lochner: Associated Press journalist in Berlin from 1924. He accompanied the German army into Poland in September 1939, and his reporting won him the 1939 Pulitzer Prize for correspondence. He then accompanied the German army in the Netherlands, Belgium, and France. In 1942 he published *What About Germany?* attacking Nazism, and *The Goebbels Diaries* in 1948.

Elsie Mendl: Mendl was a celebrated American socialite and heiress, who, when in France, lived at her home at the Villa Trianon on the grounds of the Palace of Versailles.

Edward R. Murrow: Murrow was the most prominent radio journalist of the war years, working for the Columbia Broadcasting System and followed at home by millions of Americans. He assembled a team of correspondents, like Sevareid and Smith, who came to be known as the "Murrow Boys." He played a very significant role in reporting the Blitz.

Robert Murphy: US diplomat who spent the entire decade of the 1930s in Paris.

Quentin Reynolds: A prolific author and journalist, New York–born Reynolds was based in London as associate editor at *Collier's Weekly* from 1933 to 1945.

William Russell: A consular clerk in the US embassy in Berlin who has left a delightful account in *Berlin Embassy* of his time in the heart of the German capital as the security of the world swiftly unraveled between August 31, 1939, and April 10, 1940.

Jimmy ("Vincent") Sheean: Illinois-born Sheean was a writer and journalist who reported across Europe from 1922 through 1940.

Howard K. Smith: A young Rhodes scholar and journalist who first encountered Nazi Germany in 1936 and was deeply repelled by everything that this abhorrent ideology represented. He recorded life in Berlin throughout all of 1941, up to the point at which Germany declared war on the United States, and graphically captured Hitler's personal hatred of Roosevelt.

Charles Sweeny: A wealthy American, champion golfer, and nephew of American soldier of fortune Charles Sweeny. He married into British society and founded and funded the Eagle squadron of US fliers in the RAF.

Raymond Gram Swing: Print and broadcast journalist, a leading American voice from Britain during World War II.

Eric Sevareid: A CBS journalist who was one of the "Murrow Boys." He reported on the fall of France in 1940 and later helped bring daily life in the London Blitz to millions of Americans.

Etta Shiber: American widow who had lived in Paris since 1936, living at 2, rue Balny d'Avricourt, Paris, with her friend Catherine ("Kitty") Bonnefous, the British-born wife of a French wine merchant. With Madame Bonnefous, Shiber ran an escape network (réseau) for British servicemen following the withdrawal at Dunkirk, sending over 150 men into the Unoccupied Zone. Many made successful "home runs" to Britain. Both Shiber and Bonnefous survived the war.

William ("Bill") Shirer: Journalist who gained fame through the publication in the 1960s of *The Rise and Fall of the Third Reich*. Originally a foreign correspondent for the *Chicago Tribune* and the International News Service, Shirer was the first reporter hired by Edward Murrow. He broadcast from Berlin from 1933 through 1940, and his vivid images of the time were captured in his *Berlin Diary*.

Lothrop Stoddard: A popular writer on racial subjects who held that America needed to retain its Nordic-derived racial makeup. He toured Germany for four months between late October 1939 and February 1940, receiving preferential treatment by the Nazis—presumably because of his support for eugenics—and interviewed many senior Nazi figures, including Hitler.

Leland Stowe: Pulitzer Prize–winning journalist noted for being one of the first to recognize the expansionist character of the German Nazi regime, captured most presciently in his 1933 *Nazi Germany Means War*. Most commentators at the time laughed him off as a warmongering eccentric.

Tracy Strong: Secretary General of the World Committee of the Young Men's Christian Association (YMCA) between 1926 and 1938. In 1940 he went to Geneva on behalf of the European Student Relief Fund, helping to organize Prisoners' Aid and to escort Jewish students to Switzerland.

Drue Tartière: Born Dorothy Blackman, "Drue Leyton" (her stage name) left Hollywood to marry Jacques Tartière in 1938 and moved to France. At the outset of war she joined the shortwave radio station Paris Mondial. After the fall of France she made her way to Barbizon, where she spent the war years working for the Resistance. Nearly two hundred escaping and evading Allied servicemen managed to flee France by her efforts.

Dorothy Thompson: Journalist and broadcaster, who in 1939 was recognized by *Time* magazine as the second most influential woman in America next to Eleanor Roosevelt. She is notable as the first American journalist to be expelled from Nazi Germany in 1934 and as one of the few women news commentators on radio during the 1930s.

Al Wedemeyer: Between 1936 and 1938, Wedemeyer was one of two US Army officers who attended, as exchange students, the Kriegsakademie in Berlin.

John G. Winant: US ambassador to Britain following the return of Joe Kennedy, from March 1941 to April 1946. A stark contrast to his predecessor, he played a significant role cementing American support for the last remaining democracy in Europe to stand up to Hitler.

CHAPTER ONE

"Nazi Germany Means War"

January 30, 1933. It is a typically cold, midwinter day across northern Europe. In London, the world's largest city, fresh winds blow. Across southern England intermittent rain, sleet, and snow keep people indoors. In Germany that night a political winter sets in that is to last for more than twelve years and encase the entire world in its frozen embrace. In the *Times* (London) the following day Canadian-born journalist Matthew Halton described the previous night's events in Berlin, when the Nazi Party under Adolf Hitler had taken control of the Reichstag. A man now on a crusade against the new totalitarianism taking root in Germany, Halton pulled no punches. "Strutting up the Chancellery steps is Hitler, the cruel and cunning megalomaniac who owes his triumph to his dynamic diabolism and his knowledge of the brutal corners of the human soul," he wrote in his memoir, *Ten Years to Alamein* in 1944, using language that made many in the West consider the journalist one of those alarmists who naively saw the world through a simplistic, sensationalist, and self-righteous lens:

Surrounding him is his camarilla of braves: the murderous fat Goering, a vain but able man; the satanic devil's advocate, Goebbels; the cold and inhuman executioner, Himmler; the robustious radical, Roehm, organizer of the Brown Shirts. . . . Their supporters were decreasing in numbers; but by intrigue and a trick, Germany is theirs. Supporting this terrible elite are the brown-shirted malcontents of the S.A., nearly a million of them, and the black-uniformed bullies of the S.S., the praetorian guard. And the whole structure is built on the base of a nation whose people are easily moved by romantic imperialism, by the old pan-Germanism, in new and more dynamic form, by dreams of Weltmacht [World Power] and desire for revenge, and even by nostalgia for the jungle and for the tom-toms of the tribe.

Halton, the *Toronto Star*'s London-based Europe reporter, was to prove one of the most prescient journalists of the age. The language he had begun to utilize when describing what he was seeing around him during his visits to Germany was urgent, prophetic, full of warning for what would happen to Europe, and the world, if it ignored what was happening at great speed to Germany. Laying aside journalistic convention, Halton became one of a tiny group of prophets who began urgently to warn the world of impending doom. "The things I saw being taught and believed everywhere in that nation," he wrote in one of his reports from later in 1933, "the superiority of one race and its destiny to rule—will one day become the intimate concern of all of us."

Halton was in no doubt about what Hitler's ascent to power meant for Germany. He visited twice that year, first in January and then, more extensively, in the fall. From the very first instant he suspected that the name Hitler had given to his political party—the National Socialist German Workers' Party—was merely an enormous, brazen hoax, designed for one end, and one end alone: an aggrandizing, racist agenda that would attempt to place Germany ahead of every other country of Europe, with force if necessary. From what he could see, Hitlerism was neither national nor socialist, nor, for that matter, about the workers. It seemed to him to be about the creation of a racially pure

Germany (in which Jews, Gypsies, and Slavs were obvious disposable imperfections), disciplined, obedient, militaristic, and imperial. Most worryingly of all was that the fabulous lie inherent in the banality of the name of this political party was widely believed, and constituted the basis of Hitler's ascent to tyranny. To the fanatical few, the believers, the National Socialist German Workers' Party was a means to an end, the first step of which was the assumption of total, dictatorial power, after which the principal themes of the February 24, 1920, Declaration—racial purification from within and territorial aggrandizement outside to form a Grossdeutschland (Greater Germany) of eighty million Germans, in which *Lebensraum* (living space) was to be achieved—would be acted out, with legal violence if necessary. The name therefore fooled lots of Germans, as well as much of the watching world, few of whom ever bothered to read (or knew where to look for) the defining articles of Nazi faith. The lie was carefully concealed within other myths of Germanhood, ones that enjoyed a widespread appeal, particularly among a people humiliated by defeat in 1918, confused by the political uncertainties of the Weimar years, and pauperized by the collapse of Wall Street in 1929. It was the latter, much more than the impact of 1918, that lit the path for Germans, and Germany, down the road to the gates of a Nazi Valhalla. With a shock Halton understood that the Nazi creed was not being foisted unwillingly upon a reluctant population. Many in Germany welcomed the Nazis with open arms. "Germany enters a nightmare," Halton wrote. "I feel it in my bones. She has heard the call of the wild."

In the comfort of his English home, H. G. Wells dismissed the Nazi coup d'état that placed Hitler on the chancellor's chair as a "revolt of the clumsy lout," a charge that led to the Nazi burning of his books—among thousands of others—in Berlin's Opernplatz on May 10, 1933. Wells underestimated the simplicity of the Nazi program, the ferocious tenacity of its adherents, and the unchallenging acquiescence of the mass of the population. His accusation proved to be naively offhand, akin to the view among the aristocracy in the *Heer* (i.e., the German army: together, the German armed forces were known as the Wehrmacht) that they could control the "little Corporal." Wells gave no thought to the consequences that the rise to power of the lout he described would have for Germany, or the world for that matter. This was no schoolyard bullying that would disappear with the maturity of age. That Hitlerism was ever able to so dominate European and global politics to the extent that it did for twelve hellish years, sending the world screeching into a cataclysmic war from which it escaped only by the skin of its teeth, battered, bloodied, and changed forever, is no mystery now. In the early 1930s, however, the fast-approaching catastrophe wasn't so obvious to everyone. Even though Europe was awash with North American journalists reporting back fearfully about the developments in the heart of Europe, where the Enlightenment legacy of centuries—before which lay the Reformation and before that the Renaissance—was being buried by a darkness so unfathomable as to be unimaginable, few read the warning signs correctly. That the warning bells were ringing, loudly, in every country of Europe and indeed across the world is indisputable; what seems so shocking is that few bothered to lift their heads to listen.

One of those who noisily rang the alarm bells, and who was roundly ignored, was the *New York Herald Tribune* journalist Leland Stowe, whose fears were succinctly articulated in a small book published in London in December 1933 with the uncompromising title *Nazi Germany Means War*. Stowe, who had received a Pulitzer Prize in 1930 for his reporting of Great War reparations, was as shocked as Halton after he spent two months in Germany that year. He concluded that Germany had two voices. One was a public voice meant to pacify the fears of outsiders, and spoke repeatedly of peace. The other was for internal, German consumption, and spoke relentlessly of martial values, social discipline, the needs of the state eclipsing those of the individual, Germany's requirement for living space, self-evident German racial superiority among the nations of Europe, and the imperative to achieve a homeland for all Germans, not just those who currently had the good fortune to live within the present boundaries of the Reich. What this meant for Austria, and for large slices of Poland and Czechoslovakia, was clear to the Nazi propagandists, and a message preached diligently and persistently every day. These ends would be achieved, Hitler asserted in *Mein Kampf*, "by a strong and smiting sword." "Hitler declares that Nazi Germany wants peace at the very moment when Nazi Germany is busy, with an appalling systemization and efficiency, preparing its 65,000,000 people for perfected martial co-ordination such as has never existed before," Stowe warned. "This, in its logical sequence, can finally lead only to war."

Stowe's book flopped. Neither buying public nor politicians wanted to spend money on a tome that suggested that on its current course war was inevitable, and confirmed that their persistent "ostrichitis" was a terminal illness. Equally, Halton's reporting of his two-month tour of Germany in the autumn of 1933 for the *Toronto Star* was regarded to be so alarmist that he was dismissed by many as an exaggerator, a warmonger. He was criticized for reading into situations and events a meaning far beyond their reality. For suggesting, for example, that the Nazis and their followers were not Christians, truly following the sayings and precepts of Christ, he incurred the wrath of Catholics and Protestants alike, who accused him of ignorance. Germany was, after all, the most observant country in Europe. It was factually erroneous, the argument went, to suggest otherwise. The dominant theological worldview across western Christendom in the 1930s was pacifism, which, although it attempted to express politically Christ's blessings on the peacemakers and the instruction to "turn the other cheek," seemed to assume that simply believing in nonviolence would somehow persuade an enemy to think twice about using violence at all.

Halton, and others like him, were accused by Germans of not understanding the country or the German hunger for a new political settlement and an honorable place in the world. It was a common enough accusation. Although Halton robustly dismissed the Western reactions to his warnings, he nevertheless worried at the time that well-meaning ignorance of Nazism abroad was almost as bad as Nazism itself. If people only knew what hatreds lay at the heart of the Nazi creed, he thought, they would oppose it just as strongly as if they were fighting a burglar in their house. But because Nazism was cloaked in a cunning disguise, few people could see it for what it was.

Indeed, he believed that the fox was already inside the chicken coop. The German people, or at least large numbers of them, had embraced ideas they would have regarded, in another political or cultural milieu, as desperately irrational. Vast swathes of Germany now espoused nonsensical racial views about their own superiority over other varieties of humankind that had no place in rational or scientific thought and which, as Halton observed, "one would have expected children to laugh at." What had happened to the most intellectual country in Europe? He concluded despondently that it seemed apparent "that the Germans were the least intelligent, if the most intellectual, of Western peoples." Using the same analogy, they were also the most religious, if unchristian. Shockingly, the crazy notions of Aryan supremacy propagated so assiduously by the Nazis had already received academic and intellectual legitimacy, and had been translated into notions that had quickly become widely accepted by otherwise thinking people, taught in schools and subsumed into common, everyday thought. He noted the prolifically published arguments of men such as geographer Professor Ewald Banse, whose *Military Science: An Introduction to a New National Science*, published in 1933, argued among other things that

> War is both inevitable and necessary, and therefore it is imperative, and the nation's mind must be directed towards it from childhood. Children must learn to infect the enemies' drinking water with typhoid bacilli and to spread plague with infected rats. They must learn military tactics from the birds, hills and streams.

How was it possible for the most cultured society in the world to embrace such extremism? Why—and how—could otherwise deeply intelligent, well-educated, rational men and women embrace such nonsense? Halton observed the transformation of the German mind at first hand. The recipe was simple. If one lived within a lie for long enough, it didn't take much to fail to distinguish the lie from the truth. Ultimately, the power of the lie would trump reason and the exercise of rational thought. Indeed, one began to believe the lie. In 1930 he had made several friends in Germany during visits when a student at the University of London. His new acquaintances were all socialists and internationalists, and laughed at the Nazi buffoons clowning around on the outskirts of politics. Three years later, after Hitler's rise to power, he went to meet one of these men, living with his parents in the Rhineland town of Bonn. Halton was relieved to learn that this man had not supped from the Nazi cup, but was disquieted to hear that two of the others had become Nazis. Five years later, he returned to the family home during the Bad Godesberg conference in September 1938. "What a pity you should have come up from Godesberg" the man's mother exclaimed when she saw Halton at the door, "because Friedrich is there! He commands a detachment of the S.A. which was sent from here to the conference." All that was required was time, and the repeated articulation of the lie.

Leland Stowe's experience of living in Germany in 1933 shocked him with how diametrically different it was from ordinary life in France, Britain, or the United States. In Germany, for instance, uniforms abounded. A packet of cigarettes he purchased in a café included a gift of a picture of a soldier sitting behind a machine gun. In restaurants, the music was a mixture of popular airs, an occasional waltz, and the obligatory quota of Nazi marches:

> I saw more uniformed men on the streets and in the public places of Berlin than I had seen in any foreign city from London to Constantinople. I witnessed more parades and marching troops in three weeks than I had seen in Paris in nine months. I heard rousing military bands at eleven o'clock in the morning, going by the office window, or on Hermann Goeringstrasse at eleven o'clock at night. I saw long columns of boys and girls in their teens, uniformed and carrying flags and marching somewhere at all sorts of unexpected hours. Often they sang and their voices were clear and high and in striking unison. I saw great swastika or imperial flags hung out everywhere; thousands of them, outdoors and indoors—always flags.

Three years later, when 22-year-old Rhodes scholar Howard Smith arrived in Germany through the port of Bremen, he was overwhelmed by the militarization of society:

> It took my breath away. I had read about Nazi rearmament, but to me it was still a word, not a sense-idea. In New Orleans, I could sum up in a figure of two integers all the uniforms I had ever seen. Before our boat docked in Bremen I saw a big multiple of that figure, sailors of Germany's war navy, walking up and down the long wharves. The railway station in Bremen, and later every railway station I saw, was a milling hive of soldiers in green uniforms in full war-kit and with rifles, getting off trains and getting on them. Farther inland, towns looked like garrisons, with every third or fourth man in uniform. On trains, all day long, one passed long railway caravans of camouflaged tanks, cannon and war-trucks lashed to railway flat cars, and freight depots were lined with more of these monsters hooded in brown canvas. In large towns, traffic had to be interrupted at intervals on some days to let cavalcades of unearthly machines, manned by dust-covered, steel-helmeted Men-from-Mars roar through the main streets on maneuvers.

In 1933 Stowe commented on the catchy little musical ditty played during intermissions in radio programs, which proved to be the popular song "Volk an's Gewehr" (People, to Arms!). On the streets, young boys dressed in Hitler Youth uniforms played with wooden cannons in the parks and practiced throwing hand grenades as part of their school curriculum. At the time Halton, among many others, was concerned about the vast gulf that existed between what the Nazis said they were doing and the interpretation of these things by newspapers, politicians, and observers in other, far distant places, especially those safely cushioned in the protective cocoon of Western liberal democracies, who thought that all systems of government operated similarly, and where bad people were constrained by the law and the structures and systems of civilization. But it wasn't only wishful-thinking Western intellectuals and politicians who harbored delusions about the Nazi program in Europe. In a 1933 interview with Goering, Halton was struck by how deeply the Nazi leadership had itself drunk from the cup of its own delusions. What was worse than believing their ridiculous racial bigotries, especially against the Jews within and the *Untermenschen* without, was their unfounded conviction that the policymakers in the West secretly supported them, even if they couldn't express this support openly. After all, it wasn't a secret that it was Western capital—sourced through London and Wall Street—that was financing the rebuilding of Germany, and which by necessity was close to the Nazi economic program. The interests of both sides were therefore closely aligned. If the outcome of Versailles was to be reversed, Goering asserted, Britain and France would be sensible. Both countries knew that Germany was Europe's bulwark against the specter of Soviet bolshevism. "Germany will save Europe and Occidental civilization," he blathered. "Germany will stop the rot. Germany will prevent the Untergang des Abendlandes" (a reference to the book *The Decline of the West*, published by Oswald Spengler in 1926). Goering was well briefed about attitudes in the West. The well-read man or woman on the street in London and New York was already saying, and believing, some of this. Those in Warsaw, Prague, and Paris were less inclined to do so, however. The unbelievers were widely ridiculed in their own countries. In Britain, Winston Churchill was the most prominent of those who did not accept this worldview, but for the most part the political establishment ignored and reviled him in equal measure. Churchill was, at the time, like a biblical prophet crying out in the wilderness, scoffed at by those who considered him a warmonger for advocating robust responses to the militaristic posturing of the totalitarian states.

Yet all it needed, argued Halton, was for people—in Germany and the West—to read. The 25-Point Program of 1920 was unequivocal (see Appendix 1). It was the Articles of Faith of a new religion, and held to fanatically by true believers. This was the foundation stone upon which all else was being built. Hitler mapped out these plans for rebuilding Germany in this image in *Mein Kampf*, but wisely refused his publishers permission to have the rambling tome translated into English. It would give the game away. When Halton interviewed Albert Einstein at a secret location on England's south coast in September 1933, he asked the famous scientist whether it was Hitler's plan to destroy European Jewry. "Jewry?" Einstein retorted. "Jewry has less to fear than Christendom. Can't you people read?" When Halton asked him what the ultimate result of the Nazi project would be, Einstein immediately responded, "War. Can't the whole world see that Hitler will almost certainly drag it into war . . . [?]" They couldn't. Most Western diplomats and statesmen in 1930s Europe made the mistake of misunderstanding Hitler's true nature and ambitions. After all, these—articulated in *Mein Kampf*, in repeated public utterances in Germany, in speeches and interviews—were so fantastical, outrageous even, that most reasonable men and women did not consider them viable, and so dismissed them utterly. This was the underlying reality of appeasement: sane politicians and statesmen believed that Hitler likewise was rationally calculating what he could secure by beating the war drum without taking his country and people into a ruinous war. When they visited Hitler in person, the German Führer mollified them with honeyed lips. He was a man, the representatives of the democracies believed, with whom they could do business. Did he not repeatedly assert that he wanted peace? The appeasers did not realize—until it was too late—that if Hitler could not secure peace on his own terms, he would do so by means of war.

Halton visited Dachau in the late summer of 1933, at a time when carefully escorted visitors were still allowed, and he came away—even in these early days of the Nazi concentration camps, before they had become mass killing machines—shocked not so much at the casual brutality of the place but at the political and social environment that sent people there in the first place. The inmates needed social reeducation, the guards explained, and training them to learn social discipline and civic obedience was an essential part of the program. The prisoners had only themselves to blame: if they had not behaved in a socially irresponsible way—demonstrated by their dalliance with communism, or Seventh Day Adventism, or whatever their personal weakness had been—they would not have had to be punished. Brutalism was the new creed. The following year Dorothy Thompson, who had been reporting from Berlin on and off since 1925, recorded for *Harper's* magazine the sight of what appeared to be a delightful Hitler Youth summer camp at Murnau. On first arrival, she was much taken by the sight and sound of six thousand adolescent voices singing in unison. Then she saw, on the hillside above the camp, in stark, black letters, a banner proclaiming ominously YOU WERE BORN TO DIE FOR GERMANY. Self-sacrifice on behalf of the state was a lifelong expectation. A brutal life would precede a brutal death, all in the name of Greater Germany. She found herself driving away from the place at the unprecedented speed of sixty-five miles per hour, so desperate was she to put it behind her. The Reverend Stewart Herman of the American Church in Berlin listened every Sunday morning in 1936 as the bells of all the surrounding steeples rang out at church time:

> And almost every Sunday morning when the bells were inviting people to service I would hear the sound of tramping feet and singing voices marching down the converging streets into the near-by square. When I went to the window, as I often did, to see what was going on, the same scene always met my eyes. Columns of boys in brown shirts and dark-blue shorts—ski pants in winter—with heavy boots on their feet were parading along under banners and flags. They marched three abreast just like the regular infantry and they tried to take long steps like the soldiers they wished to imitate.
>
> They were not marching to church, as they frequently used to do before Hitler came to power. These were the Hitler boys and they were going into the movie theatre just across the street to practise singing their songs of hatred and war and to be exhorted once more that to live and die for Germany—the greatest nation on earth—is the noblest aim in life. Other nations, they were informed, were trying to destroy the Fatherland but the Fuehrer had rescued the country just in the nick of time.

If the Germans accepted brutality among themselves, Halton observed, it would be easy, when the time came, to accept it as necessary for others. "Loutish brutality was being coldly cultivated as an instrument of national policy," he concluded. The behavior of many otherwise sane, intelligent Germans towards their enemies during the war that was to come had its roots deep in the common acceptance of such ideas long before hostilities were ever declared and German men donned their Hugo Boss–designed black or gray-green uniforms and goose-stepped to war.

Brutalism extended to the deliberate trampling of other social sensitivities and age-old cultural and religious proscriptions. On one occasion during their tour of Germany, Halton and his wife visited a summer camp at Vaterstetten a few miles east of Munich, housing young women being groomed to be "brides of Hitler." Their duty was to couple with carefully selected local soldiers—tall, strong, fair-haired, and blue-eyed specimens of racial superiority—to produce sound Aryan stock with which to populate the lands that Grossdeutschland would one day encompass. The young women they interviewed believed this mission, passionately. Here was the evidence that the Nazi plan, even in its infancy, was acting out the program first laid out in 1920. The inevitable consequence of *Lebensraum* was the subjugation of the *Untermenschen* who already lived in these territories, and their displacement by true, racially pure, German stock. No stigma was attached to the Hitler-brides' production of children out of wedlock. Indeed, the regime encouraged and applauded their efforts. "The body of the German girl must be steeled and hardened like that of the German man," recited one young woman they interviewed. "Only the sound health of millions of German women can guarantee the vitality of the German people and the historical greatness of the German race." The idea of the Hitler-bride, Halton recorded, was "to become as rarefied and mystic as anything in theology." Piece by piece the old Germany was being destroyed and reshaped into a different, more terrifying, image.

Stewart Herman was later to equate the encouragement of Aryan procreation with the careful and deliberate slaughter of the old and the mentally and physically infirm:

In August, 1940, a German pastor, boiling with helpless indignation, told me that the Gestapo planned to disembarrass the nation of three-quarters of a million mental and physical invalids who were eating German food and absorbing the energies of healthy German doctors, nurses, and guardians. Some next-of-kin were the startled recipients of notifications that their relatives had "died" shortly after being transferred, without warning, to one or the other of three institutions which quickly became notorious. Other next-of-kin were frantically trying to withdraw their relatives from public hospitals and homes.

The destruction of these "useless mouths," Herman noted, helpfully provided "extra space for the additional tens of thousands of babies which German mothers were to be prevailed upon to bear."

A year after Halton's tour of Germany, the journalist William ("Bill") Shirer and his wife, Theresa ("Tess") Stiberitz, an Austrian photographer, returned to Berlin after an absence of several years, in the employ of William Randolph Hearst's Universal Service. Shirer was profoundly shocked by what he found, and staggered around for the first few days in a fog of depression. Where was the old Berlin he had known and loved only a few years back? The stimulating conversations of yore in the "care-free, emancipated, civilized air" of an age now lost to history, where "snub-nosed young women with short-bobbed hair and the young men with either cropped or long hair—it made no difference—who sat up all night with you and discussed anything with intelligence and passion" had been replaced by the depressing paraphernalia of a police state. It was now September 1934. Uniforms were everywhere. Heels clicked. Bloodred swastika flags adorned windows and lampposts. Posters depicted steel-jawed soldiers defending the Fatherland, or rapine Jews rubbing their hands over ill-gotten (German) booty. Troops marched. A favorite song was "Siegreich Wollen Wir Frankreich Schlagen" (Victoriously We Must Smash France). The ubiquitous Heil Hitler grated. It was increasingly dangerous not to acknowledge, using the Nazis' preposterous raised arm salute, marching troops and banners on the street. Likewise, the journalist Janet Flanner watched this new cultural norm spread across Germany like an inkblot.

[T]he Roman arm salute (originally a password among his militia),
soon became the social greeting de rigueur among Germany's civilians, and was officially called "the German greeting" in distinction
to the old Bürgerliche Gruss, or bourgeois Guten Tag. In Bavaria,
where the greeting used to be "Grüss Gott" Hitler's name has been
substituted for that of God. As most German aristocrats still click
their heels, kiss the ladies' hands, and, if in uniform, add the old-
fashioned military salute, these, plus the Nazi arm-flinging, make
modern German salutations fairly acrobatic affairs.

Shirer found himself ducking into shops just to avoid these increasingly frequent occurrences. He gritted his teeth. He had a feeling that
things were going to get much worse before they got better. Two days
later, following the long train ride south to Nuremberg, he recorded
his first ever Nazi Party parade. It was only the fourth of its kind in
history, and yet this party of gangsters now ran Germany. Where
would they take it? Would the German people allow it, or would sense
and rationality return after the nightmare? He watched Hitler ride into
the ancient town like a Roman emperor "past solid phalanxes of
wildly cheering Nazis who packed the narrow streets," but he was
surprised at the dullness of the man. Dressed in a worn gabardine
trench coat, Hitler did not present an imposing figure. He had none
of the self-conscious grandiloquence of Mussolini, fumbled with his
cap and stared blankly at "his Germans," as he liked to call them,
as the crowds cheered in ecstatic adulation. It was all rather confusing.
The man who had transformed the political dynamic in Germany so
dramatically, and was a demigod to many, appeared to have none of
the personal charisma that Shirer expected to be a prerequisite for
such a figure. "He almost seemed to be affecting a modesty in his
bearing," he was forced to conclude. "I doubt if it's genuine." Yet that
night he watched as a "mob of ten thousand hysterics . . . jammed
the moat in front of Hitler's hotel, shouting: 'We want our Führer.'"

The young Howard Smith was equally confused. He caught sight of
Hitler close up at the opera in Munich in 1937, and observed that the
spectacle was impressive because Hitler was not:

He was a short, very short, little, comical looking man. Had his eyes had the firm, warm glow of Lincoln's or the dash of Kaiser Wilhelm's, it would have been different, but his eyes were beady little black dots with timid circles under them. Had his moustache the boldly turned up ends like that of Hindenburg, it would have been otherwise. But his was a laughable little wisp of hair not as broad as his crooked mouth or the under-part of his nose. That was what, after you smothered your first unconscious smile, alarmed you, and brought back in its fullest strength the haunting fear of the Myth. This was the thing that had built a party in impossible circumstances, taken over control of a nation and created the mightiest army in the world. This, the "apotheosis of the little man," was what I saw as the blood-spitting, fire-breathing monster of the future. This funny little figure with its crooked smile, flapping its hand over its black-coated shoulder in salute, was God the omnipotent and infinite, Siegfried the hero of Nordics, and Adolf Hitler, the coming ruler of a destroyed world.

Shirer thought that the behavior of these frantic disciples reminded him of religious enthusiasts he had once met in the Louisiana backwoods. These Germans certainly considered Hitler to be their messiah. The outstretched arms of thousands of devotees reached to the sky. It was thus in a flash of understanding that Shirer understood the truth. Nazism was, of course, a religious creed as powerful as any in history. Hitler was the God of this faith. Dorothy Thompson likewise saw this in 1934 when she was expelled from Germany, remarking, "As far as I can see, I was really put out of Germany for the crime of blasphemy. My offense was to think that Hitler was just an ordinary man, after all. That is a crime in the reigning cult in Germany, which says Mr. Hitler is a Messiah sent by God to save the German people—an old Jewish idea. To question this mystic mission is so heinous that, if you are a German, you can be sent to jail." Hitler did not force Christianity to kneel at the altar of National Socialism. With a few exceptions it did so willingly, understanding only too clearly that the German people now had a choice of religions, and that Hitler was as attractive as anything the liberal German Church could offer. Here was gorgeous pomp; glorious ritual; dramatic heraldry fluttering over the medieval streets; bands playing Hitler's own "Badenweiler Marsch," with its resonating cymbals and heavy drum beat, and the magical feast of black uniforms (designed by party member Hugo Boss), shining swords and polished helmets. It was a martial heaven, as the Nazis always intended it to be. Unbelievably, the spectacle went on for a week. By the end Shirer was exhausted, physically, mentally, and emotionally. But he now realized the hold that Hitler had "on the people, to feel the dynamic in the movement he's unleashed and the sheer, disciplined strength the Germans possess."

The relentless diet of propaganda inside the borders of the Reich was accompanied by the strangulation of unbiased news from abroad. In an age before mass travel, few knew anything about what was happening outside their country other than what they were told. Only the friendliest of foreign newspapers were allowed to circulate freely in Germany, one of which was London's *Times*, which Shirer observed to have an immense circulation in January 1936. As time went on, however, the German state attempted to secure a monopoly of news, and listening to foreign radio stations, the most popular being the German-language programs of the BBC, Radio America, Radio Moscow, and the Swiss Beromünster, rapidly became criminal offenses.

—m—

On May 21, 1935, Shirer recorded in his diary that Hitler had made yet another masterful speech in the Reichstag proclaiming his desire for peace. Yet, like Halton, Stowe, and Thompson, among others, Shirer saw clearly through the noisy charade. Hitler was in fact calling for war, under the cloak of demands for concord. It was the assassin's knife: hidden until it was plunged, deep and red, into the body politic of Germany's enemies. Shirer was now convinced of Hitler's remarkable powers of oratory: what he lacked in visual presentation he made up for in his fantastical speeches. He held his audiences spellbound, but the demands he made that night in exchange for peace revealed that in fact they were impossible for Europe to accept. And what did he get for this drum-banging? Fear.

In Western capitals politicians did not want to stand by the provisions of the treaties jointly made at Versailles in 1919 and Locarno in 1925, and were afraid to resist the demands for a reasoned, rational, adult conversation about Germany's proper place in the world. After all, she was merely exerting her natural rights, the argument went, and Versailles was embarrassingly—and unnecessarily—harsh. We would do the same, surely, given similar circumstances. Give the Germans some leeway. They are no threat to us. Using these arguments, at a stroke Great Britain allowed Germany at the Anglo-German Naval Agreement in London to break free of the Versailles straightjacket, providing it with the ability to build as many submarines as the British. "Why the British have agreed to this is beyond me," remarked Shirer, unpersuaded of the argument that embracing Germany would make it more peaceful. "German submarines almost beat them in the last war, and may in the next."

At a speech to the Reichstag on March 8, 1936, Hitler revealed this inherent—though carefully hidden—contrast between his demand for peace and his desire for war. After a diatribe against the threat of bolshevism, Hitler told Germany—for the first time—that he was unilaterally rescinding the Versailles treaty with respect to the demilitarization of the Rhineland. At the same time, he repudiated the 1925 Treaty of Locarno. This was all in pursuit of peace, but one that was this time favorable to Germany and her interests. It mattered not whether these conflicted with those of her neighbors: only Germany mattered. Shirer found himself in the Reichstag watching Hitler's performance, marveling at the consummate manner in which Hitler controlled his baying crowd as they shouted out in synchronized union the "Sieg Heil" chant invented by Hitler's half-American foreign press chief, Ernst "Putzi" Hanfstaengl (so Hangstaengl claimed):

> Now the six hundred deputies, personal appointees all of Hitler, little men with big bodies and bulging necks and cropped hair and

pouched bellies and brown uniforms and heavy boots, little men of clay in his fine hands, leap to their feet like automatons, their right arms upstretched in the Nazi salute, and scream "Heil's" the first two or three wildly, the next twenty-five in unison, like a college yelk Hitler raises his hand for silence. It comes slowly. Slowly the automatons sit down. Hitler now has them in his claws. He appears to sense it. He says in a deep, resonant voice: "Men of the German Reichstag!" The silence is utter.

Hitler then dropped the bombshell none were expecting:

In this historic hour, when in the Reich's western provinces German troops are at this minute marching into their future peace-time garrisons, we all unite in two sacred vows.

He could go no further, Shirer recorded. The noise was deafening:

It is news to this hysterical "parliamentary" mob that German soldiers are already on the move into the Rhineland. All the militarism in their German blood surges to their heads. They spring, yelling and crying, to their feet . . . Their hands are raised in slavish salute, their faces now contorted with hysteria, their mouths wide open, shouting, shouting, their eyes, burning with fanaticism, glued on the new god, the Messiah. The Messiah plays his role superbly. His head lowered as if in all humbleness, he waits patiently for silence. Then, his voice still low, but choking with emotion, utters the two vows:

"First, we swear to yield to no force whatever in the restoration of the honor of our people, preferring to succumb with honor to the severest hardships rather than to capitulate. Secondly, we pledge that now, more than ever, we shall strive for an understanding between European peoples, especially for one with our western neighbor nations. . . . We have no territorial demands to make in Europe! . . . Germany will never break the peace." It was a long time before the cheering stopped.

It wasn't just the Reichstag that cheered Hitler. The repudiation of Versailles was endorsed by most Germans, even those who had no time for their country's leader. Rhinelanders, who certainly didn't want another war with France, as Shirer reported, had also caught "the Nazi bug" and were hysterical about this supposed recovery of Germany's sovereignty, self-respect, and self-determination. The "Nazi bug" had a particularly military air to it, as Howard Smith observed:

> Every fiber and tissue of the social fabric was strained towards that single needle-point goal of war. Newspapers screamed belliger-ency and hate every single day. The objects of the belligerency altered with expediency, but the screaming tone was unvaried. "We have been wronged by A; we are being threatened by B; we will right those wrongs and eliminate that threat, and Heaven help any misguided individual who stands in our way!" Children were taught it in schools; we were given a milder dose of it in the university. Soldiers had it drilled into them as another reflex. Art was nothing but war posters. Germany clearly and unequivocally wanted war and told the world so in tones so distinct that it was criminal to disbelieve them.

Peace! It was that simple. Hitler prefaced all his military actions with the claim that his ultimate purpose was peace. He was right, of course, except that this wasn't what it seemed. Germany would accept peace *after* whatever war was necessary to reassert the rights due to it by its ancient birthright. Indeed, Hitler preached peace long and loudly. So much so that any accusation that he in fact wanted war sounded deliberately argumentative, even subversive. Yet *Mein Kampf* made it explicitly clear that Hitler saw war to be inevitable, and that peace was acceptable only on terms favorable to Hitler's concept of Germany's manifest destiny. Indeed, the one thing that the Nazi elite held to fanatically was the twenty-five demands of the "Program of the National Socialist German Workers' Party" signed on February 24, 1920, the first four being:

We demand the union of all Germans to form a Great Germany . . .

We demand equality of rights for the German People in its dealings with other nations, and abolition of the Peace Treaties of Versailles and St. Germain.

We demand land and territory (colonies) for the nourishment of our people and for settling our superfluous population.

None but members of the nation may be citizens of the State. None but those of German blood, whatever their creed, may be members of the nation. No Jew, therefore, may be a member of the nation.

Hitler's claims of peace were therefore, as Halton described them, hollow, "pap for his own people—and ours—and . . . the most blatant mockery to anyone who sees Germany now." Yet on the streets of Berlin, London, and New York, the wide-eyed and closed-minded repeated the mantra that Hitler wanted peace, and was seeking merely self-respect for the Fatherland. What country did not want this for itself? Why could the Versailles victors demand one thing for themselves and something completely different for their vanquished foe? For how long was Germany going to be punished for losing the Great War? Did this not violate every principle of natural justice?

Few American visitors to Germany in the mid-1930s failed to see that Germany itself was not at peace. As Dorothy Thompson reported during a visit in 1934, the traditional courtesy of Germans remained, but now it was a façade for fear: of being watched and reported on, and having to talk within the constraints of a new orthodoxy. There could be no criticism of Hitler, the National Socialists or their dream for a new Germany, or indeed anything that might be construed as being anti-German. People could no longer speak freely; there was no freedom of the press; telephones were monitored; strikes were forbidden; dissenters disappeared, sometimes forever, into hidden jails run by the trench-coated Gestapo. Fear seemed to stalk the streets. People became careful about what they said, where, and to whom. Josephine ("Josie")

Herbst returned to Berlin in 1936, where she had first lived in 1922, and saw through the cover of cleanliness, order, and discipline:

> For anyone who knew Germany in former years, it is a changed and sick country. Perhaps it is cleaner than before. The country-side is peculiarly orderly and beautiful . . . Yet silence is over the countryside, in little inns where one is sharply scrutinized, in trains, along streets. Talk does not bubble up anymore.

In a series of articles published in the *New York Post* in 1935, Herbst pulled no punches in her analysis of Nazi-run Germany: The daily abuse of the Jews, the omnipresent propaganda defining bolshevism as the greatest threat to the nation, and black-hearted Jews being the manufacturers of communist perfidy. In the *Nation* on January 8, 1936, she asked:

> How long will the psychological reasons for submission to Hitler hold in the face of continuing economic instability for the great mass of people? Hitler has been successful in selling to the Germans the idea that he saved the country and all Europe from bolshevism, and that bolshevism is a destructive force, a strictly Jewish movement. Lately the term bolshevism with too much use has begun to lose its sharp edge. The Catholics also have been accused of bolshevism. The result has been to throw them into the opposition movement. In the Saar one of the illegal papers of the underground movement appears with the hammer and sickle combined with the Catholic cross. A priest about to be arrested was warned by the underground route; his house was surrounded by workers and peasants from the neighborhood, few of whom were Catholic, and the troopers coming to arrest him turned back at the sight of the dense crowd.
>
> The existence of the underground movement is denied in the legal press, but twenty illegal papers come out regularly in Berlin alone. Hundreds of others appear irregularly. The papers are distributed by children and by workers during their working

hours. The penalty for distributing such contraband may be the concentration camp; it may be death. Strikes are treason, and leaders are punished by death at the hands of a firing squad or by sentences to concentration camps. Yet strikes go on. Dozens occurred last summer, especially in the metal trades. Sometimes the strike consisted in a passive laying down of tools for an hour. Sometimes work was merely slowed up, "sticking," as they term it, "to the hands." Demonstrations used to be made for the release of [Ernst] Thälmann, the Communist leader, but lately there have been none, and it is not known for certain whether he is alive or dead. Only Germans who get their information from the legal press have any illusions about the so-called "bloodless revolution" of the Nazis; blood has flowed and is flowing.

—m—

The shocking dissonance between the young men of his own age in Germany and his upbringing in New Orleans startled the youthful Howard Smith when he visited Germany in 1936. Together with a friend they decided to cycle from Heidelberg to the ancient city of Worms on the west bank of the Rhine, following the reoccupation of the Rhineland, to see what they could see. It proved to be a revelation:

The town was not in war, yet, but it was the best imitation of a town-in-war I have ever seen. The streets were filled with soldiers. On every corner forests of new sign-posts told the way to parking grounds for motorized units, regimental headquarters, divisional headquarters, corps headquarters, field hospitals. We elbowed our way the length of the main street and saw not another man in civilian dress. That evening we spent in a beer-hall, in whose upper stories we had rented rooms. The beer-hall was packed with fine-looking young officers, drinking, shouting, and singing. The tables were wet with spilled beer and the air hazy with blue cigarette smoke. I do not know what it was, except that the turn of this reaction was logically due—it was perhaps partly that the beer had loosened up my imagination—but watching the faces of these men, my own age, my own generation, caused me to think of their military culture, for the first time, in terms of me and my culture. For the first time I thought of Germany, not as an academic subject studiously to gather facts about for discussion at home, but as a real, direct and imminent threat to the existence of a civilization which gathers facts and discusses. A schism deeper than the Grand Canyon separated my world from that of the young man across from me, whose face bore fencing scars and carried a monocle over one glassy eye. The fetishes of my world, the values it worshipped, if it did not always attain them, were contained in words like "Reason," "Think," "Truth." His fetishes and his values were "Feel," "Obey," "Fight." There was no base pride for me in this involuntary comparison; rather, a terror like that which paralyses a child alone in the dark took hold of me. For, my world, with all the good qualities I thought it had, was, in terms of force, weak; his was mighty, powerful, reckless. It screamed defiance at my world from the housetops. One had to be deaf not to hear it.

—⁂—

By September 1937, the Shirers had decided to move their home to Vienna, Tess's home city, and far—they thought—from the stultifying repression of Berlin. In his diary Shirer summed up his experience of the previous three years. The good things—the theater (when it stuck to pre-Nazi plays); their many friends; the lakes, parks, and woods around the city, "where you could romp and play and sail and swim, forgetting so much"—were cancelled out by the horror of the Nazi regime, wherein "the shadow of Nazi fanaticism, sadism, persecution, regimentation, terror, brutality, suppression, militarism, and preparation for war has hung over all our lives, like a dark, brooding cloud that never clears."

The world did not understand the real Germany. Wallace Deuel wrote in the *Chicago Daily News* in February 1941, that one "of the chief reasons why much of the outside world has failed to understand the Nazis and what they have been doing and are planning to do is that people simply cannot believe that the Nazis are the kind of men they are." This truth lay at the heart of appeasement, and accounts in major part for its failure. Well-meaning visitors wanted to believe that Hitler and his henchmen were merely healing Germany by restoring its self-respect after the horrors of humiliation and the subsequent worldwide financial crisis. They were also imposing discipline following chaos. Surely no one, not even Hitler, wanted war? Was that not self-evident from Hitler's repeated speeches? It was ridiculous to assert that Hitler, now he was in power, would take Germany down the path of the extremist nationalism he had espoused in his immature political youth. This view was superficial and naive, Shirer considered, because it saw the extent of Nazi politics only through the dangerous self-limiting prism of Western wishful thinking. Germany was, he believed, hard set on a path that would lead it to inevitable conflict with all—states, groups, and individuals—who opposed him, and the evidence was everywhere. Like a rabid dog, Hitler would keep on slathering and biting until he was destroyed. The ultimate end of Hitler's plan for Germany, and the purpose of all his policies—Four Year Plans; "guns before butter" speeches by the Nazi elite; and every evidence of the obvious resurgence of the Reichswehr (the army Germany was allowed to keep by the Treay of Versailles)—was total war, he thought: there was no other rational explanation. Despite the strictures of Versailles, none of which were being enforced by the international community that had imposed them, every public parade saw new and better guns, faster tanks, more aircraft. Matthew Halton agreed. At the end of 1933 he had written in the *Toronto Star*: "During the last month in Germany I have studied the most fanatical, thoroughgoing and savage philosophy of war ever imposed on a nation. Unless I am deaf, dumb and blind, Germany is becoming a vast laboratory and breeding-ground for war . . . They are sowing the wind."

But few at home paid him any attention. It wasn't politically acceptable in the West to believe that war was the ultimate political ambition of Nazi philosophy, and of the new Nazi government. It was too preposterous for words. The failure of liberalism in the 1930s was the naivete to accept that any sane, rational human being *wanted* to be illiberal.

CHAPTER TWO

Paris in Springtime

Since the days of the Marquis de Lafayette, Paris has been a magnet for Americans of every economic, political, social, and sexual hue seeking another place to live, if only for a time. Many scores of thousands of Americans had, since the earliest days of independence, identified with Thomas Jefferson's suggestion that the second place "for every travelled inhabitant of any nation" (the first place, of course, being home) was France. The industrialization of personal transport and communications in the late 19th century brought large numbers to France aboard fast steamships. Newspapers, connected by the telegraph, kept them in touch with home. The Great War, and the arrival of the two million doughboys of Pershing's American Expeditionary Force in 1917, rekindled an affection between nations that had begun 141 years before. By 1939 there were some thirty thousand Americans living in the French capital, down from a height of perhaps forty thousand at the end of the previous decade. It had dropped as low as 13,500 when the American dollar had been dramatically revalued in 1934, but numbers steadily grew again as the decade progressed. In addition, several hundred thousand American tourists descended on Gay Paree every year, brought over literally by the boatload. In 1939 American tourists arrived in record numbers, to the extent that London newspapers, jealous of the surfeit of dollars that accompanied the visitors, talked of the "invasion of France." Paris far exceeded London as *the* European destination for Americans seeking to explore lands and cultures beyond their shores.

For most Americans living there, "France" was synonymous with "Paris": indeed, most expatriates lived in or around *La Ville-Lumière*, although for the celebrities of the day the Mediterranean coast held as much allure as it does today. Even with war clouds descending, the Great Depression lurking in the hinterlands of recent memory, and the turbulence of French domestic politics, Paris—or rather a somewhat artificial creation of an idealized Paris, one inhabited in the main by foreigners who made their own rules and created a place after their own imaginings—retained its extraordinary magnet-like properties, a bright light to attract every kind of moth. There were those whose money enabled them to merge into the amorphous new aristocracy of France, one defined by culture, couture, and cuisine; those who had remained from the Great War; those who had to be there because of their diplomatic appointments or business associations; those who sought cultural, artistic, or sexual self-expression or freedoms denied them at home; and those who were there for more prosaic reasons, such as marriage or employment. Many were refugees from Prohibition. Paris had an extraordinary way of welcoming those who might be considered outsiders in their own lands. It had been home for significant numbers of writers, such as Gertrude Stein, Henry Miller, Ernest Hemingway, Ezra Pound, and F. Scott Fitzgerald, who, although not a homogenous group, nevertheless formed a loose colony in the French capital between the wars. France provided for them a social status far higher than they could receive at home, and attracted writers who worked on the edge of domestic sensibilities. During the 1920s a famous long-stay resident—Gertrude Stein—held court among a menagerie of expatriate writers seeking fame and fortune in France. The Left Bank was their lure. Stein, for instance, lived at 27, rue de Fleurus, and Sylvia

Beach ran her bookstore, Shakespeare and Company, at 12, rue de l'Odéon. Homosexuals found that Paris provided them refuge from the legal restrictions and moral constraints of their homeland. Both Beach and Stein enjoyed openly lesbian relationships with long-term partners.

Josephine Baker, who arrived in Paris in 1925 and made her name and career in the French capital as a dancer, jazz and pop music singer, and actress, was one such. The "Black Pearl," one of many appellations, became famous on the Paris stage, specifically Les Folies Bergère, not least of all because of her infamous *"danse sauvage,"* a song-and-dance act in which her modesty was protected only by the flimsiest string of bananas. The artistic license this part of Paris gave Baker reflected the liberty that others also found, or gave to themselves, in the city. Ironically, the Old World of Europe seemed to possess freedoms, sophistication, culture, and anonymity denied in parts of the new. People could reinvent themselves here, in a place which had long welcomed migrants without any fear that newcomers would somehow upset the natural balance of things. Matthew Halton's enthusiasm for the France of pretty girls promenading in the latest fashions, vigorous intellectual and political debates, high couture, café culture, wonderful food, and scent of a different countryside was commonplace among North Americans of the period.

This American diaspora quickly built up in Paris all the facilities and amenities they enjoyed at home. The 120 beds of the American Hospital at Neuilly-sur-Seine looked after their medical needs, with American doctors and surgeons like Dr. Sumner Jackson and Dr. Charles Bove to care for them; American grocery shops and taverns catered to their physical needs; an American high school looked after the education of their children; and a raft of different denominations had churches in the French capital to provide spiritual succor. The main means by which the American community kept in touch was the *Paris Herald Tribune*. Its letters page, or "Mailbag," attracted literate correspondents who conversed on every subject under the sun. One of the most celebrated, Pauline Avery Crawford, corresponded in rhyming couplets about issues that exercised and amused the newspaper's readers. They ranged from items of fun and trivia, to a clear-eyed articulation of the consequences of the resurgence of violent nationalism welling up in neighboring Germany. Crawford had first arrived in the city in 1926 and lived on her own in a tiny apartment on the Rue Jules Chaplain, off the Boulevard Raspail. A medical accident at the American Hospital had resulted in the amputation of a leg. Correspondence to the *Herald Tribune* reflected the wide diversity of expatriate American opinion about Nazism. For many, Hitler and his cronies represented a disciplined way of life that had brought order and self-respect to Germans after the humiliation of war and the subsequent poverty that had ravaged the country. Crawford repudiated such arguments. For years she had watched with concern the rise of Nazism in Germany, and in the fall of 1936, she took a trip with her two sons to Bavaria to see for herself. The very act of crossing the border was sufficient to demonstrate to her the fundamental deficiencies of totalitarianism, as her French newspapers were confiscated by "heel-clicking, uniformed police who gave the party in the compartment Nazi salutes." She found the political atmosphere stifling; people no longer talked openly about political issues, and letters were censored.

—⁂—

The France that lay just below the surface of what visitors and tourists saw, and what expatriates imagined for themselves, was deeply fractured. Robert Murphy had worked as counselor in the US embassy since 1930, witnessing at first hand the tremendous political, economic, and social turmoil that marked the decades preceding the war. The many shades of left and right that colored the political rainbow, together with the intense divisions between supporters of Church and secular state, rich and poor, intelligentsia and proletariat, each category of which appeared to despise all those outside the tight confines of their own tribe, and in which activists seemed to yo-yo between extremes (the journey from communism to fascism, for instance, was a remarkably short one for many French radicals in the 1930s), served to tear the post-Versailles political settlement apart. After 1918 France was at peace in Europe, but not at peace with herself. Between 1935 and 1940 she had twelve separate premiers. Indeed, the apparent turmoil at the heart of French society seemed to show that the revolution of 1789 had continued thereafter as a perpetual phenomenon in French national life, gifted from one generation to another, although each time expressing itself in new forms. The universal terror in France during the fifteen years preceding 1939 seemed to be of each other. The bourgeoisie—whose incomes had been devastated during the Great Depression—lived increasingly in terror of Moscow-inspired communism, exemplified by the militant trade unions that expanded during the 1930s. They were equally frightened of the vast mass of working-class proletariat who inhabited the so-called Red Belt of poor-quality housing built in concrete swathes around Paris to service the new large-scale engineering plants for automobiles and aircraft. These plants had sprung up in untidy industrial accumulations at the turn of the century, and they had exploded in size in the post–Great War economic boom. Social conservatives—mainly Roman Catholic, the ancient religious power—saw the answer to the question of social cohesion, or lack of it, in terms of sacerdotal discipline, but the proponents of anti-priestly secularism were terrified at the prospect of a reemergence of rule by the Church, and by extension the Vatican. Big business hated small business, and vice versa, and both elements at opposite ends of the economic spectrum sought to emasculate the other in defense of their own prerogatives. Political life fragmented into a multiplicity of cabals, some of the Left, some of the Right, some a schizophrenic cross-pollination of the two, all struggling against each other in a daily battle for the oxygen of political expression and public support. Some were noisy but restricted their debates to the political sphere: others, of both left and right, marched, organized, and even armed themselves against the coming Armageddon. No house divided against itself, as the priests relentlessly taught, could stand. The only question, in the short history of the Third Republic since 1870, was, Who would survive?

It wasn't just political separation Murphy witnessed but a deep fissure in the heart of French society so severe that Professor Julian Jackson refers to the period between 1934 to 1944 as a civil war. At the heart of this struggle was an existential quest for the meaning of "France." The Great Depression meant that a hoped-for healing of France's social divisions by means of increased and redistributed wealth never materialized. The dramatic drop in agricultural prices impoverished the peasants in an economy still dominated by the land. No consensus as to the solution could be obtained. Those who saw the answer lying in direct action began to organize and march. Some demanded the end of liberal democracy, which they considered to have failed by the political chaos it appeared to have engendered. The right-leaning Croix de Feu commanded by Great War veteran Colonel de la Roque boasted over 300,000 members at the end of 1935. On the Left, Léon Blum's Popular Front, an amalgam of communists, radicals, and socialists, came together to oppose fascism, and won the May 1936 elections, propelling Blum into the premiership. His government survived a year, which was a lifetime in the febrile atmosphere of the time. Ironically, the advent of a socialist government did not calm the Left but rather served to empower workers in their grievances against employers. Social tension and chaos increased: in the year following the PF's victory, the state was incapacitated by strikes, some twelve thousand all told, involving 1.8 million strikers, all enthused by the apparent accession of "workers" to power. The massive growth in trade union membership—into the millions—followed.

For conservative worriers about this transformation of power, the advent of the Spanish Civil War exacerbated their worries about uncontrolled and uncontrollable change. Fearful of the end of life as they knew it, the bourgeoisie armed themselves against rule by the proletariat. The old cabals returned, in militant form. On the Right, the Cagoule (literally, "Hooded Ones") stockpiled weapons for the inevitable clash with the forces of radical communism. Politics in France, fractured bitterly before 1936, became dramatically polarized after this date, the advent of the Popular Front acting inadvertently both to radicalize the Right and to give focus and purpose to the Left. To this mix needs to be added the widespread impulses in France towards pacifism, instincts it shared with many well-meaning souls in Great Britain and the United States. Indeed, the liberal West was riven through with pacifistic impulses that were ultimately proven to be both dangerous and naive. Dangerous, because they dampened efforts to arm and defend oneself adequately, and naive by their inability to persuade enemies or potential enemies to adopt the same pacifistic ambitions. For France, the primary driver for the pacifist impulse was the experience of the trenches, and the determination among many who had shared the agonies of the Great War that servitude was better than death. Totalitarianism exploited such impulses ruthlessly.

Murphy counted thirty-seven separate governments in France during the ten years of his assignment. The truth was that France, when war came in September 1939, was split so comprehensively that a unified response to aggression—the nation thinking, behaving, and acting as one, under determined political leadership, in resistance to unprovoked aggression—was impossible. For Murphy and his wealthy, Francophile ambassador, William "Bill" Bullitt, the task was to ensure that American interests were maintained in France, that intelligence about the state of political affairs in Paris and further abroad was analyzed and presented in a timely manner to Washington, and that insofar as it was possible, the statesmen of Europe would be persuaded to follow the paths of peace.

—⁂—

Bullitt was appointed US ambassador to France in 1936, a few short months following the German reoccupation—in contravention of Versailles—of the Rhineland. French fear of German drum-beating was high, but French government indecision was so decisive that no action was taken to enforce the treaty obligations Germany had made in 1919 to keep the region demilitarized. Bullitt, who had begun his working life as a journalist and novelist, was a long-term friend and political ally of the president, Franklin D. Roosevelt. The friendship was to end in 1941 primarily because of bitter disagreement over Bullitt's actions during the French government's withdrawal from Paris. However, for the four years that preceded the cataclysm of 1940, Bullitt diligently fed back a vast daily diet of information, intelligence, and gossip to Washington. An intelligent, gregarious, sociable man (he was also extremely wealthy), Bullitt's diplomacy centered on befriending everyone of influence, regardless of political hue, so as to interpret the swirling eddies of the Third Republic for FDR. "Mr. Bullitt was terribly, terribly popular with everybody, particularly the French politicians," observed the writer Clare Boothe Luce when she met him for the first time in April 1940. "Without exception, every living ex-Premier of France called him by his first name and gave him his deepest confidence," she noted. He fluttered unashamedly around every bright light across Europe, drawing in views, ideas, and intelligence, which he faithfully (if somewhat loquaciously) reported back to the president. His apartment at 2, avenue d'Iéna in the 16th arrondissement and a rented château at Chantilly became welcoming oases that excluded no branch of political opinion. The embassy's invaluable contacts, according to Robert Murphy, extended "from the extreme left of Maurice Thorez, Jacques Duclos and Marcel Gachin, through Léon Blum, Vincent Auriol, Pierre Got, Gaston Bergery, Edouard Herriot, Paul Reynaud, Edouard Daladier, Camille Chautemps, Yvon Delbos, Jules Jeanneney, Georges Bonnet, Pierre Laval, Pierre-Etienne Flandin, Georges Mandel, Raymond Patenôtre, Albert Sarraut—even Marcel Deat and Colonel de la Roque." Bullitt's black-tie diplomacy was made easier by the fact that he had been on intimate terms with the country since childhood, spoke the language fluently, and had an easy knack for creating confidences, many of which became genuine friendships. His ultimate purpose, and that of the president he served, was to use American influence with the French political classes to persuade France to patch up its differences with Germany, and by so doing avoid a return to war in Europe. Perhaps his only naivete lay in not fully appreciating Hitler's aggrandizing pretensions, although in this regard he was in good company. From the beginning Bullitt believed that the United States need not—indeed, should not—become involved in a future European imbroglio. He only changed his tune when he heard Nazi jackboots marching across Europe, realizing that he had been hoodwinked. Until this time his belief was that Europe needed to solve its own problems, without interference from the United States. America had already expended much blood and treasure in 1917 and 1918: over 320,000 Americans had become casualties in the Great War, and the country, Bullitt believed, should not be asked to do so again.

As the German saber rattling grew louder, Bullitt was the obvious person for French politicians to turn to in their hour of need. After all, America was the world's bastion of democracy, "the land of the free," the leading protector of the idea of individual freedom and representative democracy, not to mention industrial potential. It helped that Bullitt was likeable and wealthy enough to entertain both politicians and commentators. As he hated both communist and fascist excess, no serious French politician was excluded from his counsel. By the time war had been declared, his neutrality was nuanced by his belief that America needed to do everything in its power, short of joining in the fighting, to assist France in the defeat of the Nazi aggressor. The days, pre-Munich, in which he could be described as an appeaser were long past. In 1938 the writer and journalist Janet Flanner painted Bullitt perfectly for the *New Yorker* as a man who believed in ideals and considered them worth fighting for. He was unashamedly partisan, she wrote, and as such was ". . . a fighter, an unembarrassed patriot, and an explosive romantic. . . . Headstrong, spoiled, spectacular, something of a nabob, and a good showman," she observed, "he has complicated ambitions which are a compound of his devotion to his own notions of idealism, his interest in his career, and his faith in the ultimate fate of the human race." In 1940, his spirited advocacy of France and French interests, together with his increasingly urgent appeals to Washington to engage meaningfully in the new European war—short of declaring war herself—placed him in a role akin to that of the French ambassador to Washington and ultimately led to his breach with FDR.

When Bullitt first arrived in Paris to take up his appointment in 1936, Léon Blum, the Jewish leader of the left-of-center Socialist Party, headed the Popular Front coalition, which held tenuous power. The Popular Front included two other leftist parties, the Moscow-leaning communists under Maurice Thorez, and the much smaller Radical Party led by Edouard Daladier. Arrayed against these parties was a vociferous variety of rightist, Royalist, and Catholic groups. On February 6, 1934, street fighting between several of these factions in Paris led to the spilling of blood, with fifteen dead and hundreds wounded. It was a defining moment in the disintegration of prewar French social and political cohesion.

On October 24, 1936, Bullitt had lunch with Blum and faithfully reported its outcome to FDR. The premier, far from being a radical leftist, had middle-of-the-road political views akin to those, Bullitt reported, of the US president. This did not prevent him from being widely distrusted in France by the political, religious, and economic Right, who feared that any form of socialist government was tantamount to opening the floodgates of bolshevism. It didn't help that Blum was, to many, a reviled Israelite. France's problem, Bullitt believed, was a dearth of real leadership, on either side of the political spectrum, able to dominate and control a single party sufficiently to enable it to have a majority in parliament. Instead, weak leadership produced the shaky coalitions of political opportunity that came and went with destabilizing and depressing regularity. Bullitt considered, however, that despite the violence of the words between them, the differences between Left and Right (considering the events of February 6, 1934) would not inevitably lead to a civil war. France already had one on her doorstep in Spain, and trembled at its ferocity. "The whole of France has been shocked by the civil war in Spain," he noted. "The lower middle class, which in the last election in considerable measure voted Communist, doesn't want that sort of thing in France."

Instead, the fear on every mind was the possibility, once more, of war in Europe, following Germany's unilateral actions to reoccupy the Rhineland. Blum, he reported, was at least interested in trying to reset France's relationship with Germany. Bullitt believed in the rationality of statesmanship, and was convinced that "the nub of the problem of European peace is still—as it has been for so long—reconciliation between France and Germany." He was concerned to note, however, that Europeans were as wont to talk about war as they were about peace. On November 24, 1936, he warned FDR that every political conversation he had had was suffused with the talk of war. The reoccupation of the Rhineland had shaken everyone. "Everyone in France, including Blum and the British Ambassador," he told FDR, "is convinced that war is about to arrive. . . . Everyone is convinced that war will come by the Spring or Summer of 1938." The crux of people's concerns was Czechoslovakia, which Bullitt considered to be "the next item on Hitler's menu" because of the large number of ethnic Germans residing in its western provinces. France had recently signed a treaty with Czechoslovakia offering military solidarity in the event of attack, but would France have the political will to use force if the time came to challenge Germany militarily? They had failed to do anything over the Rhineland, on France's border. Why would they do anything to support Czechoslovakia, so far away? There were those, he suggested, like the Belgian ambassador to Paris, who believed that treaty or no, France would never risk a war with Germany merely for the sake of Czechoslovakia:

> I have, however, discussed the same eventuality with a number of Frenchmen, and they say that France would march, knowing perfectly well that, when France began to be beaten by Germany, England would have to come in on the side of France.
>
> My own guess is that there would be a hair's breadth decision, and that no one can predict with certainty as to whether or not France would march in support of Czechoslovakia.

What could the United States do, Bullitt asked the president, to preserve peace in Europe? On December 8, 1936, Bullitt recorded Blum's view that the only way to contain an aggressive Germany was to bind Britain, France, and the United States in an alliance based on a reappraisal of the post-Versailles settlement. Bullitt warned Blum in return that the United States would categorically not involve itself in another war in Europe but would commit itself to securing peace, and to "stopping the deluge which is approaching. I am still convinced that the only possible method of stopping it is through direct negotiations between Paris and Berlin. But I am not at all sure that such negotiations can succeed because I suspect that the Eastern frontiers of Germany fixed by the Treaty of Versailles remain just as unacceptable to Germany as the day they were decreed."

But not everyone accepted that the march to war was inevitable. The British ambassador to Washington, Philip Kerr (Lord Lothian), a high-profile appeaser, told Bullitt that he was "convinced that Hitler will not accept peace except at the price of domination of Eastern and Central Europe and the Balkans" and that this was a price Europe should be prepared to pay to ensure stability in Europe. Bullitt reported that many on the French Right agreed with this view. He conversed with Czechoslovakian ministers who wanted Europe to unite in securing an "understanding" with Germany, and if not, Czechoslovakia would "make her own deal with Germany rather than wait to be crushed." On May 10, 1937, Bullitt reported that Blum was "more or less in despair with regard to the possibility of keeping Austria and Czechoslovakia out of the hands of Germany. Hitler has the ball and can run with it in any direction he chooses." On November 23, 1937, Bullitt told FDR of Hitler's chilling comment to the Duchess of Windsor: "Our buildings will make more magnificent ruins than the Greeks'."

The one thing that Bullitt worried endlessly about was the state of British and French aircraft production, believing that the future war would be determined by the side with the best, and greatest number of, aircraft. Most military observers at the time, following the attack on Guernica in Spain in 1937, feared for the safety of their cities, and emphasized the threat from the air. Many of Bullitt's missives to Washington were replete with warnings about the advanced state of German aircraft design and production, and the distance France and Britain would have to travel to catch up if they were ever to compete with the Luftwaffe. A visit to Berlin enabled him to gauge the public mood. He was taken aback by the arrogant exuberance of a nation that apparently was no longer cowed by the defeat of 1918. Their joie de vivre had returned. "The Germans are confident and cocky," he wrote, "sure that time is working for them; sure that they can get exactly what they want and determined to get it." The exact response of Britain and France to German expansionist rhetoric—and to a lesser extent that of Poland and the Soviet Union—exercised him daily:

I am less sure than I was a few weeks ago that France will actually go to the support of Czechoslovakia in case of a German attack. I still believe that France will do so but there is a considerable possibility that if the Germans begin their attack by a revolt of the Germans of Bohemia, the French will communicate at once with London and ask if Great Britain will support France in defending Czechoslovakia and the British will reply by advising France to refer the matter to the League of Nations and adding that until the League has decided on appropriate action they will do nothing. This may prevent the French from taking any action until Germany has overrun Czechoslovakia.

In the meantime, Bullitt was clear that no one should be under any doubt that bringing into the Reich all Germans living contiguous to it—including those in Czechoslovakia and Austria—remained a vital German foreign policy goal, a point reinforced by a meeting in Germany with Herman Goering in November 1937. What would France do, Bullitt asked himself, if Germany acted on this policy? Opinion in Paris seemed starkly divided between attacking Germany preemptively, to forestall a German move against Czechoslovakia, and doing nothing that might put French blood and treasure at risk. Bullitt's view was that anything was preferable to war. He argued as much to FDR on May 20, 1938, writing that it would be better for the Czechs to give in to Hitler rather than risk general war in Europe. A war over Czechoslovakia would make the "slaughter of the entire younger generation of France . . . certain and every city in France could be levelled to the ground by German planes. The French, even under such circumstances, would hold out and the war would be a long one, involving England and all Europe. There could be only one possible result; the complete destruction of western Europe and Bolshevism from one end of the Continent to the other." What Bullitt failed to consider in his analysis was what would happen to a Europe under the harsh subjugation of Nazism if no one was prepared to stand up in defense of the new countries that emerged from Versailles. On June 13, 1938, he told FDR that he felt "like a participant in the last days of Pompeii."

The full truth about Hitler's territorial ambitions only gradually illuminated Bullitt's political consciousness. He had, earlier, believed that war could be averted by France and Germany burying their hatchets and embracing peaceful cohabitation in Europe. He had not taken into account the missionizing imperatives of Nazism. He did now. On March 23, 1939, he told FDR:

> Tonight Hitler is on his way to Memel [in Lithuania]. He will soon be making plans to visit other spots in Europe. Someday someone will have enough guts to pull a trigger and the affair will begin. The British seem to be awake at last and the French definitely are awake.

Memel represented a damascene conversion for Bullitt. The common people whom he observed now also realized the fatuousness of attempting to placate someone who was intent on war. Hitler's march into the Sudetenland "convinced every French man and every French woman that no promise of the dictators was to be relied on; that words were useless; and that Hitler could be stopped by nothing but force. As a result, there is a curious *serenity* from one end of France to the other. There is no vacillation or mourning. The spirit of the people is incomparably better than in 1914 and far better even than the spirit last September."

Bullitt presciently laid out the consequences of continued German aggrandizement in Europe, understanding implicitly that Poland would be next and—if the Poles should cave in—France would follow. It was at this point that Bullitt's tune began to change, from one in which splendid isolation amidst the sound of the war drums in Europe was the urgent imperative for the United States, to one which now accepted that someone needed to stand up to Hitler, or else all of Europe would be swallowed piece by piece, thus placing the United States in a difficult strategic position:

> The moral for us is that unless some nation in Europe stands up to Germany quickly, France and England may face defeat and such

> defeat would mean the French and British fleets in the hands of
> the Germans and the Italians. We should then have the Japs in the
> Pacific and an overwhelming fleet against us in the Atlantic.

In other words, as he explained to FDR, even though Americans did
not want to confront Germany militarily by entering another war in
Europe, time would demonstrate that they would have no choice. From
this point on, his warnings to FDR were about the dire threats to the
United States if America did not take up the cudgels against Nazism in
support of the weakly defended European democracies. Robert Murphy
expressed the same fears following a visit back home just before the
outbreak of war, when many "American acquaintances chilled me with
the bland assertion: 'Let Europe settle its own problems. This time we
will stay out of it.' The seductive assumption that we had the power
of choice accounted for the sense of security amazingly possessed by
most Americans at that time."

Virginia Cowles soaked up the physical glories of Paris when she
returned in August 1938 after several harrowing months in Spain
observing the trauma of her Civil War. The City of Light was a haven
of peace and beauty following the horrors of hungry, war-torn Madrid.
The sun shone through the parade of mighty chestnuts that stood sen-
tinel on either side of the Avenue de Champs-Élysées, while the Seine
glistened serenely in the sunshine. But sinister darkness threatened
this otherwise bucolic scene. She admitted feeling fear clutch at her as
she walked the streets of the French capital, wondering for just how
long peace would prevail. On the outside people appeared unconcerned,
life continuing in the graceful, carefree manner that defined Paris as
the world's most elegant city. The news had arrived days before that
reservists in the German army had received their mobilization orders,
the latest escalation in the verbal battering levied by Berlin against
Czechoslovakia. With Austria subdued, the only hope for the protection of the sovereignty of any country in Europe against the threats

from Germany was international law, and the determination of the world—led in Europe by France and Britain—to stand by a threatened sovereign state in her hour of need. But would the European democracies defend in one another the freedoms they themselves held dear, or would they instead attempt to avert the threat of all-out conflagration by appeasing Berlin, and giving in to her aggrandizing demands? Cowles was frightened. As the year went by, during which she had a roving commission for London's Sunday *Times*, she described watching "the lights in the death-chamber go out one by one."

In France, the government asked the people to prepare to fight to defend their country. The state visit of King George VI and Queen Elizabeth, for whom Parisians turned out in large, excited numbers, and for which the bands played "Rule Britannia" as enthusiastically as if they'd been on Pall Mall, was now a distant memory. War was on everyone's minds. Would the Entente Cordiale survive to defend Europe's liberty? Cowles seemed sure that it wouldn't. She could see no widespread willingness by politicians or people to stand up for democracy, either in their own country or abroad. Peace was dying, she thought, looking around her. "In their hearts people knew it, but the actual fact was so appalling they clung desperately to hope. They kept a vigil in the death-chamber, clasping the patient's cold hands and refusing to admit, even to themselves, the growing pallor of her face." Two months later, following Chamberlain's abnegation of international law at Munich, Bill Shirer visited Paris and agreed with Cowles's conclusion. He knew Paris well, and had watched Paris tear itself apart in the February 1934 riots that had nearly destroyed the Third Republic. He confided to his diary:

> Paris is a frightful place, completely surrendered to defeatism with no inkling of what has happened to France. At Pouquet's, at Maxim's, fat bankers and businessmen toasting Peace with rivers of champagne. But even the waiters, taxi-drivers, who used to be sound, gushing about how wonderful it is that war has been avoided, that it would have been a crime, that they fought in one war and that was enough. That would be okay if the Germans,

who also fought in one war, felt the same way, but they don't. The guts of France—France of the Marne and Verdun—where are they? Outside of Pierre Comer, no one at the Quai d'Orsay with any idea at all of the real Germany. The French Socialists, shot through with pacifism; the French Right, with the exception of a few like Henri de Kerillis, either fascists or defeatists. France makes no sense to me anymore.

Shirer would undoubtedly have known of the "party crowd" in Paris, those for whom money enabled them to float above the common preoccupations of politics, survival, and the poor. Far above the struggle of millions of the working and lower middle classes, who just about managed to survive at the bottom of the economic food chain, the rich elite played. France was the stage on which rich Americans and Europeans enjoyed their wealth while France and the French people acted as stagehands and bit-part actors scurrying about to change the endless stage and scene settings for their reveries. Charlie Scheips observed that Bettina Ballard, the American *Vogue* Paris editor, called the 1939 social season "the most brilliant Paris has seen since the carefree late 1920s," noting that the only enemy discussed at the series of frenetic and lavish parties during the last two weeks of June was the weather. In September, the French edition of *Vogue* carried photographs of the greatest party of the season. The world had turned upside down. No matter. The 81-year-old American heiress Lady Elsie Mendl (née de Wolfe) threw an extravagant, surreal "Circus Ball" for Parisian society on July 1, 1939, at her home, the Villa Trianon château on the grounds of the Palace of Versailles. War clouds were on the horizon, but the ostrichitis that had removed the moral compass of many European politicians simultaneously made the rich of Paris pretend that whatever nastiness was occurring elsewhere would never affect them. The wealth that protected them in peace would be the fence that kept the dogs of war at bay. Or so they thought. Or perhaps it was just a chance to make one last hurrah? Some seven hundred of Paris's most exquisite creatures turned up in white tails and fabulous gowns for what Scheips describes as the city's "Last Frivolous Gesture," to dance the night away in the company of elephants, clowns, tightrope walkers, jugglers, a Hawaiian guitarist playing from a boat in the swimming pool, and a blind accordion player, who strolled amidst the guests. It was tantamount, as Scheips acknowledges, to "dancing atop a Volcano." Such foolishness was an attempt to fend off reality, to maintain the partying traditions of a moneyed elite. The event was the talk of the town, and fodder for the Parisian magazines, in the few months remaining before Damocles' sword was loosed from its horse-hair thread and fell, fatally, on all of France, rich and poor, resident and refugee alike, on September 3.

But to ordinary visitors, those who did not receive the gilded invitations to Château Trianon, superficially Paris continued to hold its allure. It did so for Matthew Halton, who, even on the verge of the war he had been prophesying for six years, regarded it as still one of "earth's most civilized and beautiful towns."

> Children still laughed [a]round the pond in the Luxembourg Gardens. The policeman on point duty still whistled *Le Madelon*; the occasional *chômeur* still begged a franc to buy *un pain*; it was still pleasant to sit under the trees at the foot of Sacré Coeur to drink your coffee and wine. Midinettes [salesgirls] still danced down the streets without benefit of that garment which the French with marvelous euphemism call a "sustain-throat." And as it was St. Catherine's Day when I got there just after Munich, when unmarried girls over twenty-five pray to the saint for a husband, the Catherinettes were going to church.

But underneath lay a sense of frustration, depression even. That night he dined with three army officers at Le Relais de la Belle Aurore, a restaurant established in 1789—a time of great upheaval in a previous era—at 6, rue Gomboust, Ci-devant Rue de la Corderie St. Honoré:

> "We are about to reap the fruits of blindness and stupidity," said the younger major.
> "The fruits of venality and selfishness," said the other.

"Worse," said the colonel. "The people are not rotten. The France of Verdun has not rotted in twenty years—except at the top. C'est la trahison. France—and England—are being betrayed from within the gates."

Writing to the *Herald Tribune*, Pauline Crawford captured the essence of the problem in verse. Repudiating appeasement, she warned that unless the free countries of Europe dealt with the dictators, America would have to come to the rescue again:

In 'thirty-five bad Ethiopia Was "civilized into Utopia"
In 'thirty-six the Spanish border
Was bravely crossed to "Maintain order."
In 'thirty-seven the Chinese died
In order to be "pacified."
In 'thirty-eight a neighbor nation
Gave Austrians "self-determination."
In 'thirty-nine Memel was "freed,"
And Czechs and Slovaks "guaranteed."
And small Albania from descendants
Of Romulus won "independence."
And other nations, so it's stated,
Are hoping to be "liberated."
So 'ere another state's selected
And by dictators is "protected,"
It might be wise to send this very
Clear note in their vocabulary:
Dear Sirs: If you do not behave, you
Will face ten million Yanks to "save" you.

CHAPTER THREE

The Gathering Storm

B y the beginning of 1938 Hitler had become greatly emboldened. His repeated demands for the so-called racial "self-determination" of the estimated ten million German speakers who lived outside the borders of the Reich, even though most of these had never been part of a united German state—the very first demand of the 1920 Nazi Party Declaration—became daily more strident. The reaction by Britain and France to both his rhetoric and his actions during the previous eighteen months had been derisory. Many politicians—of every ilk—believed sincerely that to oppose Hitler would be to enrage him and bring about the very situation they were trying to avert. Hitler, it was believed, was like the bull in the matador's ring. It was the skill of the bullfighter, not the strength of the bull—or its fevered determination, in all its rage and fury, to gore its opponent—that would, in the end, bring the situation to a conclusion. In March 1938 Paris and Moscow offered the Czechoslovaks the promise of military support if they were threatened. London refused to make any similar commitment. As it turned out, France's pledge proved to be entirely hollow. Most politicians in

France and Britain did not believe that the Nazis' radical agenda was real, and was, rather, a mere ploy for domestic power. Once that power had been attained, like any other rational man, Hitler would follow a more statesmanlike course, especially where his neighbors were concerned. Provoking Nazi anger would, so their argument went, only encourage the fanatics who believed this hegemonic nonsense about German racial superiority. In any case, Nazism wasn't bolshevism, and the greatest fear of property-owning democracies in Europe since 1917 had been that of communist revolution in their own countries seeping out of the unrestrained violence that had overwhelmed the old Russia. Little did they realize that Nazism and bolshevism were not opposites but rivals for the repression of liberty, competing as to who would wear the jackboots. Accordingly, none had lifted a finger to prevent the remilitarization of the Rhineland, in contravention of Versailles. France watched supinely, deep fractures in her political system preventing her acting with unity and authority. The previous year the United States had enacted the so-called Neutrality Acts, legalizing America's descent into isolation from political entanglements abroad—specifically Europe—by making it difficult to trade with any warring country regardless of the righteousness of the cause. European democracy could expect no help from the United States if it was threatened by totalitarianism of any kind. If the European democracies were unwilling to back even their own treaties, Hitler judged—correctly, as it transpired—they'd be unwilling to withstand demands that had no direct consequences for their own sovereignty or security. For those countries with significant Germanic populations, such as Austria and Czechoslovakia, or indeed any country that did not cede to Germany's demands, the implication was clear. Complete and unequivocal acquiescence to Hitler's requirements was his term for peace in Europe. If he could not secure what he wanted, war would be the result. In the twisted logic of the governing Nazi elite, the resulting war would be the fault of those who failed to acquiesce.

Captain Al Wedemeyer of the United States Army was on a two-year exchange with the German army in 1937 and 1938, attending the famous War College in Berlin alongside some of the best middle-ranking officers in the *Heer*. It gave him an unparalleled insight into the German army. During the second week of March 1938 he was skiing with his class at Obersdorf in the Bavarian Alps, when the war college course came to an unceremonious halt and his German colleagues were ordered to return to their units. They were told that the course had been put on hold but would resume soon. On the morning of March 12, the small group of overseas students was offered leave during this unexpected interregnum in their studies. "It was a curious experience—the evening before in good camaraderie, arms linked, drinking wine and singing songs; this morning an ominous secrecy, a charged atmosphere," he recalled. "Could it be war? Living in Germany at this particular time one had mixed feelings, almost always tension, occasionally an exciting eruption of some kind. I wondered what had happened to cut short the ski trip which had at least one more week to go."

Wedemeyer made the most of this unexpected holiday by travelling to Montreux in Switzerland to visit his two sons, who were attending boarding school. It was as he entered Switzerland on the train later that day that he learned from excited passengers that the German army was marching into Austria. Spending a couple of days with his sons, he decided to fly to Vienna to see what he could of this so-called annexation—Anschluss—for himself. Everywhere were parades, German troops goose-stepping down cobbled streets packed full of excited people:

> The Viennese, who were outwardly exultant, cheered lustily. But I wondered. Somehow the Viennese cheers sounded unnaturally lacking in spontaneity. It soon became apparent that many Germans prominent in civilian life as well as a large number of military men were greatly concerned about Hitler's hunches, his dangerously provocative moves on the international chessboard.

During his time in Berlin, Wedemeyer had become aware that not all Germans approved of their new leader or the regime that was being imposed on the country. However, dissent wasn't widespread, or loudly voiced. Nevertheless, it was self-evident to him that "the Nazi leaders were preparing for war." But, fearful of provoking the beast, free Europe did nothing about Austria. Their failure to act at a stroke signaled the end of Czechoslovakia. To those who were prepared to understand the Nazi program, the union of all Germans was an article of faith and had to be achieved, even if it entailed the spilling of blood. This was the Nazis' manifest destiny. It was, too, Hitler's personal mission. This is why fate had called him to the highest office in the German state.

In London Virginia Cowles reported that the Anschluss raised tension "to a higher pitch than at any time since the Great War." Silent crowds gathered in Downing Street to watch the cabinet ministers leaving their hastily summoned meeting, while newsboys cried out to a cold, gray world: "Germany on the march again."

> Worried speculations ran the gamut from saloons to fashionable London drawing-rooms. There was a general rush of volunteers to ambulance services and air-raid precaution organizations, and hundreds of young business men signed up with the Territorial Army. Everywhere there was a cry for more arms.

The government tried to assuage people's fear by declaring that tensions in Europe remained just that: issues for Europeans, and not for the British. Otherwise intelligent, rational commentators bent over backwards to demonstrate that everything was not as it seemed. "The *Times* ran leading articles emphasizing the enthusiasm with which thousands of Viennese welcomed the Nazi regime," noted Cowles, "and the Archbishop of Canterbury rose in the House of Lords to say that Hitler should be thanked for preserving Austria from a civil war. 'Why all the gloom?' cried Lord Beaverbrook, and the catchword stuck. 'Why all the gloom?' echoed the public, and settled back in its comfortable illusion of peace."

In Berlin, an astonished Shirer watched the world—which was failing comprehensively to understand these ideological certainties—attempt to placate Germany. The thing they feared most was a return to the horrors of the Great War, so in their panic they allowed themselves to ignore their democratic principles, together with their international commitments—including their promises to protect Czechoslovakia—in the headlong flight to avert a war. Ironically, war was made more certain by their failure to demonstrate to Hitler the folly of using force. Under inexorable pressure from Berlin, the only option seemed to be to encourage this new-age bully's victim—Czechoslovakia—to give in to its persecutor. If, by making territorial concessions, Czechoslovakia could prevent central Europe from falling into war, surely that would be a good thing, for which the entire world would be grateful? The argument fell, Shirer believed, on many points, not least because of the relentless militarism of the German state. Every day evidence appeared on Germany's streets of a march to war that would not be removed by the forced kowtowing of states being bullied by Berlin. But even Shirer was beguiled by the rationality of his own logical mind. In Geneva on September 9, 1938, watching the ineffective and deeply divided League of Nations do nothing about the looming Czech crisis, he dismissed the idea that Germany would fight to recover the Sudetenland, first because "the German army is not ready; secondly, the people are dead against war." Neither, however, were obstacles to Hitler. Berlin pumped out grievous propaganda that daily traduced, belittled, and mocked Czechoslovakia. Hermann Goering shouted during the Nazi Party's annual rally at Nuremberg: "A petty segment of Europe is harassing human beings. . . . This miserable pygmy race [the Czechoslovakians] without culture—no one knows where it came from—is oppressing a cultured people and behind it is Moscow and the eternal mask of the Jew devil . . ."

The very real fear of war wafted across Europe in September 1938 like a cloud of poison gas. In Britain, newspapers predicted millions of deaths from bombardment from the air. On September 12, Hitler, in a speech to the party faithful in Nuremberg, raged at the Czechoslovaks, demanding that the slavery the "German" population had suffered at the hands of their culturally impoverished overlords was ended by means of ethnic Germans being able to secure their self-determination. By this he meant, of course, that these regions should be transferred to Germany, regardless of the principles of national sovereignty or international law. His demand was the "return" of all parts of Czechoslovakia where at least 51 percent of the population considered itself "German." Ed Beattie of United Press watched with horror and anger the carefully orchestrated scenes at Nuremberg, concluding that it was "virtually impossible for any American who has the slightest conception of what is going on, to feel anything but hatred for the present regime."

> Hitler stood alone . . . one third of the way down the long narrow congress hall. Behind him, blood red, were banked the hundreds of standards of the stormtroops of the whole Reich. Before him was a handpicked audience, Germans, Austrians and a big block from Sudetenland, which he knew would respond to every note he sounded.
>
> First he hurled the West Wall in the faces of France and England. Then he talked of the German army and air force, and of the great stocks of food and raw materials which he said would make Germany invulnerable to blockade. Then he turned to Czechoslovakia, and brought the crowd to its feet with the most biting attack he ever made on any nation, and the mob roar surged and broke against the red-draped rostrum.

Meanwhile, the German press pumped out its carefully orchestrated anti-Czech vitriol:

> WOMEN AND CHILDREN MOWED DOWN BY CZECH ARMOURED CARS
> BLOODY REGIME—NEW CZECH MURDERS OF GERMANS
> POISON-GAS ATTACK ON AUSSIG?
> EXTORTION, PLUNDERING, SHOOTING—CZECH TERROR IN SUDETEN
> GERMAN LAND GROWS WORSE FROM DAY TO DAY!

"Because they never got a chance to hear anything else," observed Beattie, "big sections of the population began to believe that the Czech really were a nation of rapists, baby beaters, gunmen and assorted habitual criminals." What chance did ordinary Germans have of seeing the truth through this heavy veil of lies? During the national elections in Czechoslovakia during May 1938, German propaganda was intense. Beattie watched, horrified, as "the scream of the German propaganda rose and grew hoarser each week, and the stiffness of the Czechs gradually went out of them as the pressure increased and their allies grew more evasive and jittery." He saw a change that summer of a country that in May was ". . . a small country sure of itself, well-armed, aware of its danger, and willing to fight" to one which by mid-August knew that it was "as good as sold out." During these elections Virginia Cowles travelled to Aussig in northern Bohemia to follow the progress of electioneering by Konrad Henlein's pro-German party. The rally she attended, with 6,500 others, was, she recalled, "a nightmare of flags, swastikas, banners, photographs of Henlein, posters of Hitler, and ear-splitting 'Heils.'" Their hatred of all things Czech—whom they referred to as ". . . a race of emigre peasants"—aligned them unequivocally with Hitler's Third Reich regardless of the Nazi Party's other policies. Their attitude was "Germany good or bad." Many Germans in Czechoslovakia "protested bitterly against discrimination and complained that their people were constantly subjected to irritations by officials who could speak only Czech," she wrote, although "on looking back it seems astonishing that anyone could have solemnly argued the pros and cons of the German case, when the latter had already suppressed their own minorities with unequalled savagery."

The danger that Hitler faced was moving too quickly, and by so doing provoking war with France and Britain. To get his way, he turned up the notch gradually. He wanted them to acquiesce in his plans not by force but by a style of diplomacy that said one thing and did something entirely different. As the late summer days of September went by, it was clear that both France and Britain had determined—for reasons of keeping the peace in Europe—to seek compromise with Germany, and not to contest Germany's demand for the Sudetenland if the only alternative was war. The sovereign territory of Czechoslovakia was to be the sacrificial lamb for "peace" in Europe. On September 15 Hitler made his argument to Chamberlain at Berchtesgaden for the so-called self-determination of the Sudetenland, after which the British prime minister, with the agreement of France, proposed the transfer of some Czech territories to Germany. Czechoslovakia was not consulted. Suddenly national sovereignty, the rule of international law, and the self-determination of states (as opposed to that of people-groups within those states)—especially those in far distant places—was of no import.

Jimmy ("Vincent") Sheean and his English-born wife, Dinah Forbes-Robertson, were in Prague throughout that awful summer. In early September, they drove out to visit the Sudeten areas, accompanied by Matthew Halton, who had arrived in Prague from London on September 15, the day that Chamberlain flew to Berchtesgaden, determined secretly not to commit British blood to the defense of an ally. Chamberlain left the meeting with Hitler with the understanding that Britain, France, and Germany would work together to develop a proposal for the gradual transfer to Germany of all those areas of Czechoslovakia that had a population in which the majority was ethnically German. Halton recorded that most Czechoslovak people he met still had no inkling (although some were now guessing at it) that they would be sold down the river by their allies. They remained full of heart, willing to fight, in the knowledge that fearsome though it was, Hitler's Wehrmacht was no match for Britain, France, and Czechoslovakia together. According to Sheean:

> The most frightened citizenry in Europe during the Czech crisis were the Germans, the least frightened were the Czechs . . .
>
> That day I saw a crowd of men standing before the statue of John Huss to vow resistance: "We have had twenty years of freedom after centuries of oppression. We will maintain it or die." The city which cradled Protestantism and was a birthplace of the Renaissance had become freedom's central keep and knew it . . .
>
> But a few days later Chamberlain was to speak of the Czechs as a "faraway people of whom we know nothing." It is a phrase which will have a prominent place in any anthology of blindness and shame. [8 P.M. BBC broadcast, September 27, 1938]

During their two-day journey through Karlovy Vary (Carlsbad) and Eger, the Sheeans and Halton saw a proud people quietly determined to resist any infringement of their territorial integrity, although what they also saw of Sudeten sentiment spoke of pro-German belligerence:

> We passed girls cycling along with gas-masks on their arms, and driving through the Czech defence lines we saw soldiers lounging round [sic] haystacks which hid concrete pillboxes. "Bestial people, the Czechs," said Sheean, "they are preparing to defend themselves." At a wayside inn the Czechs clinked their glasses and sang to a tune from La Bohème, "Come in, Adolf, we're ready." The people were splendidly brave. They expected war, and knew what they would suffer during the first months, but they believed that among their great allies the i's were all dotted.

The travelers returned to Prague in time to hear, on Wednesday, September 21, the announcement over loudspeakers in central Prague that President Edvard Beneš had been forced to accept an ultimatum from London and Paris to adjust Czechoslovakia's borders. The streets were flooded with a shocked populace. This wasn't war or invasion—yet—but a wholly independent country had been forced to move its borders to placate the demands of its bullying neighbor. What would be next? If we give a little bit, said many Czechs, would not Hitler simply demand more? The popular broadcaster Raymond Gram Swing of the Mutual Broadcasting Corporation was on vacation in Prague on that fateful night. He and other colleagues found themselves in a hotel with a balcony overlooking Wenceslaus Square. "Suddenly a new sound filled the square. It was a tremendous mechanized voice that emanated from the government's public-address system in the downtown area. It was making the first public announcement of the government's decision to surrender to German demands. The voice said:

> It is not cowardice that has moved our leaders to their decision. This is a decision that has pierced our hearts. Even the bravest man must retreat before the fury of an avalanche. God knows it often

requires more courage to live than to commit suicide. God knows that no honest man can say that we were frightened and cowardly when we authorized the foreign minister to tell France and Britain: "We have chosen to sacrifice ourselves for the peace of the world, just as the Saviour sacrificed Himself for the welfare of mankind."

Later that night, before he began his journey to Vienna, Swing met up with three friends, all Jews—Olga Forrai, the leading soprano of the Prague State Opera, her husband, Frank Demant, and Peter Herman Adler, conductor at the Prague State Opera—to urge them to flee while they had the chance. Who knew when the Germans would arrive? All three agreed and made it to safety in the United States.

Walking through the milling crowds in Wenceslas Square at dusk, Sheean detected not an angry, noisy response but a "general feeling of disillusionment, distrust and unease." Women wept, men sat disconsolately, and young men sang patriotic songs. It was akin to a funeral, and in many respects it was precisely this: the death of a young and democratic state whose life had been extinguished on the altar of ugly, unprincipled realpolitik.

> Never have I seen an assembly of people so instinctively moved to grief. Hope was to revive again later, and again to be betrayed, but on that Wednesday, September 21, the sure instinct of the people perceived the whole tragedy at once and mourned over the passing of their nation.

Perhaps half the population of Prague—as many as 500,000 men, women, and children—flocked to the National Parliament that night, united in peaceful, quiet grief for their collapsing democracy. The preeminent emotion he observed was tearfulness, many "thousands of these people were weeping all through the night. I even saw a policeman in tears."

> Those who witnessed it, in whole or in part, know that it was a truly spontaneous expression of the grief of a people; in years of

experience of such matters I have never seen anything like it. . . .
The cry of the people of Prague on that night was from the heart.

But amidst the anguish existed a determination to fight. Most people expected Prague to be razed to the ground like Guernica, but believed nevertheless that the Czechoslovakian army's thirty-five divisions would put up a strong fight against an advancing German army. The country duly mobilized and prepared for war.

—⁂—

Janet Flanner arrived in Vienna on September 5, 1938, six months after the Anschluss. She wanted to see what effect the German occupation had had on what had once been one of the great capitals of Europe, now relegated to the provincial capital of the Third Reich's latest province of Ostmark. On the surface, not much appeared to have changed. People still drank their hot chocolate in the sidewalk cafés. Few people bothered with the recently imported "Heil Hitler," and on the streets she observed a sense of normalcy. While whipped cream and pastries could still be enjoyed—at a price—in the Viennese cafés, some foodstuffs were already running scarce. It was also clear that Hitler's policy was to win the vast mass of good Aryan workers to his cause:

> Over three hundred thousand modest Viennese, principally of the working class, have already applied for a K.D.F., the midget German motorcar that bears as its name the initials of the Kraft Durch Freude movement it is to exemplify. When it comes out, it will cost only 950 marks, which may be paid in installments of 5 marks weekly. It will go 14 kilometres on a litre of gas and use an eighth of a litre of oil per 100 kilometres. People who earn 500 marks or more monthly will be forbidden to buy the car, which is intended for the small earner. In Vienna, an annual vacation of two weeks with pay has been instituted by the Nazis, and waiters now work nine instead of fourteen hours a day. Hitler's increasing concern for the proletariat generally and his growing harshness

toward their bosses have placated the masses as much as they have frightened the owner class.

The most obvious manifestation of Nazi ideology, however, was a display in the vast Nordwestbahnhalle. It was called "The Eternal Jew":

There prints, photographs, models, electric signs, graphs, fine typography, and sales talks are used not to make consumers buy a product but to make the public boycott a race. There is a movie, with loudspeaker comment, of a kosher calf-killing. There are ethnological wax masks, and photographs of living international and local Jews, the latter grouped according to those spheres of activity the Viennese Jews governed, apparently without the slightest difficulty—the theatre, law, medicine, the dress trade, violin playing, banking, etc. As the founder of Bolschewismus, Karl Marx Mordechai, so-called, gets a whole wall; as, apparently, the equally reprehensible founders of Kapitalismus, the Rothschilds get two walls, one of which displays their increasingly distinguished family tree. Among the pictures of the international intelligentsia to be shunned are portraits of Charles Chaplin, Heine, Mendelssohn . . .

Looking around her in Vienna, Flanner observed that the signs of this ideological racism were now widespread. On shop doors belonging to non-Jewish businesses could be found swastikas, accompanied by a sign announcing ARISCHES GESCHÄFT (ARYAN BUSINESS). Those shops without this ethnic passport were clearly Jewish. Jewish doctors and lawyers were slowly being deprived of their right to practice, although for the time being Flanner was still able to buy from Jewish shops, many of which continued to trade.

—⁂—

Flying into Bad Godesberg on September 22 in his Lockheed Electra, Chamberlain was shocked to discover that Hitler now rejected the arrangement agreed to at Berchtesgaden. Instead of launching plans to deescalate tension, Hitler now ratcheted up the pressure on London and Paris by issuing an outrageously one-sided ultimatum (disguised as a "Memorandum") demanding that the Sudetenland be ceded to Germany no later than September 28. If the Czechs failed to see sense, Germany would intervene to "protect" the Sudetens by force. So much for the agreement the previous week. Hitler wasn't now talking about "adjustment" but wholesale absorption of part of the sovereign territory of Czechoslovakia into the Reich. The terms Hitler insisted upon, of course, all favored Germany. Chamberlain refused. Prague, naturally, also rejected this threat, while France mobilized 600,000 soldiers, and Britain placed the Royal Navy on alert. Perversely and prematurely the German press congratulated Hitler and Chamberlain for their diplomacy, all in the pursuit of avoiding war in Europe. Hitler's reaction to the rejection of the Bad Godesberg proposals led to what Matthew Halton, listening to the German leader talking to a crowd of twenty thousand whipped-up party faithful at the Berlin Sportsplatz on Monday, September 26 (he had flown back from Prague for the occasion), considered "the most impassioned or apoplectic one I ever heard him make, and probably the most lying and ferocious tirade ever made by the head of a State. His body trembled with emotion and he sobbed with melodramatic heartbreak and slavering ferocity . . . [threatening] that Europe had only four more days to live unless his demands were granted."

> "This oaf of a Beneš wants to exterminate the German race," [Hitler] roared brokenly. "He has succeeded to some extent . . . Now comes the day of freedom and revenge. I call you, my Germans! Come with me! March with me! Man for man, woman for woman, raise your hands and swear this sacred oath: Our will shall be stronger than our need and danger. We have decided. We are ready. Let the robber Beneš choose!"

"Sieg Heil! Sieg Heil! Sieg Heil!"
Sick at heart, Bill Shirer in Berlin watched a motorized division lumber through the streets apparently on its way to the east at dusk on Tuesday,

September 27. War seemed close. If Hitler wanted peace, the troops would still be in their barracks. But Shirer was surprised—and pleased—at the lack of any demonstration of support by the Berlin populace:

> I pictured the scenes I had read of in 1914 when the cheering throngs on this same street tossed flowers at the marching soldiers, and the girls ran up and kissed them. The hour was undoubtedly chosen today to catch the hundreds of thousands of Berliners pouring out of their offices at the end of the day's work. But they ducked into the subways, refused to look on, and the handful that did stood at the curb in utter silence unable to find a word of cheer for the flower of their youth going away to the glorious war. It has been the most striking demonstration against war I've ever seen.

It was at Munich, on September 29, that Hitler got what he wanted. Chamberlain and Daladier met with Hitler and Mussolini and agreed that Germany be allowed to take the Sudeten Province from Czechoslovakia. Chamberlain, as Ronald Blythe has observed in *The Age of Illusion*, seemed "privately determined to confront the sordid dictators with the whole armour of a nineteenth-century Christian liberal English gentleman. The pity, of course, was, it was not his own other cheek he turned for the blow." He gave up the strong line he had taken at Bad Godesberg against the Memorandum. The result, as Halton observed, was a pantomime:

> We were begging Hitler to take what he wanted—if only he wouldn't shoot—and Chamberlain was being hailed as nothing less than a saintly knight-errant for doing the begging. Britain and France were imploring Hitler to take those things which would make him master of Europe and make it necessary for Britain and France to prepare for a gigantic conflict in which victory was less certain than in 1938.

On September 30, the Czechs learned that despite their own wishes France and Britain had handed the Sudetenland to Germany. There would be no war, as Czechoslovaks had no choice in the matter: London and Paris had told Prague that if it wished to fight, it would have to do so on its own. Beneš resigned, and the Wehrmacht marched. It was "peace in our time" according to Chamberlain, who was greeted by ecstatic crowds when his Electra 14 touched down in Heston on September 30. Churches had been packed across Britain, people praying for peace. Many in Germany also believed that Chamberlain was right, and thanked God for the peacemakers. But as Shirer, Beattie, and others prophesied loudly and often, the sad truth was that few in the West realized that Munich, far from removing the potential for war, confirmed its imminent prospect. Czechoslovakia was not as far away as Chamberlain supposed, nor was the quarrel of no import. Either London and Paris gave in to Hitler every time the German dictator wanted to secure peace on his one-sided terms, or they would have to fight. Giving in to the tyrant on one occasion would not improve the bully's behavior. It merely forced them to choose whether to continue to give in or to make a stand. It was easy to give in when the interests they were being asked to defend were far off, and separated by vast distances of geography, culture, and history. But when those interests came closer to home, the choice suddenly became much more difficult.

—m—

On September 30, Matthew Halton landed in Regensburg after flying from Paris to London and thence to Berlin, with permission to accompany the German troops preparing to advance into the Sudetenland the following morning. Arriving at the Park Hotel Maximilian after midnight, he noted grimly the line of German jackboots sitting outside each of the hotel doors, waiting to be polished. "The boots of the Prussian grenadiers are clopping down Europe again, but this time unopposed," he told his diary despondently. At dawn, along with Bill Shirer and several other journalists, Halton was collected by black-uniformed SS men and driven down the Danube and through Passau, on their way to the border, and into a new chapter in the history of human aggression. After Passau, they:

continued along the river, then turned into the lush green hills of the Bohemian Forest and hurried towards the frontier where the German troops awaited their signal. We drove through fifty kilometres of mountain villages and through thousands of troops. The slow peasants ploughing on the hillsides and the old men drinking their *helles* or *dunkel* in the roadside inns seemed detached, almost scornful. Over the Christ of a wayside shrine a swastika had been attached, with the words: "In this sign ye shall conquer."

At two o'clock in the afternoon, with Colonel Karl Schoerener and five hundred German troops, we stepped over the frontier into Czechoslovakia. The troops occupied the customs house and dynamited a hole through the tank traps. A pioneer unit with portable electric saws cut through the trees which had been felled across the road and severed the wires of remote-control mines under the bridges. Josef Schwarzbauer, the Sudeten Nazi burgomaster of Sarau, kissed the hand of Colonel Schoerener. Cheering girls and wine-gladdened old men threw flowers and five hundred soldiers had flowers garlanded around their necks.

"The Sudeten Germans had come home," to quote the German papers, or, to be more accurate, the Sudeten Germans had become Reich Germans for the first time since the Holy Roman Empire.

"Heil Grossdeutschland!" shouted the girls. "Sieg Heil! Sieg Heil! Sieg Heil!" "It was an unwritable and unheard-of heart jubilation," raved the German papers the next day, which was somewhat less false than their vicious concoctions during the previous weeks about "indescribable fire, terror and murder in Beneš's Soviet State." The Free Corps of Sudeten Nazis marched with the troops. The leather-faced old Burgomaster Schwarzbauer, dressed in his Sunday black, made a little speech about the "liberation" and another old fellow was so gladdened by liberation or new wine that he had to be carried away.

As dusk fell over Sarau there was the clean nostalgic smell of pines and earth. The soldiers made their bivouacs. An old woman yelled in rage at a goat that would not march, and two soldiers went into the woods with two girls. Three thousand yards away, on the other side of the Moldau River, Czech soldiers were camped, preparing to withdraw the next day. In St. Wenceslas Square in Prague at that moment angry, despairing crowds were shouting: "It is still not too late to give us arms." But the Bohemian bastion was gone, and it was now an utter certainty that "the last war was only the beating of the drums of the storm which was to overwhelm our century."

They returned to Regensburg that evening by bus, Halton sitting with Shirer, both "speechless with gloom."

—m—

On October 4, Jimmy and Dinah Sheean drove the eighty-five miles from Prague to Carlsbad to watch the triumphant entry of the German legions and their Führer. Their journey took them slowly through the marching ranks of the men who only days before had been preparing to repel a German invasion. "The Czech army, retreating down the road, dispirited and not in good order, let us pass with only the cursory glances at our documents," Sheean recalled. "We went through a kind of continuous mob of them of all the different varieties, eating their breakfast and slogging along home. They were an unhappy and beaten lot, beaten without having had the chance even to fight."

Reaching Carlsbad at 9:00 A.M. they were struck by the effort that had been made to welcome the new owners. The town was covered in an explosion of fluttering Nazi flags and vast crowds of delirious inhabitants giving the Nazi salute and nailing swastikas wherever they could. Carloads of German officers crept slowly into the town, surrounded by a small but ecstatic crowd in which young girls were prominent, running forward to offer them flowers. Walking through the town square, the Schmuckplatz, and through the tight, steep streets, the Sheeans were struck by the warmth of the welcome being afforded the new German masters, despite the intermittent drizzle that fell throughout the day. The rain failed to dampen the public display of affection these new members of the Reich showed for the author of their deliverance. Many of the townsfolk were "weeping for sheer joy. 'This is the happiest day of my life,' they told you when you gave them a chance," he said. Those who did not wish to welcome "Hitler as the new master of Europe" made themselves scarce. Preparations for the Führer's arrival went on all morning. Truckloads of infantry arrived, wearing flowers in their helmets and in the ends of their rifles, and courted by girls in the streets eager to touch the hands of a German soldier. More flags were hung and swastikas nailed up. Then in rumbled the light tanks, their tracks clattering on the ancient cobblestones, before the army provided a display of precision goose-stepping to the adulation of the crowd. They had now been told that the Führer himself was on his way. When he finally arrived at 2:00 P.M., accompanied by martial music and steel-helmeted troops lining the streets, "the cheering was continuous," Sheean reported. "We could hear it starting afar off, out of sight, by the Eger bridge presumably, growing stronger as the cars surrounding the Fuehrer pushed their slow and would-be majestic way through the streets." Hitler came into sight, "rigid in his long military coat and cap, his hand at the military salute." For the assembled populace, the cry they had been encouraged to shout rolled out across the square: "*Wir danken unserem Fuehrer* [We thank our leader]," interspersed with the ubiquitous "Sieg Heil, Sieg Heil, Sieg Heil!" Once the cheering had died down—five full minutes of screaming adulation—Hitler spoke, affirming to the Sudetens, "That I would be standing here one day, that I knew."

—m—

In Germany, the Nazi squeeze continued slowly but surely, like the python slowly compressing the life from its prey. Ed Beattie was in Berlin on November 9 to witness the carefully marshaled response by the authorities to the murder in Paris of the young German consul, Ernst von Rath. "They are giving the Tauentzienstrasse a going over" was the phone message he received in his apartment on the Olivaerplatz that evening. Donning his overcoat, he went out to look. It was just after midnight. He walked east for a mile towards the shopping area of the Tauentzienstrasse, full of high-end shops, many owned by members of the Jewish community, the streetlamps casting their eerie glow on the sidewalks. The streets were largely empty, a few late-night drinkers strolling home from the restaurants and beer halls. Most of Berlin was in bed. He could hear the commotion long before he saw it. On the Tauentzienstrasse a gang of men had begun systematically smashing up and looting shops, one after the other. They knew exactly what buildings to attack. When Beattie got there, they were pillaging a famous jewelry shop:

> They had broken through the ornamental night grill on the big window; and were already inside. Somebody had been thoughtful enough to bring along a couple of crowbars, which was fortunate. A lot of the silver pieces like coffee urns and loving cups would have stood up pretty well under ordinary battering.
>
> There were a dozen men and boys at work, smashing every-thing in sight, jumping up and down on the ruins to make sure nothing escaped. Someone concentrated his activities on the big mirrors and the glass showcases, hurling heavy silver pieces at them to make sure they were adequately broken. I saw one man slip some small object into his pockets.
>
> The burglar alarm was ringing steadily, and there were other bells going, on down the street; but of course nobody came.
>
> Twenty or thirty people stood on the pavement outside watching a big policeman who stood helplessly shouting through the window at the wreckers. "My God, are you human?" he was crying. Nobody inside paid any attention to him.

Sickened, Beattie strolled further along the road to where it became the Kurfürstendamm, heading back in the direction of Olivaerplatz. The same systematic, organized looting and despoliation was taking place there too, but on a much larger scale. It was clear that this was organized, centrally controlled pillage, undertaken by members of the SA and Hitler Youth:

The terrace of a Jewish-owned cafe was smeared with some tarry, foul-smelling concoction. Jewish windows as high as two stories above the street were smashed. The stocks in stores were either ruined or looted. If the proprietor lived on the premises and happened to resist, he could always be beaten up.

Somebody set fire to a synagogue, and the Berlin fire department, which is very efficient, saw to it that the flames did not spread to the good Aryan buildings on either side. The fire in the synagogue attracted a lot of the ordinary wreckers, who stood around and chatted gaily and agreed that this was the sort of stuff to give them.

Back on Olivaerplatz he saw that, in his absence, the gangs had looted a grocery, the contents being strewn all over the roadway. "Even the little drug-store, whose proprietor had sometimes given medicine to people who had no money, was wrecked. It was a grand night, all over Germany, for the party riff-raff." The following day he continued to walk the streets:

The next day, they got around to the Unter den Linden shops. In sections like the Grosse Frankfurterstrasse, the gangs went around making sure they had left nothing undone in the darkness. I saw one old Jew, just off Kurfustendamm, chased by about twenty men. It was all in a spirit of good fun, and he was allowed to escape after he had been knocked down a few times. On the Tauentzienstrasse, they carried out the body of a man who had shot himself.

This was all undertaken with no resistance or opposition by ordinary Berliners, the vast majority of whom either felt no compassion for the victims or were too frightened to stand up for them. Beattie saw only one man who made the slightest effort to halt the outrages.

Of course, the Jews lost their shops to "politically reliable" Aryans, and there was an oppressive fine, and they were forced out of homes which were considered too good for them, and they were informed that they were considered incapable of driving a car, and there was forced liquidation of all sorts of valued personal possessions. And they were forced to adopt given names which henceforth would stamp them as Jews. But that was all more or less in the routine.

"The Jews naturally find such a life intolerable and long to emigrate," concluded the writer Lothrop Stoddard. He continued:

> But that is most difficult because they can take almost no money or property with them, and other countries will not receive them lest they become public charges. Their greatest fear seemed to be that they might be deported to the Jewish "reservation" in southern Poland which the German Government is contemplating.
>
> The average German seems disinclined to talk much to the foreign visitor about this oppressed minority. However, I gathered that the general public does not approve of the violence and cruelty which Jews have suffered. But I also got the impression that, while the average German condemned such methods, he was not unwilling to see the Jews go and would not wish them back again. I personally remember how widespread anti-Semitism was under the Empire, and I encountered it in far more noticeable form when I was in Germany during the inflation period of 1923. The Nazis therefore seem to have had a popular predisposition to work on when they preached their extreme anti-Semitic doctrines.
>
> The prevailing attitude toward the Jews in present-day Germany reminds me strongly of the attitude toward the Christian Greeks and Armenians in Turkey when I was there shortly after the World War. The Turks were then in a fanatically nationalistic mood; and, rightly or wrongly, they had made up their minds that the resident Greeks and Armenians were unassimilable elements which must be expelled if they were to realize their goal of a 100 per cent Turkish Nation-State. . . .
>
> In Nazi Germany, the resolve to eliminate the Jews is further exacerbated by theories of race. The upshot, in Nazi circles, is a

most uncompromising attitude. If this is not oftener expressed, the reason is because they feel that the issue is already decided in principle and that elimination of the Jews will be completed within a relatively short space of time. So, ordinarily, the subject does not arise. But it crops up at unexpected moments. For instance, I have been stunned at a luncheon or dinner with Nazis, where the Jewish question had not been even mentioned, to have somebody raise his glass and casually give the toast: Sterben Juden!—"May the Jews Die!"

Stewart Herman observed that, over time, "the anti-Semitic threats of the most virulent Nazi Jew-baiters had been divested of the unreality of prophecy and clothed with the actuality of history. It was not to be expected that the rigours of war would bring any alleviation of the sufferings of the German Jew; but it was not inconceivable that German ingenuity, preoccupied as it was by a full-scale conflict, would have postponed temporarily the pleasure of devising new tortures for a paltry half-million non-Aryans, who were already scared almost to death. On the contrary, the ingenuity and famous organizing ability of the Germans proceeded with the systematic extermination of the Jews just as though it was their only concern."

—◊—

On March 15, 1939, Hitler completed the occupation of Czechoslovakia that he had begun with the post-Munich occupation of the Sudeten provinces. At a stroke the Czechoslovak state established in 1919 was dismembered. This action propelled Europe—and the world for that matter—into the Second World War. Those who had attempted thus far to appease Hitler now realized that they had been wrong. He could not be trusted, as his foreign policy did not follow any rational, observable course (it did, of course, if they had read *Mein Kampf* or the 1920 Program of the National Socialist German Workers' Party, or had bothered to have taken Hitler at his word). Thus, Britain and France were forced to offer Poland guarantees for its own security, which meant that if

Germany continued its process of military aggrandizement, Britain and France were firmly and formally committed to war. It meant that Hitler now had a choice: to give up any further territorial claims or risk war with the West.

George Keenan, a veteran American diplomat well versed in European affairs, had arrived in Prague the day before German troops had converged on the Sudetenland the previous October. His first and over-riding impression of the city had been the widespread weeping among the people crowding Wenceslas Square. In the weeks and months that followed, the loss of Czech freedom was most keenly felt by those whom the Nazi regime hated and were hunting down: socialists, communists, evangelical Christians, social reformers, and Jews, among other opponents of totalitarianism. When, on March 15, 1939, Nazi Germany swallowed up the rump of Czechoslovakia, the first people to seek refuge at the ill-equipped American Legation—not much of which could be given—were those who lived in fear of the Nazi state. Keenan recalled one occasion:

> Two disheveled men, ashy-pale with fear, came up to ask for asylum. They had been Czech spies in Germany, they said, and they were known to the local Gestapo. Their faces were twitching and their lips trembling when I sent them away. They were followed by two German Social Democrats, fugitives from the Reich. They seemed almost dazed with terror. They seemed to accept my statement that I could do nothing for them, but they wouldn't leave. They refused to believe that they had to leave that building, where they still could not be touched, and to go out into the streets where they were no more than hunted animals. A Jewish acquaintance came. We told him that he was welcome to stay around there until he could calm his nerves. He paced wretchedly up and down in the anteroom, through the long morning hours. In the afternoon, he decided to face the music and went home.

The snow was falling thickly on the streets that evening when, at seven o'clock, Keenan went out into the town to see what was going on. People were rushing around aimlessly. The next morning a line of desperate people stretched out of the legation building, far too many for the tiny staff to manage. At 10:00 A.M. the news arrived that German troops were in the city. Keenan went to have a look in the legation car:

> Driving up the hill on the Nerudova, just before my own apart-ment, we met a German armored car stopped in the middle of the narrow street. The driver was evidently trying to find the German legation and had stopped there, by the Italian legation, to ask the way. A crowd of embittered but curious Czechs looked on in silence. The soldier in the turret sat huddled up against the driving snow, nervously fingering the trigger of his machine gun as he faced the crowd.

Seeing German tanks trundling over ancient Prague cobblestones was harrowing, for in the swastika-covered panzers Keenan could see all too clearly the end of the rule of law in central Europe. Without any attempt by those countries strong enough to protect the right of weaker countries to their own sovereignty, further bullying and aggrandizement by Germany could only ensue. By the end of the day Prague's ancient cobblestones reverberated to the sound of hundreds of snow-clad armored vehicles. That night, the only people on the streets were German soldiers, as an 8:00 P.M. curfew forced the frightened populace indoors.

The helplessness many Americans in Europe experienced when faced by the full horror of Nazi aggression was exemplified for Keenan by an experience at the height of the Munich crisis:

> One morning, only three or four days after my arrival, there burst into our office an attractive young lady wearing a collegiate Amer-ican fur coat and tossing, in her indignation, a most magnificent head of golden hair. Without further ado, she proceeded to burn us all up for our sleepy inactivity. The advance of the Germans into the Sudeten area was causing the Czech inhabitants of that region, she said, to flee by the hundreds of thousands. Within a

day or two these hordes would be descending on Prague. No one was making any provision to feed them, to house them, to care for them. It was time for us to bestir ourselves. "Why," she demanded to know, "don't you do something about it?"

It was Martha Gellhorn. Wearily, Keenan attempted to explain that the Legation simply did not have the wherewithal to look after itself, let alone hordes of refugees. But he acknowledged that Gellhorn was right. What was America doing? Did it think it could simply wash its hands of state-sponsored iniquity when that iniquity was being levied on people in a land far away and therefore of no moral responsibility for Americans? Gellhorn thought not, and Keenan agreed. In Prague in March 1939, however, he lacked the wherewithal to do much more than protect himself, let alone the hundreds of thousands who now found themselves at the mercy of Nazi terror.

The occupation of the remainder of Czechoslovakia and its subsequent dismemberment was, Keenan considered, an utterly foolish move by the German leader, because it made slaves of the Czechs. In asserting pan-Germanism Hitler and his Nazi cronies had given no thought to what the *Untermenschen* would think when they suddenly found themselves to be slaves. What was certain was that they would not take this newly imposed, uninvited status lying down. Indeed, as the Germans in 1939 and 1940 had no interest in the survival of the Czechs as a race, nation, or even functioning state, their "brutal and reckless destruction of the status quo" created determined enemies in the Czechs. His reports to Washington described "the utter failure of the Germans to win any sympathy among the Czech population; the growing bitterness and cynicism of those Czechs whom the Germans left, almost contemptuously, as helpless figureheads in the Protectorate government; the shameless financial corruption and economic plundering of the province by the new German masters; and finally, the establishment in the minds of the Czechs of the possibility of a world war as the only hope for liberation and a better future." His warnings were prescient, not just for the future of Czechoslovakia but for all countries that were to have the misfortune to be overrun by the Wehrmacht and subsequently administered by the Nazi machine. "Time and again," he wrote, "I was forced to emphasize this psychological failure of the Germans, and its significance not just for the future of this particular area but for the prospects of a successful Nazi hegemony in Europe generally . . . Inflation, impoverishment, economic disruption, bitterness, lack of confidence, and the moral disintegration of public administration can reap no good harvest either for victors or vanquished. . . ."

In May 1939, only two months after the occupation, he warned that:

> . . . the Germans will find themselves forced in the end to sweep away the last figments of Czech autonomy, to place their reliance solely on their bayonets and to attempt to crush by sheer force the powerful Czech nationalism which they have hitherto tried to exploit. In this case, it is outright war: an undeclared war in which imprisonments, shootings, deportations, intimidation, and bribery on the one side would be pitted against passive resistance, sabotage, espionage, and conspiracy on the other. If it comes to this, the Germans will probably hold the upper hand without undue difficulty as long as the broad basis of National Socialist power remains intact. But they will have no happy time of it, and if the tide ever turns, Czech retaliation will be fearful to contemplate.

In Prague, the summer was full of the sort of portents that would have had medieval priests hastening to their knees. Frequent and destructive electrical storms swept the country, causing massive destruction to harvests. Society was crippled, a paralysis overcoming the people as they awaited the next calamity:

> Everything is in suspense. No one takes initiative; no one plans for the future. Cultural life and amusements continue in a half-hearted, mechanical spirit. Theaters and public amusements attract only scanty and indifferent crowds. People prefer to sit through the summer evenings in the beer gardens or the little parks along the rivers, to bandy the innumerable rumors in which they

themselves scarcely believe, and to wait with involuntary patience for the approach of something which none of them could quite describe but which they are all convinced must come and must affect all their lives profoundly.

The future for Czechoslovakia under German military rule soon became clear. At the daily press conference for foreign journalists in Berlin on November 18, 1939, it was announced matter-of-factly that nine Czech students at the University of Prague had been shot. "Why?" asked Bill Shirer. The question bored the German spokesman, who replied that the students had staged anti-German demonstrations in Prague on October 28 and November 15. He added, as if these effete American liberals with their discredited notions of individual liberty had no idea of the social discipline required of a nation-under-arms, "There can be no joking in war-time." Later in the day the Germans announced that three more Czechs, two of them policemen, had been shot for "attacking a German." "I would bet my shirt," observed Shirer, "that in the twenty years that three million Sudeten Germans lived under Czech rule not a single one of them was ever executed for taking part in any kind of demonstration." The killings had begun, and in the full light of the international press, the Nazis were not ashamed.

CHAPTER FOUR

"A Long, Agonizing Illness"

T o most North American observers in 1939, London—the largest city in the world, with a population of some eight million—was a hive of confusion. No one knew what Hitler's real intentions were, and the dominant political agenda was to do anything to keep the little man with the comical mustache happy. Certainly, no one wanted another war. Those who called for rearmament were lazily dubbed "warmongers," and the few who opposed the government's policy of appeasement—something accepted by most of Westminster and the vast bulk of the population—were considered nutcases. The noisy Conservative, Winston Churchill, was the most prominent of a tiny few who, in Parliament and the civil service, saw the looming storm clouds for what they were. The problem with London, considered Martha Gellhorn, was that the people seemed to have no idea of the danger they were in.

When Virginia Cowles arrived in 1937, an article she had written on the situation in Spain for the *Times*—which was editorially in support of the principle of appeasement if it served to prevent Britain from going back to war—caught the eye of Sir Robert Vansittart, permanent Under-Secretary of State for Foreign Affairs in the Foreign Office. One of the loudest anti-appeasement voices in the British government, his admonitions made him one of a few in London arguing against negotiating a compromise with Hitler. He agreed with Cowles's argument that allowing Germany and Italy to wage war unchecked in Spain was tantamount to letting the bully terrorize the playground. Indeed, he considered British neutrality on Spain to be craven, because Britain chose not to police the Non-Intervention Agreement it had signed with Italy, Germany, Russia, and other European countries in August 1936, while Germany, Italy, and Russia, in the full lens of world publicity, blatantly ignored it. Vansittart's philosophy was that described by Ronald Blythe in *The Age of Illusion*: "Ever since the advent of Hitler the Government's policy had been that of the man busy stamping out such sparks and brands of his maniacal neighbour's bonfire as should drift into his garden. There was never the ghost of an attempt to dowse the bonfire itself or restrain the incendiary neighbour. Out of such rooted cravenness bloomed the dead nettle of Munich and the policy of non-intervention." International law, not to mention the safety of any states unable to defend themselves against an aggressor willing to use force against them, was equally threatened. Germany and Italy were "trying to lead the world back to the Dark Ages," Vansittart told Cowles. "And if we don't wake up in time, here in England, they may succeed in doing it." Cowles recognized that his—as well as Churchill's—voice was being drowned out by the noise of those who believed that peace needed to be given a chance, and at a price that preserved the safety of the majority. Unfortunately this approach served merely to embolden Hitler, who increasingly saw what the threat of violence could achieve in the face of political timidity. The direct consequence of this pusillanimity in 1936 was the sacrifice of Austria, then Czechoslovakia, and finally Poland. The route to war was, in retrospect, given the green light by British and French cowardice with respect to the issue of neutrality in Spain. Vansittart was unable to swim against the current of lawlessness sweeping the Continent, and he was removed from his job as head of the Foreign Office at the end of 1937.

Britain's problem was that vast swathes of opinion makers had fallen for the rubric that suggested that rearmament would invariably lead to war, while simultaneously divorcing themselves from any comprehension of the motives and inclinations of the users of force. Put another way, the argument was that the possession of strong armed forces would invite retaliation, and therefore be the progenitor of war, not its eradicator. What the advocates of this belief failed to appreciate was that in the hands of a free and democratic nation, strong armed forces serve as a deterrent to aggression. Strong military forces in a peaceful country on the whole mean more, not less, peace, while strong armed forces in a country in which peace is not valued will invariably have dangerous consequences. A country inevitably makes itself weaker if it cannot respond to military aggression by another. To counter threats, military power needs to be sufficient to deter a potential aggressor. It is important that a rational decision maker is never given a positive answer to the question, Do I think I can gain an advantage by my neighbors' military weakness or unpreparedness? In other words, equality in the balance of power is required. The Labour Party, for instance, campaigning in the British 1935 general election, used the slogan "Armaments Mean War—Vote Labour" and in 1938 used the similar slogan "Stop War. Vote Labour." It was well meaning but completely wrong, a denial of the experience of history and a profoundly erroneous view of the reality of human nature. Dorothy Thompson saw this clearly in 1934, when she observed that one of the most dangerous illusions in the Anglo-Saxon mind was "that all peoples love liberty, and that political liberty and some form of representative government are indivisible." Many centuries of political culture in both Britain and America, where individual liberty was the fountainhead of social existence, had blinded both peoples to the reality that not everyone thought like them. This was the fundamental error at the heart of British policy making in the 1930s, an error built on the remarkably widespread influence of pacifism in the period, a characteristic it shared with the United States and France. In 1939 the imbalance of power in Europe was such that the aggressor nations—Germany, Italy, and the USSR—were emboldened by the pacific nature of the European democracies, which smaller nations had trusted for their defense. The politics of wishful thinking would never survive in a collision with a Nazi worldview built on completely different principles.

—∞—

When Martha Gellhorn arrived in Britain on assignment for *Collier's* magazine, she was asked to write an article on the attitude of ordinary people to the threat of war. Virginia Cowles accompanied her on a journey around the country, asking this question. The dominant response was incredulity. Why would there be war? The nasty Mr. Hitler might provoke conflict on the Continent, but why should it involve Britain? It was a faraway drama, they were told, to be fought out by belligerents in countries whose names Britons couldn't spell. Any idea that the beating of these far-off war drums represented an existential struggle for the future of democratic freedoms the world over played no part in the public conversation about government policy:

> To direct questions, such as "Would you fight for Czechoslovakia?" we received a confusion of replies. The waiters in a cafe in Leeds said they would fight if the Government had signed any obligations, but had the Government signed obligations?

Martha was furious with this wooly thinking, and could not understand why Britons everywhere were not up in arms to defend the rights of fellow workers in Spain, Austria, and Czechoslovakia, who did not enjoy the freedoms to which they—in Britain—had long been accustomed. Where was their feeling for their fellow man?

—∞—

The gorgeous weather across western Europe during the summer of 1939 extended to Berlin, the warm sun bathing the city in its soft, tranquil rays, belying the violent darkness of the political atmosphere as the German government thundered threats against the grotesque mistreatment of German interests by the criminally minded government in Warsaw. How many innocent Germans were fated to die cruel and barbaric deaths at the hands of illiterate, uncivilized Poles while Germany stood idly by? Wodan's war drums continued to hammer their insistent beat, loudly seeking revenge for the humiliation of Versailles: the wicked treatment of the German minority by the Poles, which was caused by the illegal division of Europe in 1919, was the casus belli. The emasculation of Germany after the Great War had been an outrageous piece of revenge politics, so went the argument, which had resulted in millions of pure-born Germans being subjected to low-born slave masters in an oppressive Slav state. Natural justice demanded that this intolerable situation be reversed. Berlin was offering the Poles the opportunity to do so voluntarily. If not, the threats were clear to those who listened carefully enough. The manufactured hysteria describing "Last Warnings," "Unendurable Outrages," and "Murderous Poles" had been splashed over the front pages of the newspapers for much of the year. There is no doubt that the Polish mobilization in April had exacerbated the mud-slinging, although by late August most newspaper-reading Germans were exhausted by this talk of war.

On June 18, 1939, the 23-year-old Joseph Kennedy Jr., son of the American ambassador to Great Britain, wrote to his father from Berlin, during a visit to Germany:

> One is immediately impressed here by the lack of talk about war. In nearly every other place I have been this is the only conversation but here they appear unconcerned about it. It seems it was the same way in September. The propaganda on encirclement is very strong and may serve [to unite] Germany as sanctions did in Italy. The material condition of the people seems nominally good. There is a shortage of coffee and they say flour is difficult to obtain. It is hard if you are entertaining to get good things and in large enough quantities. However, it is far from bad and it is thought that they are canning tremendous amounts in case of war. Although there is grumbling amongst the workers there seems no possibility of any [kind] of a revolt even if they were led

into war. In the last analysis the German does what he is told. As far as I can gather the average German is very much against the policies of the Nazis—and the German worker complains of the numerous taxes he has to pay. Also there are collections from time to time in the restaurants by the brown shirts which takes more and more from them. Hitler is regarded by many people as a God and there is no doubt of the difference between him and the rest.

There is a tendency with the terrific shortage of labor to replace most of the easy positions by women. A young girl who wanted to take a vacation the other day went to police headquarters to get her visa and was asked whether she was working or not. She said no that she was on a vacation. They said get a job in two weeks or we will get you one.

I should think Hitler is backed by at least 80% of the people. Many of them disagree with the policy against the Jews but on the whole are with him.

That seemed to be the crux of the entire problem.

For William Russell, a consular official in the American embassy, the onward march towards war had an awful inevitability about it. In the first days of September, Berlin was caught up in a confusing cacophony of war talk, war preparations, rumor and counter-rumor. While *hausfrauen* (housewives) ran from shop to shop stocking up on the foodstuffs they expected soon to be in scarce supply, tanks, trucks, and artillery pieces rumbled through the city as the barracks emptied. In the clear blue sky overhead, Luftwaffe transports lumbered, fighters swooped, and scores of black-crossed bombers droned purposefully eastwards, flying in precise, silvery formations towards destinations at which those observing on the ground could only guess. The air was so thick with aircraft that it seemed to Russell that all the bombers in the world had congregated to fill the air above the city. At the railway stations, anxious foreigners struggled to find seats on the trains heading north, south, and west, to Denmark, Holland, France, and Switzerland. Scattered clumps of children stood waiting calmly for their evacuation trains, blue labels hung neatly around their necks, as weeping mothers and stoical fathers said farewell to their progeny.

In the absence of real news—other than the crass propaganda that filled the papers, which most people, even the most heavily indoctrinated, regarded for what it was—rumors flourished. Frightened, ignorant, the people waited fearfully for what was to come. "Oh, Herr Russell, what are they thinking of?" his maid, Hana, exclaimed to him one day. "Are they all crazy? What do we Germans want with another war, what will we do if war comes?" He could only answer that war seemed inevitable, despite his German acquaintances on the street, such as the traffic policeman who always had a comment on the political issues of the day, insisting that the genius Führer—who of course only wanted peace (was he not always telling them so?)—would sort it all out somehow. But to Russell—like Cowles—the signs all pointed in one direction, and one direction only. One giveaway was that throughout the tumult, the discordant sounds of Richard Wagner constantly filled the airwaves. *Gotterdammerung* seemed an apt summation of the atmosphere. William Shirer noted that no one outside Germany ever understood the effect the music of this man had on the Nazi spirit. It provided a cacophonic backdrop to war. "Whenever it was necessary to rouse the people into a fighting spirit, German radio stations trotted out their most stirring recordings of Wagner," argued Russell. "Blustering old Wagner, as German as any German, with his violins shouting and his horns locking with each other."

Russell's job in the American embassy gave him a grandstand view of the Nazi state's policy regarding the unwanted of Europe, as the racial detritus of Germany—primarily Jewish—washed up on his doorstep in the Immigration Section. People wanted to flee to America at this early stage in the war not necessarily because they had been threatened with violence but because of the repeated, low-level harassment they suffered merely by attempting to live. "Nothing was too petty for the mighty German government so long as it could do some harm to a harried Jew," he observed:

The Germans practiced persecution not only by committing the major crimes at which they were past masters—murder, unjust imprisonment, arson, robbery. The Nazi government stooped to the smallest things: petty persecutions such as special yellow park benches for Jews to sit on; special restricted shopping hours for Jews, special laws for Jews; newspapers attacking Jews, which were pasted up on bulletin boards all over Germany. As terrible as were the beatings and the killings, I sometimes thought that it was the little things which hurt the average Jew most. One day he was a respected citizen of Germany; the next day he had to pack his belongings and move on somewhere.

—⚝—

Howard K. Smith returned to Berlin from a stay in London on New Year's Day, 1940. His first impression on returning to the German capital was that unlike the confused and chaotic London he had just left, Berlin had slipped calmly and easily into the war. From what he could see, the city was organized and disciplined, its people obedient and dutiful. It was as though being at war was a natural, expected state. Under the circumstances, and considering six years of relentless propaganda, this was not surprising. In his absence seven million German men had been mobilized for the war against Poland, and the impact on the streets seemed wholly unnoticeable. His heart sank when he realized the truth of the words spoken to him by a German officer, with whom he was walking down Unter den Linden: "Look around you, Herr Smith. Nowhere a sign of war. Not the slightest difference from two years ago. Is that not the best argument for our strength? We shall never be beaten."

In his diary, Bill Shirer charted the march to war in Berlin throughout August 1939. He noticed a remarkable dichotomy in the minds of the people. On the one hand, they did not want war, as Joe Kennedy Jr. had noted earlier in the year, and believed their Führer's repeated protestations of peace. But on the other, they had begun to absorb the belligerence—and intransigence—of their leaders. They also believed in the manifest destiny of Germany to dominate Mittel-Europa—mid-Europe—and in recent years under their Führer they had, in the words of Lothrop Stoddard, "marched with giant strides toward the realization of one of their oldest dreams . . ." On August 9, Shirer had a conversation with an old acquaintance, a man who had fought in the Great War. Initially opposed to war, the veteran seemed suddenly to have drunk from the Nazi cup:

> He became violent today at the very mention of the Poles and British. He thundered: "Why do the English butt in on Danzig and threaten war over the return of a German city? Why do the Poles provoke us? Haven't we the right to a German city like Danzig?"
> "Have you a right to a Czech city like Prague?" I asked. Silence. No answer. That vacant stare you get on Germans.
> "Why didn't the Poles accept the generous offer of the Führer?" he began again.
> "Because they feared another Sudetenland, Captain."
> "You mean they don't trust the Führer?"
> "Not much since March 15," I said, looking carefully around before I spoke such blasphemy to see I was not being overheard. Again the vacant German stare.

"Embattled Poland was the last local obstacle to Mittel-Europa," observed Stoddard, who spent three months in Germany from late October 1939. "By a series of amazing diplomatic victories, Adolf Hitler had taken all the other hurdles without firing a shot. This led the average German to believe that the Fuehrer would complete the process without recourse to arms."

The parallels with Czechoslovakia would have been uncanny had it not been obvious that Berlin's pattern of threats and intimidation to foreign states she was trying to cow followed a distressingly similar pattern. The newspapers first cried out all sorts of absurd indignities against the enemy, accusations, brazen for their falseness, in which the truth was subverted for a lie. On August 10, for instance, Shirer noted the newspaper headlines:

ANSWER TO POLAND, THE RUNNER AMOK AGAINST PEACE AND RIGHT
IN EUROPE!

WARSAW THREATENS BOMBARDMENT OF DANZIG—UNBELIEVABLE
AGITATION OF THE POLISH ARCHMADNESS!

Two weeks later the propaganda continued to pour out:

COMPLETE CHAOS IN POLAND—GERMAN FAMILIES FLEE—POLISH
SOLDIERS PUSH TO EDGE OF GERMAN BORDER

THIS PLAYING WITH FIRE GOING TOO FAR—THREE GERMAN PAS-
SENGER PLANES SHOT AT BY POLES—IN CORRIDOR MANY GERMAN
FARMHOUSES IN FLAMES

Shockingly, most Germans, including his friend the Great War
veteran, believed this nonsense. On August 11 Shirer visited the Free
City of Danzig (Gdansk), and despite the huge volume of military traffic
on the streets of the old seaport reported that "the local inhabitants
don't think it will come to war. They have a blind faith in Hitler that he
will effect their return to the Reich without war." The people certainly
wanted to be allied to Germany, but not at the expense of war or the
loss of Polish trade.

Shirer's view was that Poland—like Czechoslovakia before it—was
threatened with extinction as long as she presented herself as a threat to
a resurgent Germany. Hitler simply could not have a strong Poland—
or a strong Hungary, Romania, or Yugoslavia, for that matter—on
his eastern border. Berlin's demand to regain sovereignty of Danzig
in the cause of pan-Germanism was partly a pretext for subjugating
the threats against her to the east, but also a genuine expression of the
long-term Nazi demand for *Lebensraum*.

On August 23, the entire world changed. The Nazi-Soviet Pact was
announced to the amazement of everyone outside of Hitler's inner
circle. The Soviet Union had always been the "evil empire," and to
find one's country allied to its erstwhile and bitter enemy was, at the

very least, confusing. But it was immensely popular, especially with the traditionally left-leaning working classes, principally because the people assumed that it meant the absence of war on two fronts, ever the haunting specter of German strategy. People began visibly to relax, and to enjoy the uncommonly hot weather.

But for Shirer, the signs continued to point unerringly to war. The bar at the Hotel Adlon on the Unter den Linden was empty, the last of the British journalists having left the city. Another was the implementation of strict rationing, which began on Monday, August 28. "This will also arouse the people from their apathy," he thought, noticing that Hitler had suddenly begun to ramp up the warnings about the state of the international situation. Food was severely rationed: meat, 700 grams per week; sugar, 280 grams; marmalade, 110 grams; coffee or substitute, one eighth of a pound per week. As for soap, 125 grams were allotted to each person for the next four weeks.

From then on it became difficult to hide the preparations for war. The big question for Shirer and the handful of American journalists in Berlin was whether France and Britain would stand by their promises to Poland after the way they had behaved towards Czechoslovakia the previous year. Troops filled the streets in a variety of commandeered nonmilitary transports, all heading east. The centers of power on Wilhelmstrasse sought to alleviate the fears of their western neighbors—Belgium, Holland, Luxembourg, and Switzerland—by assuring them that their neutrality was sacrosanct. By Tuesday, August 29, Shirer reported a dramatic shift of public morale from elation at the prospect of no war to abject dejection at the near certainty that war was imminent. Hitler had now escalated his demands, just as he had done with Czechoslovakia, noisily demanding the return to Germany of not just Danzig and the Corridor but all ex-German territories ceded to Poland by Versailles. Carefully controlled by Goebbels, the newspapers provided a daily barometer of the temperature of war. Hitler formed a war cabinet. The news arrived that the Poles had ordered a general mobilization. By all objective means, war looked daily more inevitable, although the desperation of the people to avoid another conflict seemed to rise in direct proportion to the belligerency of the news reports. How, Shirer thought on the morning of August 31, could a country with a people so resolutely set against war, do so? He was soon to have his answer.

—⁂—

Matthew Halton was on holiday on the shore of Lake Annecy when he read one morning in *Le Petit Dauphinois* that "the German Foreign Office announces that Herr von Ribbentrop will go to Moscow to conclude a non-aggression pact with Russia." In an instant he realized what it meant: Germany was securing its eastern flank in order to do what it wished with Poland. Germany was about to go to war.

> My first thought was of my two young brothers, ripe for this war, and of an older brother, who had been ripe for the other. The next was of my daughter in London. I looked at three Dewoitine aircraft which were skimming the lake; and decided we could go rowing once more, and perhaps have lunch on the dark, cool, wooded point half a mile away. Then I telephoned to Annecy for reservations on the night train to Paris, and we went upstairs to pack our bags.
>
> "Is there such a rush?" my wife asked.
>
> "Just a war, that's all; perhaps before we get to London."
>
> "We shall fight, of course?"
>
> "Oh, yes. . . . By God, we're finished if we don't!"

On their way to London the Haltons had a last look around Paris, sure that all the omens spelled war:

> Paris was beautiful that day, and completely calm. We went into the Louvre for a last look at the Winged Victory. For the last time we paused in the Tuileries Gardens to look at Gambetta's statue and read [George Danton's] . . . words: "L'audace, encore l'audace et toujours l'audace!" . . . and the day has come. We gazed for the last time at the matchless view of Place de la Concorde and Champs-Elysees. We walked all the way to the Luxembourg Gardens and for the last time had coq au vin at Ducottet's in the Street of St. Bernard's Ditches. We walked all day, indefatigable, bemused. A

last visit to Ste. Chapelle. Then a taxi to the Gare du Nord, just to watch the women of France saying good-bye to their men.

—ᵐ—

A week or so before the Haltons fled France, Virginia Cowles took the train to Berlin. She wanted to gauge the temperature at the heart of the Nazi state for herself, staying at the famous Hotel Adlon on the Unter den Linden, where all other foreign journalists in this city of four million met to talk, eat, drink, and exchange gossip. She had never visited Berlin before, and was struck by a feeling of menace in the air. "The pavements were crowded with uniforms and the streets resounded to the sound of tanks and armored cars," she recorded. "Even the somber grey buildings had a forbidding look." It was a strong contrast to the still gay atmosphere in Paris. Instinctively she considered Germany to be the enemy of world peace. Although she was far from home, she concluded that Czechoslovakian sovereignty was no different from American sovereignty. An attack by Hitler on one country in contravention of its independence represented a threat to the very foundation stone of all free states.

The lobby of the Adlon was filled with brown and black uniforms, and although in the Grill Room, where the foreigners congregated, conversation was loud and febrile, the atmosphere was uncomfortable. Cowles was conscious always of "guarded conversations and a feeling of being watched. Most of the telephones were tapped and you could often hear the click of the recording machines." Russell concurred. The principal impression of his several years of working in Nazi Germany was "the fear, the continual whisper, look over your shoulder before you speak, whisper, whisper, whisper. This nation-wide fear discourages any attempt to form a secret movement within the Reich. A man who fears that the Gestapo has information concerning his telephone calls, the contents of his letters, his private conversations with supposed friends—whether he is actually guilty of any wrongdoing or not—hesitates to work secretly against the Nazis. He is afraid that his first slip, however small, will result in his arrest and that the Nazis will use all of their accumulated Gestapo information to put him away permanently."

The time she spent in Berlin was sufficient for Cowles to dismiss the claim that Hitler was attempting to defend Germany from those wishing to ravish her. Hitler's plans for Europe had nothing to do with defending the culture of Western civilization from the bolshevist barbarians of the East. The threat of bolshevism, she argued in her newspaper column, was to the Nazi regime merely an excuse; an ideological "straw man," a smoke screen for something entirely ulterior—namely, the expansion of Germany in Europe at the expense of her neighbors. Was war coming? Unless Britain and France stood together to protect those states unable to protect themselves against Germany's threats and bullying, it was inevitable. She would describe the terrible twelve months that led to September 3, 1939, as a long, agonizing illness in the body politic of European democracy, when "every type of medicine—hope, treachery, idealism and compromise—were feverishly injected in her veins in a desperate attempt to keep her alive. Her recovery at Munich was an artificial one. After that she went into a coma and a year later died." The truth of Nazi ambitions was observed by Lothrop Stoddard in 1940:

> Not once did I hear a single German, high or low, rich or poor, suggest even in the most confidential talk that the Reich should throw up the sponge and accept peace terms in accordance with British and French war aims. To give up Poland, Czechoslovakia, and Austria, for example, seems to most Germans quite impossible. By gaining control over these lands, the Germans believe they have got what they have long wanted—an unshakeable economic and political supremacy in Central Europe.

—◆—

In London at the end of August Matthew Halton found himself walking with Viscount Cecil through St. James's Park, a delightfully bucolic scene. "Ducks squabbled under the little bridge; flamingoes poised themselves on one leg with disdainful grace; pelicans gazed solemnly at the white towers of Westminster Abbey. Children raced between the thick velvet lawns and bugles rang from the nearby barracks of the

Household Cavalry. Visible over the Admiralty Arch, Nelson squinted from his pedestal in Trafalgar Square; and in the Horse Guards Parade water bubbled from the little memorial fountain with its inscription, "Blow out, ye bugles, over the rich dead . . ." The conversation with Lord Cecil was about the epitaph that would soon be written to the disastrous end to two decades of the failed policy of appeasement. "Perhaps the coming war will teach the world," he mused, "that mankind's first line of defense is its conscience, and that principles are more potent than guns. Hitler can be defeated now only by guns. It may teach us to put force in the hands of law."

—∞—

On the morning of September 2, 1939, Russell stood in the windows of his office in the US embassy on Pariser Platz. Unable to leave their offices, the clerks opened the windows, to allow them to lean out and hear the loudspeakers relay what the country had been told would be an important announcement from their Führer. The speakers had been temporarily erected for the occasion, in the expectation perhaps that vast crowds would fill the sun-kissed streets to worship their leader. But this was not 1914, and the streets and the neighboring Tiergarten were empty. The consular staff had no radio in the office, but the quality of the loudspeakers in the street enabled them to hear the Voice clearly when the manufactured adulation in the Reichstag finally died down. The Americans had watched him drive past a short while before, a few of them suddenly guessing at the full import of what they were watching. Some continued to type away regardless, unaware of the true significance of the events unfolding around them. How on earth did this warmonger get away with it? Russell wondered. The relentless march to war, led by the heavy beating of the Nazi drum while the helpless populace was swept along by circumstances now completely out of their control, made him determined to see Hitler punished. "I had witnessed three years of his terror, his pettiness, his cruelty, his negation of every human advance. He and his heavy-booted gang had lorded it over the rest of the people far too long." Before the nation's leader came on air, the encouraging sounds of martial music reverberated through the streets, seeming to bounce off the wide boulevards and reverberate against the classical buildings of old Berlin. Then the music stopped. After a silence a tired, rasping voice began to speak. Repeating the oft-said lies of the brutalities meted out to German nationals in Poland, the same accusations levied against Czechoslovakia the previous year, Hitler told "his Germans" (as he was wont to describe them), together with the waiting world, that history was in the process of wiping out the injustices of Versailles: "Germany has answered Poland's aggression with action. Since early this morning German armed forces have been moving into Polish territory." His voice now rising to a crescendo, he barked:

> I have put on the uniform of a soldier. It will not be taken off until Germany is victorious. If I should fall on the battlefield, Hermann Goering is to be my successor. If Hermann Goering should fall, Rudolf Hess will be your leader.

At this the old formula played itself out.

"Deutschland Sieg Heil!" cried the four hundred Nazi-buttonholed members of the Reichstag in orchestrated union.

"Sieg"

"Heil!"

"Sieg"

"Heil!"

"That is how a dictator country goes to war," concluded Russell despondently. "Three 'Heils' and the discussion was over. . . ."

The embassy staff went quietly to their desks. There was no excited chatter or conversation. In the blue skies outside it was as though nothing had changed. In Poland that morning, of course, it was obvious, as the Wehrmacht rolled east, with bombers overhead, soldiers tramping along dusty roads and tanks crawling across the harvested fields, that everything now was different. Very different. That night the first blackout descended on Berlin, the populace warned of counter-strikes by waves of vengeful Polish bombers. The sirens went off first at 7:00 P.M., people scurrying to the shelters. It was a false alarm.

Strangely, Berliners did not feel particularly threatened. After the alert the streets and bars, cafés and restaurants were crowded, people talking excitedly about this change to their lives. Finishing a live broadcast at 2:30 A.M. (Saturday, September 2), Shirer struggled to make his way home through the unexpected darkness, groping through the pitch-black streets, guided by the vague light of the whitewashed curbstone. After a troubled night's sleep he awoke to bright sunshine and two questions. First, did any Polish bombers get through last night? Apparently not. Second, how would Britain and France react to this blatant Nazi aggression against a sovereign state, one whose security they had committed to protect? The greatest fear for Russell, Shirer, and many others was that the democracies would turn their backs on Poland and allow the aggressor to triumph, as they had with Czechoslovakia. Russell said farewell to one of his friends, a Canadian trade commissioner, who was leaving the country. "Maybe you'll be back in a few days," Russell said. "I wouldn't come back," he answered. "If we don't keep our word this time I would be ashamed to be seen here." On Saturday, September 2, Shirer worried that with the German attack on Poland two days old, Britain and France might yet attempt to renege on their commitments.

—◊—

The clouds scudded across the bright blue summer sky far above the city, without the faintest hint of Polish aircraft engines bringing retribution for the German "counteroffensive" that had started two days before. It was the morning of Sunday, September 3, 1939, a balmy, late-summer Sabbath. People walked slowly in family groups across the paths, gardens, lakes, and parks that dotted the center of the old Prussian capital, as they did every Sunday. To look at them, however, one would not think that Germany was at war with Poland. The only concession to the current war setting was the activity around the Bahnhofs. Two chartered railway coaches, every nook and cranny packed with departing American women and children and their luggage, left the Stettiner Bahnhof for Copenhagen. At the same time, the Berlin railway stations were packed with hundreds of young Berliners with blue tags around their necks, awaiting trains to lead them to the safety of the countryside as a precaution against Polish air attack.

In the city center Bill Shirer stood and looked up impotently at the sky, willing the sound of Polish bombers overhead, as the screeching newssheets spoke of military victories to the east. There was still nothing from London and Paris. He didn't want to admit it, but it seemed clear that the appeasers had won, as they had triumphed all too often before. Warsaw would go the way of Prague and Vienna. War was too high a price to pay for protecting the principle that sovereignty among nations was sacrosanct. Two days had passed since the first German troops began crossing the frontier. The assurances given to Poland by Britain and France appeared as worthless as those France gave to Czechoslovakia.

Shortly after noon, the loudspeakers placed along the Wilhelmstrasse were switched on, and an announcer gave the news to a bewildered and silent crowd of some 250 people out on their Sabbath-day strolls that England had declared war on Germany. They had done it! Shirer didn't feel jubilant, but he was certainly relieved. This, finally, was the end of appeasement. Britain and France had realized the truth of what Leland Stowe had insisted back in 1933, namely that Germany wanted war, and that the only way to prevent her achieving this design was to threaten her with fast, painful, retaliatory action, the strategic principle of deterrence. The story slowly emerged. At 9:00 A.M. that morning, Sir Nevile Henderson, the British ambassador, gave the German government two hours to accept the demand to withdraw her troops from Poland, having called on Ribbentrop and handing him a note giving Germany until 11:00 A.M. to do so. Henderson was glum. He had sought and advocated appeasement, expecting Germany to respond positively to the doves of peace dispatched repeatedly from London over recent years, and advising the Foreign Office that if London treated Hitler "as a pariah or mad dog we shall turn him finally and irrevocably into one." He was politely ushered from the building, returning at 11:00 A.M. to receive the German reply. He was to be disappointed. The British demand had been refused. By 11:15 A.M., London declared war.

In Paris, Robert Murphy was sitting with Ambassador William Bullitt when in walked Madame Geneviève Tabouis, a famous (if not notorious, at least in some circles) contrarian. Her recent career as a journalist (she was foreign editor of *L'œuvre*) had been to warn of the threat of fascism, and especially that of the rise of a militarily resurgent Germany. Like many others, her insistence that France act to prevent the German takeover of Czechoslovakia had branded her, ironically, as a warmonger. Warned that Chamberlain was going to announce at 11:00 A.M. whether Germany had responded to a formal note demanding withdrawal of troops from Poland, the radio has just been switched on. So it was that the people of Europe, if they were tuned in to the BBC, heard the slow and uninspiring tones of the British prime minister announcing that Britain and Germany were now at war. Like Ambassador Henderson in Berlin, Chamberlain was also glum, his hard-fought policy of appeasement crashing around him in ignominy. Within minutes the first air-raid siren began to wail over London, sending millions of people scurrying for cover. When the sirens sounded, the American ambassador, Joseph Kennedy, was preparing to leave the embassy to drive to the Houses of Parliament. The embassy did not have an air-raid shelter, so everyone rushed to the building across the street, the temporary home of the couturier Edward Molyneux, which had a basement. "A number of Americans started right then and there to holler for boats," he observed, "and a lot of women were panicky." It was, of course, a false alarm. Such was the hype that had been whipped up about the nature of modern warfare that many believed that the clouds would be instantly dark with enemy bombers. That reality would have to wait until September the following year. Howard Smith, in London when the announcement was made, was rushed into "an underground dance-hall by a zealous air-raid warden who had apparently read all the books published on his new profession by H.M. Stationery Office. Under the heading 'Panic—how to avoid same' he had obviously read that the perfect warden always smiles so that his spirit will become contagious and reinforce the spirits of all. Also, patrons should be made to sing. For an hour we sang desperately about Packing up our Troubles in our old Kit-Bag, and a dozen other themes equally cheerful."

Another alarm was sounded that night, the noise incongruous with the beauty of the night sky, stars twinkling in the firmament far above the armada of vast gray, bloated barrage balloons that sat above the city as a deterrent to low-flying enemy aircraft. "London on a moonlit night in the blackout was a place of fantasy," Halton remembered. "Thousands, perhaps millions, of Londoners saw the stars almost for the first time in their lives." Someone remarked to Quo Tai-Chi, the Chinese ambassador in London, that the sky would soon be dark with enemy bombers. "The sky is already dark," Quo Tai-Chi replied, "with the wings of chickens coming home to roost."

In Berlin, the news from London was greeted with astonishment. Why had England declared war on Germany? (Most Germans, and many Americans, referred then and now to Great Britain and Northern Ireland—i.e., the United Kingdom of England, Scotland, Wales, and Northern Ireland—simply but erroneously as "England.") It was unthinkable! Howard and Katharine Elkinton of the Society of Friends had, earlier in the year, enjoyed a meal with a group of what Howard described as "middle-aged Nazis and their wives." The Germans had all expressed astonishment at the suggestion that Germany represented a threat to any other country, such as Romania or Poland, and dismissed the notion that there would ever be war with England.

As the voice of the announcer died away, Shirer watched the look of stunned surprise on people's faces. Had not Hitler asked repeatedly for peace, and yet they were now at war—for the second time this century—with the British Empire? What had brought this about? "To-day, I think they feel that they have been led into something which may turn out to be too big for them," observed Russell. "The truth has been kept from them so consistently that surely not over two or three per cent of all the Germans know what is going on." Somehow, the propagandists in the Reich Ministry for Public Enlightenment and Propaganda found a reason to blame Britain for this unexpected situation. Without much reasoning but plenty of bravado, the evening newspaper headlines blamed Perfidious Albion once more:

GERMAN MEMORANDUM PROVES ENGLAND'S GUILT.

At Munich, a year before, Chamberlain had given way, so why did he not do so again? It was a sign of the relentless propagandizing of the Nazi apparatus of state that many people were no longer able to recognize that it was German aggression, and German aggrandizement, that was the cause of the current crisis, not the fault of the victims, or of those who had attempted to prevent war breaking out in the first place. Nazi propaganda always attempted to turn the truth upside down and inside out. It became very difficult for ordinary Germans to differentiate between truth and fiction. The last thing Hitler needed at this point was for his own people to challenge the morality or reality of the current casus belli. Better that it was wrapped in a cloak of lies: the people would understand the reason for the subterfuge when final victory had been won, but it would be a mistake to confuse them with minor details now. The important thing was to be clear about the strategic goals (*Lebensraum*, Grossdeutschland, etc.) without worrying about the little lies that were necessary if these greater goals were to be successfully achieved. Hitler loudly claimed that it was the Jewish capitalists in London and New York who were to blame for the war, and many people appeared to believe him.

In Paris, Murphy, Bullitt, and Tabouis sat silently through the weary, uninspiring, Eeyore-like tones of the prime minister's broadcast. When he had finished announcing that Britain was now at war with Germany, Tabouis gave full vent to her fears that this meant the end of France. "Finally the ambassador, who privately shared her pessimism about French preparedness, interrupted gently, 'Surely—things cannot be that bad!'" recalled Murphy. "And then he suggested that I drop Mme. Tabouis at her home on my way back to the chancery, which I did. As we stood before the door of her house on the spacious Boulevard Malesherbes, she looked mournfully at the picturesque old buildings and exclaimed dramatically: 'Tomorrow all this will be gone! Our lovely Paris will exist no longer!' And she flung out her arms despairingly, as if she already stood among ruins."

—ɯ—

Strolling back to the Adlon to seek out any other journalists who might have been hanging around on this momentous day, Shirer bumped up instead against the nonchalance of the British stiff upper lip. The few members of the nearby British embassy—empty this Sunday except for a German policeman walking up and down outside it—whom he found propping up the bar exhibited the frustrating indifference Britons tend to affect in moments of great crisis. "They seemed completely unmoved by events," Shirer observed, astonished. "They talked about dogs and such stuff." Shirer was, by contrast, pumped up by the events of the past hour, and he couldn't understand how others could not see the current state of world affairs with the same degree of clarity or perspicacity. He had forgotten, momentarily, that he was a prophet. The only other news to emanate from the German High Command that afternoon was the statement that Germany didn't see the British (and now French, also) ultimatums to be at all serious. "We won't fire first," they insisted. In other words, let's just allow all this nonsense to fizzle out. We have no offensive intentions in the West, and if the English or the French do, well, that's their problem. We don't want war, never asked for it, and will wait for London and Paris to strike the first blow.

The onset of war frightened many Americans, who heeded the advice of the US embassies across Europe to return home if they had no compelling business to remain. The American embassy in London on August 24, 1939, had warned American tourists that the "international situation has reached a point which makes it advisable for American travelers to leave England" because by "remaining longer, they are running the risk of inconvenience and possibly danger. They are also contributing to the anxiety of those at home and will, if an emergency develops, make it harder to care for those compelled to remain." The estimated thirty thousand US citizens in Paris at the outset of the war had dwindled to five thousand by the following summer. At this point, recorded Janet Flanner, Bordeaux was packed with well-heeled evacuees queuing to catch the first berth home. Funds had run short, as the ships they had expected to depart on from Cherbourg or Le Havre never appeared, such was the confusion given to shipping schedules worldwide by the onset of war. A grand migration had thereafter taken place to Bordeaux, to await ships and sailings. "Bordeaux cafes are overrun with the visitors from the Americas, and with the animated local population. Though the town is blacked out at night, gas masks have never been distributed." She recorded that "by day all shops are open and busy. Americans, French officers, and rich Brazilians patronize the Hotel Splendide's terrace bar; the more modest drinkers populate the cafes along the handsome Allees de Tourny. Among the more celebrated evacuees are Toscanini and Hubert Fauntleroy Julian, the Black Eagle, who plans to fly something for somebody in the war if he can get things fixed up in Harlem first."

—⁓—

The days that followed the momentous announcement of war with the West was, for William Russell, Bill Shirer, and other Americans in Berlin, a letdown. France and Britain had declared war, but had seemingly done so halfheartedly. No evidence that Paris or London was taking this seriously seemed to present itself to Americans living in Berlin. It appeared that many Germans, likewise, were thunderstruck by this turn of events. They had believed that the moment war was declared the skies would be black with heavy bombers raining death and destruction. A few, indeed, wished it so, as punishment for Germany's belligerence. But nothing happened, and with every day that passed it appeared that the promise to defend Poland was hollow. Why didn't both France and Britain attack Germany, or do something to support the Polish armed forces struggling against the Wehrmacht steamroller? A war with France and/or Britain would force Germany to fight on both fronts. By all accounts the Germans were making striking gains in the east, and every day that passed without any form of retaliation from the West raised German hopes. The British and French declarations of war were, after all, the bluff and bluster the Propaganda Ministry insisted they were. Little did they understand that Britain and France did not have the military wherewithal to support Poland in its fight, or the political will in France to attack in the west. The war would not be a short one.

CHAPTER FIVE

The Ninety Percent

It was late summer, the sky's opal-blue intensity only just beginning to wane as the days grew perceptively shorter and the shadows longer. It was still warm, and at midday the sun still beat uncompromisingly against the golden earth. No breeze stirred to ruffle the still-to-be-harvested sugar beet fields that stretched far out to the wooded hills on the horizon. Harvest was late because of the absence of laborers. The news was that Algerians were being conscripted to do the back-breaking work this year, as all the farmers were now soldiers. Everything was still, and quiet. There wasn't even the sound of an insect to disturb the silence. Then, to break the spell, far in the distance a faint hum could be discerned. At first it sounded like a bee, making its way among the flowers. Its dramatic acceleration in volume, however, quickly revealed this insect to be man-made. Within a matter of seconds the screaming roar of an aircraft engine was accompanied by the sight of a low-flying Dewoitine single-seat fighter, the air force's latest, racing over the roofs of the ancient stone-built village. Almost as quickly as it had come it had gone, its noisy incursion into the still of the day leaving an invisible reverberation in the air, like the ripples on water following the plop of a stone.

For the startled Virginia D'Albert Lake, the sudden excitement of the fighter's appearance was rare evidence that the country was at war. Here in the quiet farming hamlet of Dammartin, twenty miles northeast of Paris, where she'd followed her husband's cavalry regiment when the general mobilization had been called a few weeks before, Lake had seen little of the war. It was as if the entire alarum was phony. At night trains could be heard laboriously hauling troops and equipment to the front along the line that ran some three miles distant, and an antiaircraft battery had been placed on the outskirts of the tiny village. She couldn't understand why, this afternoon's experience apart, aircraft were rarely ever encountered in this part of rural Picardy. Aircraft could be heard occasionally flying southeast, but not much else could be seen, or heard. Philippe's mobilization in September when France and Britain had declared war on Germany had presaged little more than a momentary inconvenience in their married state. Virginia had immediately decided to become a camp follower and take lodging close to wherever her husband was stationed. Dammartin was a pleasant and not unduly onerous posting. She saw Philippe twice a day, and every night. He'd lunch out with his comrades but enjoyed dinner with her every evening, often with one or more of their newfound conscripted friends. There was little to suggest that this would constitute anything more than a temporary inconvenience in their carefree civilian lives. She admitted to a flush of annoyance during mass one Sunday when the elderly priest asked for divine benediction for France's victory, instead of for a rapid and peaceful settlement of the idiocy that had led to war in the first place. Europe seemed incomprehensibly to have jumped unthinkingly onto the old merry-go-round only two decades after the end of the disaster of the Great War. Around their simple table at night, enjoying hearty country fare and plentiful *vin rouge*, their friends concurred. There was no war-hunger among Philippe's comrades. The opposite, in fact. The men were civilians called back into their old-style, ill-fitting blue serge uniforms for the duration of hostilities. None wanted war. No one considered the war to be so serious as to warrant taking a German's life. If they were ever to find themselves facing their enemy, they would only shoot in self-defense, they averred, and only to wound, not to kill.

The sudden arrival of the noisy Dewoitine that afternoon in mid-October 1939 presaged a noticeable increase in military activity, as the busyness of war began to intrude on the inhabitants of this sleepy rural idyll. The fighter planes became daily more ubiquitous, the pilots flying low in mock attacks on the antiaircraft position, rolling, diving, turning, and climbing in sudden paroxysms of screaming speed, at ever-increasing angles and attitudes that convinced Virginia that the pilots driving these pulsating, graceful machines were experts at their trade. They flew so low that she could see their faces clearly as the aircraft swept by in a vortex of noise and turbulence. They even had their first air raid. A lone reconnaissance plane flew over the frontier to their east, nearly two hundred miles distant, and the alert was sounded as far as Paris. Virginia, being on the edge of town and busy in the kitchen, did not hear the siren, and was only alerted to the situation when Phillipe came bustling home, out of breath, to fetch his gas mask. The populace stood in their gardens, scanning the skies to catch sight of the excitement, but there was none.

The war was, nevertheless, getting closer. The reality of the situation in which she found herself—a young American married since 1937 to a Frenchman, in a country that was once again, for the third time in the last seventy years, at war with Germany—was brought home to her with a jolt when she saw a notice in one of the Paris newspapers on October 17, 1939:

MORTS

AU CHAMP D'HONNEUR:

—LE LIEUTENANT PILOTE DE CHASSE MARIUS BAIZE

—LE MARECHAL DES LOGIS GEORGES HADAMAR, AGE DE TRENTE ANS.

Baize and Hadamar, flying a Morane-Saulnier fighter as part of the famous 3e Escadrille, had been shot down on September 21 in a skirmish with German fighters over the Moselle Valley. They were the first French air force casualties of the Second World War. The horrible waste of these young men suddenly enraged her. She was clear whose fault it was, bringing Europe to the edge of catastrophe again. "Why is one man permitted to bring such suffering?" she thundered to her diary that night. "Why don't we go straight to him as other criminals are treated?" Hitler had bullied and threatened his way through Europe for years, and no one had had the guts to stand up to him. The ineffectiveness of international politics intrigued and exasperated her in equal measure. How was the Soviet Union able to invade Finland with such impunity? Why on earth did Norway stick to its imbecilic policy of neutrality when its neighbor was suffering the consequences of unheralded aggression? Did it not realize that it might be next? Where were the Western democracies when liberty was under such threat? She would have agreed with Vincent Sheean's scorn for American isolationism amidst this disaster for democracy, both in France and in America. "Who is neutral when the house is burning down?" he asked. "Those on the second floor, those on the third, or only those on the roof?" The pusillanimity of London, Paris, and her own Washington was too galling for words. She couldn't make any sense of Sumner Welles's much-heralded tour of the capitals of Europe on behalf of President Roosevelt. Were "we" going to allow the strong to bully the weak, and appease the aggressors currently imposing their violent will across the length and breadth of Europe? Every time she attempted to comprehend the confusing political milieu in which Europe swirled, the less she understood it. Was it right that the democracies should follow Christ's command and show the other cheek, or would this merely encourage the warmongers? In any case, she understood that Britain, France, and the United States had been too weak militarily to stand up to Hitler, Stalin, and Mussolini's bloodlust, in Abyssinia, Albania, Austria, Czechoslovakia, Poland, and now Finland. Confused, she could only conclude that the war was making her more of a pacifist than ever.

In many small ways, the war crept closer as spring slowly merged with summer. Although they had plenty of sugar, butter, and white bread, formal rationing began in earnest, restricting the availability of meat to four days each week, with limited availability of pastries, alcohol, chocolate, together with a ration of eighteen and a half gallons of gasoline a month. Were they, she wondered, experiencing what some of her neighbors were calling *"Le calme avant la tempête"*?

—⁂—

Bill Shirer, in Berlin, was sure it was. In the days that followed the British and French declarations of war on September 3 (the British at 11:15 A.M. and the French five hours later), nothing much happened to demonstrate that hostilities between the Western democracies and Nazi Germany meant anything other than a heightened degree of political standoff. On the evening of the announcement, a subdued populace, unsure why the British and French had declared war when the Führer had repeatedly made it clear that he'd nothing against the Western democracies and had no ambitions in that regard, were surprised that no bombs fell on them. They'd half expected the declaration of war from their old enemies to precipitate the mass bombing of their cities. The first blackout, causing chaos and consternation on Berlin's roads after dark, had been imposed on September 1. Could it be that this would be a new kind of war, where civilians could sleep easy in their beds at night, free from the fear of bombing? That illusion quickly passed, with news on September 4 that a small number of British bombers had dropped their loads on the port towns of Cuxhaven and Wilhelmshaven. It didn't appear serious, however; more like a token gesture. Perhaps the British and French weren't serious? If they were, surely battle would have commenced by now? Few Germans understood just how weak militarily France and Britain were. Along the length of the border with France, as well, the advent of hostilities appeared not to be taken seriously. Shirer was told on September 5 by an official of the Reich Chancellery on Wilhelmstrasse that a shot had yet to be fired between the two sides, and that the German forces on the French border were broadcasting in French to the poilus: "We won't shoot if you don't."

Despite the onset of war, Shirer never met a German—outside of the deeply politicized Nazi apparatchiks, for whom bloodletting was an essential part of their ideology—who wanted war. The long years of hunger and instability that followed the end of the Great War remained firmly fixed in the memories of all those who were not children at the time. It was a state of affairs to which none wanted to return. Wallace Deuel agreed, writing in the *Chicago Daily News* in February 1941:

> In a single generation they have gone through a major war, a starvation blockade and a catastrophic defeat; they have had two revolutions; they have had their currency wiped out altogether once and have seen it seriously threatened with the same fate again; they have had the same exhausting and disillusioning experiences of the depression the rest of the world has had; and now they have entered a new war.

But the cruel realities of war soon made their entrance, the general population unable to prevent them. Within days the German government tightened the screw even harder on the already hard-pressed working man. Taxes went up to 50 percent, and beer and tobacco—two staple items of a worker's expenditure—also saw steep rises in duty. Prices were fixed, and in a catastrophic emasculation of the unions, workers were forced to accept lower wages for new jobs. The unions seemed remarkably quiet about this social outrage, but by then their leaders were already in Dachau. The death penalty was imposed for the crime of "endangering the defensive power of the German people," and as the days went by, the newspapers printed brief accounts of individuals caught up and disposed of by this new legal dragnet. Three youths in Hanover who snatched a lady's handbag in the blackout were sentenced to death. At the same time the radio and newspapers trumpeted the astonishing triumphs of the Wehrmacht in the "counterattack" against the dastardly Poles. When, however, on September 11 the news arrived that Warsaw had fallen, this remarkable military victory—which presaged events in the west in 1940—was met with a strange indifference on the streets of the German capital. To American observers in the city it was clear that the people did not want war. Perhaps, now that the fighting was over, or nearly so, Britain and France would rescind their declarations of war? There was no public rejoicing. On the underground after work Shirer was surprised at the lack of interest people seemed to display in the glories of their armed forces. Many people appeared sullen and depressed. The bands played "Deutschland, Deutschland uber Alles" and "Horst Wessel-Lied" but few lifted their heads from the street in acknowledgement. This was a war that few had wanted. They would still fight for Adolf Hitler, Russell concluded, "but only if he pokes them in the behind with a bayonet."

But Germans now had no choice. They had sleepwalked into a police state, acquiescing in their own political self-destruction. One night in mid-September Russell was eating his meager meal of Canadian bacon and scrawny green beans in his apartment, listening to the eight o'clock news broadcast from London, when he was interrupted by Hana, who nervously announced that he had a visitor. The block warden, a bull-necked, red-faced Nazi called Herr von Uhlrich, marched in, berating him loudly for breaking the strict radio laws by listening to the hateful BBC, that dangerous spewer of liberal, capitalistic, Anglo-Saxon sewage. The volume had been loud enough for the officious fanatic to hear the dulcet tones of the BBC news presenters through the thin walls of the apartment. Uhlrich was hated by everyone in the building. He was a Hitler-lover, condemning anyone as unpatriotic who said "Guten Tag" rather than "Heil Hitler." The former was fast becoming a dangerous sign of independent thought, punishable by the state.

Listening to foreign radio stations was widespread. It wasn't a sign of rebellion, merely desperation for unbiased information. In October 1940 Howard Smith reported that the newspapers had announced that two individuals had been punished with the death penalty for listening to London. On October 30, Goebbels had published in every newspaper in Germany a list of stations to which people might *only* listen, and in November, every German citizen received, alongside their monthly ration card, a little red card with a hole punched in the middle of it so that it might be hung on the station dial of a radio set. On the card was written "Racial Comrades! You are Germans! It is your duty not to listen to foreign stations. Those who do so will be mercilessly punished!" Smith remarked that a week later houses in his neighborhood were visited by local Nazi officials to make sure that the cards had been fastened to radios and were still there. "People who had no radio sets were told to keep the cards anyhow, and to let them be a reminder not to listen to the conversation of people who did have radios and tuned in on foreign stations."

Russell successfully sent the nasty little man away with a flea in his ear, but the incident made him ponder the power of Nazism. How could a couple of million Nazis keep sixty-five million people in check? "Our apartment was a good example of how it is done," he concluded, thinking of Uhlrich. "One Nazi was sufficient to spy on the other occupants. And, of course, behind that one Nazi was the full and dreadful power of the secret police." Uhlrich was the unwitting exemplar of the Nazi machine, Russell considered. "Nazi philosophy is that if you can keep the masses from rebelling against the small and unimportant things, it will not occur to them to revolt against the big things. Peace or war, keep the people in line. Don't let them forget that they are part of the great new Germany, the Germany which will not be downed by the conspiracies of others. Germans, we must all think alike, whether we be in the great Reich or in some foreign country! Discipline. Obedience. And we will rule the world someday." One Sunday he asked a German friend—no Nazi, a member of an old aristocratic family—for the reason behind the Nazi hold on the German people. The man thought carefully before he replied. "Four percent of the people are for Adolf Hitler," he said quietly. "Six percent of the people are against him, and the other ninety percent don't care one way or the other." Germany was en route to destruction because of the 4 percent who had voted for repression and the 90 percent who had foolishly abdicated from playing any sort of role in the political process. The self-immolation of a nation that had begun on January 30, 1933, and which was to last for twelve and a half hellish years, was the result of the carelessness of an entire nation. "Germany enters a nightmare," Matthew Halton wrote presciently the day after Hitler's assumption of power. "I feel it in my bones. She has heard the call of the wild. Pan-Germanism, six centuries old, is on the march again, but in a new and demoniac form." Should the whole country be punished for the foolishness of the 90 percent? Russell thought not. If his country went to war against Germany, he wanted it to remember that most of the population "do not agree with the policies of their leaders. And there are other millions, simple people, who believe exactly what their leaders tell them—especially when they tell them the same thing day after day." Versailles demonstrated compellingly, he thought, that it doesn't work to try to "punish a whole nation, as you might punish a single criminal."

But by September 10, after a week of the new Great War, the situation in Berlin appeared to be as phony as it did in Dammartin. People's spirits began perceptibly to lift. Was this truly war? True, the British had bombed Wilhelmshaven, but only with a handful of planes, and they dropped leaflets only—leaflets!—on the industrial Ruhr. No bombs? Clearly the Western Allies were not serious about fighting, and a negotiated peace would shortly be secured. Some even began to congratulate the Führer for the brilliance of his diplomatic brinkmanship. Some also began to believe that the continued inactivity meant that Germany was invincible. In London, the visiting American magazine editor Ralph Ingersoll considered that British bombing of Berlin was a propaganda rather than a military operation. He wasn't convinced that the RAF thought it was doing or expected to do much damage to Berlin. "The idea is simply to keep the Germans in Berlin running in and out of shelters," he concluded. "The RAF bombing is concentrated on the Ruhr and military objects along the coast. On its present scale the English bombing of Germany must be no more than a very unpleasant nuisance to the Germans. It will not become more than this until the English fleet of bombers is enormously increased." Life in Berlin began to return to normal. "The operas, the theatres, the movies, all open and jammed. Tannhauser and Madame Butterfly playing at the Opera," Shirer noted. "Goethe's Iphigenie at the State Theatre. The Metropol, Hitler's favorite show-house, announces a new revue Wednesday. The papers tonight say two hundred football matches were played in Germany today." The crowd of people—mainly women—who climbed onto the underground trains following the Deutsches Opernhaus the following night "seemed oblivious of the fact that a war was on, that German bombs and shells were falling on the women and children in Warsaw." It angered him. Only years of bombing or starvation would drum the reality of what their sons, husbands, and brothers were doing even then, in the name of "Grossdeutschland," to the people of Poland. Lothrop Stoddard heard the rumors but disbelieved them.

> Some of the rumors around Berlin were very lurid. One of the most persistent which went the journalistic rounds was that the Nazis were systematically killing off all troublesome Poles; that Gestapo and S.S. men went from village to village, rounding up those denounced by resident secret agents and machine-gunning them into a common grave which the victims had been previously forced to dig. I mention this, not to assert its credibility, but to present a picture of the rumor and gossip which are passed around when authentic news is unobtainable. The general impression among foreign journalists in Berlin was that rough work was going on in Poland. If that was an unjust inference, it's the Nazis own fault for keeping out reliable neutral observers who could have written objective, unbiased accounts.

And yet in a way Shirer sympathized with the German people. They were being told enormous, ridiculous lies every day. At the heart of any mischief in Europe, even if it was transparently German-inspired or organized, it would be the British Secret Service who was invariably to blame. The *New York Herald Tribune* announced in its Paris edition on September 22: NAZIS ASSASSINATE PREMIER OF ROMANIA. On the same day, the newspaper *12-Uhr Blatt* asked smirkingly, WHO DID IT?—THE ENGLISH! On the night of September 11, one Berlin newspaper even carried the ridiculous headline POLES BOMBARD WARSAW! The louder the lie, the more believable it was even if, on calm and analytical reflection, it was demonstrably absurd. The press was very firmly an instrument of the Nazi state. Dissenting newspapers had been closed, those editors and journalists who retained independent thought had been disposed of, or were cooling their heels in a camp courtesy of the Geheime Staatspolizei. The radios blasted one-sided propaganda every day; the newspapers, once steady, objective, and proud of their independent voice, now shackled to Goebbels's Reich Ministry for Public

Enlightenment and Propaganda, churned out simplistic tosh designed to keep the 94 percent in thrall to the Master Plan. Nothing critical or detrimental to Germany, or the Nazi concept of Germanhood, could ever be, or was, uttered.

When Howard Smith first arrived in 1936, pan-Germanic propaganda was ubiquitous. It filled the newspapers, populated placards on street-corner billboards, and flowed uninhibited across the airways. It was everywhere. In Heidelberg, he heard it in his evening classes from lecturers who pumped it out. It seemed clear that this was the Nazi agenda: to unite the country under a single idea and to allow the nation then to act as one, to create a "nation of millions of human wills united in the determination to achieve a certain, definite end . . ." If that end was conquest, a "nation which is unified in means, methods and will to carry out the single purpose of waging war could, if its neighbors were not equally determined, flood the world with blood and misery unequalled. That last is what I saw in Germany. I saw it before a month was out."

Years of lies had blunted the ability of the average German to discern between fact and fiction, even to display moral judgment. Shirer was startled to have a conversation with his maid, which started with her question, "Why do the French make war on us?"

"Why do you make war on the Poles?" I said.

"Hum," she said, a blank over her face. "But the French, they're human beings," she said finally.

"But the Poles, maybe they're human beings," I said.

"Hum," she said, blank again.

She was no different from millions of her fellows, he observed. It seemed extraordinary to him that the overwhelming attitude of people in the West to the invasion of Poland—that it was an unwarranted act of criminal aggression deserving at least unequivocal condemnation—was not replicated in the consciences of the people he saw around him every day in Germany. Why? He knew no German who did not approve of the "counterattack" into Poland. German interest had clearly been battered over many years by the criminal Poles, as it had been in previous years by the criminal Czechoslovakians. All the newspapers said so. The Führer said so. Goebbels shouted it daily from the radio. It was unfair that Germany could be abused in such a way. It was time to teach the barbarian Poles a lesson, just as the dirty Bohemians and Moravians—who had spent decades treacherously oppressing the innocent Sudetens—had been very firmly squashed the previous year. Patriotism would trump conscience in Nazi Germany, he believed, and the Germans were nothing but patriotic, even if many grieving German families did not attach the Nazi tag "Died for their Führer" on the death announcements of their loved ones who had fallen in battle. The "Fatherland" was the rich emotional seam—blood and soil—that Hitler knew he could exploit with impunity. The outrage across Germany on September 21, when Roosevelt asked at a special session of Congress to repeal the neutrality laws and allow those who wanted to buy Americans arms (he'd Britain and France in mind) to do so, was genuine. Why didn't Roosevelt want to sell arms to Germany? It was outrageous favoritism, engineered by the German-hating Jews who financed America.

While Bill Shirer was in Berlin, his young wife, Tess, and newborn baby daughter were safely tucked out of sight in Geneva, although even the sanctity of that long-neutral country could not be guaranteed in the face of relentless German rapine. On October 10, he managed to enjoy three days of rest with them both and with Demaree Bess, the *Picture Post* correspondent in Switzerland. The journey down the eastern bank of the Rhine by train provided the first startling revelation: there appeared no military confrontation with the French armies arrayed on the western bank. And yet the two countries were at war! The train chugged south in peacetime safety. The crew told him that not a shot had been fired since the declaration of hostilities. "Queer kind of war," Shirer thought. He couldn't make out the military inaction by Britain and France. If Europe was again at war, why weren't London and Paris bombing Germany? Why wasn't there at least shooting across the Rhine between the two entrenched armies, one in the Maginot Line and the other hunkered down in the Siegfried? "What can England and France be thinking of?" William Russell and his colleagues in the US embassy likewise asked themselves. "Why don't they attack Germany now so she will have to fight on two fronts?" Attack, attack, attack! Shirer listened nightly to Ed Murrow's broadcasts from London on the BBC—forbidden now to ordinary Germans, an act punishable by death—and concluded that the Allies were exaggerating their claims of action on the western front. Was it because they did not have the means to fight, or the will? Perhaps it was both? For the Nazis and their consummate propaganda machine, this was a gift. The radio, press, posters, and speeches were worked overtime. Germany, too, didn't want war, the Nazis argued, so clearly Britain, France, and Germany were closely aligned: they all wanted peace.

Shirer was even more astonished when the train passed the interminable passport controls at the border and rolled sedately into Geneva. The differences with Berlin, even in the five weeks since the beginning of the war and in the six weeks of his current assignment, were stark. Switzerland was a land of milk and honey. There was no blackout: the lights shone brightly across the towns and cantons, and cars drove with their headlights on. Food was plentiful. On his second day, in Basel, he and Demaree, he wrote, "stuffed ourselves shamefully with food. We ordered a huge dish of butter just to look at it, and Russian eggs and an enormous steak and cheese and dessert and several liters of wine and then cognac and coffee—a feast! And no food cards to give in." When he returned to Berlin two days later, his diaries were heavy with comments about the lack of food, and the rapidly declining stocks of clothes in the city.

While Shirer was in Geneva, William Russell observed the giddy reaction in Berlin to the certainty heralded across the great city of four million on October 10, 1939, that the war was over. The telephone rang in his apartment. Someone had called to say that peace was to be announced at 3:00 P.M. that day by the Führer himself. The British Cabinet had fallen, Chamberlain had resigned, and King George VI abdicated. The news spread across the city like wildfire. Crowds gathered on street corners. The telephones buzzed with excitement, news hacks calling each other expectantly for the next tidbit. You need to wait. The Führer will reveal all. Be patient! Hana rang him. Was it true? She wanted to believe it. He told her that he didn't know. The streets outside were alive with an excited buzz. Nobody knew the details of the peace deal: all they knew was that as Mr. Chamberlain had said at Munich the previous year (and had endeared himself to many Germans for saying so), there would be peace in their time. "It's all over bar the signing," a Nazi acquaintance of Russell told him. The Nazi had taken a day off to celebrate. The bars were full. The drinks flowed. The people appeared to have gone wild with joy. But still there was no confirmation. In his heart of hearts Russell distrusted the rumor. He also wanted it to be false. He did not want Nazi aggression—in the Rhineland first, then Austria, followed by Czechoslovakia and now Poland—to succeed unchecked. He was ashamed to be a citizen of a free country that refused to lift its hands to defeat tyranny elsewhere. "God, why doesn't somebody stop him?" he'd blurted out on the news when the Wehrmacht had marched triumphant into Prague on March 15, 1939. He knew that he would despise himself for the failure of the democracies to stand up to this naked, unrepentant, and exultant aggression.

Walking through the crowded streets, he observed a marked uplift in people's spirits: where there was no celebration over military victories in Czechoslovakia and Poland, there was happiness at the hope of peace. The *hausfrauen*, soldiers home on leave, young office workers, and workmen: all were smiling. He hadn't seen such public jubilation since the Anschluss with Austria in March 1938. Outside Hitler's Reich Chancellery on Wilhelmstrasse, a large crowd waited expectantly for the Great Leader to speak. Russell moved on to the Potsdamer Platz, where, at "this busiest intersection in Berlin I saw people who had gone crazy with joy."

Strangers grabbed strangers by the arms to tell them the wonderful news.

Peace, brother, peace!

Other people grabbed strangers and embraced them in a delirium of joy.

It looked like New Year's Eve in the daytime.

Everyone was repeating it.

"Hitler speaks at three."

"Peace, peace, peace, wonderful peace!"

"Praise God and Heil Hitler!"

Of course, when Hitler finally spoke, the Voice said nothing of peace. Speaking for forty-five minutes, the Führer urged people to donate more to the Nazi scheme for Winter Relief—one of many official fleecing operations—in order to support their brave soldiers at the front. He signed off with a martial fanfare.

Sieg Heil! Sieg Heil! Sieg Heil!

The letdown was unimaginable. Again, the dastardly British Secret Service was outed as the rumormonger. That night the darkness descended once again over Berlin. But the darkness was greatest, Russell observed, in German hearts. The war, for what it was, went on.

CHAPTER SIX

Le Drôle de Guerre

As the French army mobilized, the nation could not make up its mind about what it thought of the war, or its potential outcome. On the one hand defeat was unthinkable. France had the most powerful army in Europe, or at least this was what the country told itself. Etta Shiber had watched the Bastille Day parade on July 14, 1939, where the impressively strong French army had marched down the Champs-Élysées, "followed by tanks which shook the ground and made the air vibrate with their roar," and in which, "from the sky behind the Arc, 600 planes swooped down above the procession." France was blessed, too, with two other precious items in her armory, on which the people had come increasingly to rely: the physical majesty of *La Ligne Maginot* and the personal majesty of the eighty-four-year-old Marshal Philippe Pétain. When war was declared, the nation seemed to mobilize to a well-orchestrated plan. Driving from Bordeaux to Paris, Janet Flanner saw preparations for war: ". . . big green auto-buses from Paris waddling along country roads, piled with furniture for barracks, or with soldiers' kitbags, or with fodder for horses. We saw big guns being drawn by sextets of superb Percheron stallions. We saw lines of whippet tanks, painted in camouflage, rattling along forest highways. In chalk, on the necks of the tanks, the drivers had scrawled their best girls' names—Lulu, Marie-Louise, Simone, Beb. In name, anyhow, the girls, too, were all going off to war." All this was a chimera, asserted American soldier of fortune Charles Sweeny, who told Abbott Liebling the following year that the French army would collapse at the first push. The army was rotten, he argued, "because the officers were afraid to work the men hard; energetic officers were curbed by their superiors, who lived in fear of politicians." Sweeny was a man with strong opinions and a colorful past. What did he know? Liebling ignored him.

On the other hand, few wanted the war, and even fewer felt that it was worth sacrificing their lives to protect French freedom in the face of German aggression. The country wallowed in depression. When Sumner Welles toured Europe on behalf of President Roosevelt in a search for peace that he recalled in his 1944 account, *The Time for Decision*, he was profoundly shocked at seeing firsthand the extraordinary weakness of French politics. "One could almost sense in every house," he remarked, "the feeling of sullen apathy which marked most of the faces that one passed in the nearly deserted streets. There was a sensation of general waiting: of an expectation of some dire calamity." When Clare Boothe arrived in Paris in April 1940, she was surprised to observe that public discourse was not about military tactics and issues of national defense but about politics. The country was now at war, and had been for six months, but she found that when people talked about *"la guerre,"* they were not discussing stratagems to defeat the enemy; they were having political arguments about the governance of the country. The focus of the people of France, their politicians, and their political institutions was not on winning the war in which they found themselves but on continuing the discussions and divisions that had characterized the body politic in peacetime. France remained as politically and socially divided in wartime—admittedly a war it did not want—as it had been in peace.

The country had ended the Great War exhausted, physically and emotionally. France crept wounded, hesitant and without assurance,

into the years of peace, little thinking that within the span of a generation the old animosities with Germany would reemerge once more, or so
quickly. It had no stomach for the fight and was hopelessly unprepared—
politically as well as spiritually—to withstand the challenge posed by a
renewed and reawakened Germany, especially one with an ideology so
hostile to the concepts of liberty, equality, and fraternity. The country
was bitterly divided. Political animosities were severe. Governments
came and went with ridiculous regularity, placing personal and party
advantage over national unity. Leaders likewise came and went, most
attempting merely to survive in a dysfunctional political merry-go-
round. The prospect of yet another life-and-death struggle against Germany and the loss of another million young French lives was anathema
to all. Robert Murphy saw this at first hand a few days after the onset of
hostilities when he went to the Gare du Nord to watch the mobilization
of the French army. He was shocked to observe that most of the men—
conscripts—were slovenly presented, slouched along glumly, many
drunk. They didn't want to be there. There was no rousing send-off, no
bands and no encouragement to the poilus that the country was behind
them and supported their sacrifice. It was hardly what one expected to
see of an army departing to defend the Motherland. Of course, these men
reflected the mood of the nation, one in which, in Vincent Sheean's words,
the "wives and dependents of conscripts, the conscripts themselves, the
workers in war industry and the ordinary bewildered, overtaxed citizen
all alike felt imposed upon, maltreated or ignored; life had become very
difficult for the largest classes of the population; and there was no hint
of fervor, or of anything approaching fervor, about the war."

In addition, an inexplicable complacency existed across France about
the consequences of war, especially the possibility that Germany might
win. This attitude was repeatedly summarized in public in the West,
especially in France, during the late 1930s, with syllogisms that followed this pattern:

1. Germany attacked France in 1914 and was eventually defeated.
   In 1914, the Allies were not prepared for war but had time on
   their side and ultimately prevailed. If Germany were to do the

same again, it was inevitable that she would again, in time, be defeated.

2. Germany was a totalitarian state. Economic processes in these states are far less efficient than free-market economies. Therefore, the democratic capitalism of France and the Western democracies would once again prevail in the long run, even if it entailed another long, bloody, and expensive war.

Americans in France in 1940 observed and heard repeated syllogisms that demonstrated logically that war would not come, but that if it did, Germany was bound to lose. Clare Boothe for instance noted that the famous British commentator on military affairs, Captain Basil Liddell Hart, preached the message that to achieve victory, Germany would require a military superiority of at least three-to-one. It did not have this superiority. Therefore, Germany could not win. Liddell Hart had fallen into the error of reducing the complexities of mortal combat between nations to a mathematical rule. Those people who pointed to the dramatic German success in Poland were dismissed as simpletons who clearly failed to appreciate that Poland was weak and unprepared before the German Blitzkrieg fell on it, and that France had the strongest army in Europe and lay safely behind the incomparable defenses of the Maginot Line.

Then, sixteen days after the German attack, the news broke that the Soviet Union had invaded Poland. The two great European dictatorships had carved up Poland between them. Confusion reigned. In France, the prevailing attitude among those on the Left was shock. How could Moscow collude so outrageously and opportunistically with Fascist Germany? After all, the two had only just sheathed their swords in their proxy war in Spain.

It only got worse. In the first winter of the war, France was progressively drained of its stock of national joie de vivre. It had not sought conflict with Germany, and for most, the prospect of renewed conflict with its neighbor represented a severe blow. Indeed, the early days of the war in Paris were frightening. No one knew what would happen. It was expected, however, that the Luftwaffe would soon arrive, as it had done to Guernica and was even now doing over Warsaw, to rain bombs down on the helpless population of a largely undefended city. The air-raid sirens wailed repeatedly, but no enemy bombers came. Eric Sevareid recalled the siren sounding one night and a French colonel, one of his neighbors in the Continental Hotel, knocking on doors shouting with fear, *"Les avions! Les avions!"* But as time went by, Sevareid was sickened by Paris. Life seemed to continue in all its relentless futility, the people refusing to take life seriously, or to prepare for the sacrifices that war would inevitably demand. Why did they not think that the horrifying destruction that Poland was even then experiencing would not one day embrace them, destroying their comfortable isolation? After the shock of the declaration of war had died down, Paris returned to a kind of normality, attempting to retain its air of sophisticated nonchalance towards the grubbiness of the international events that threatened to shatter its golden cage. At the outset of war, Elsie and Charles Mendl, fearing the consequences of the draft on their servants, moved with a small entourage of staff and secretaries into the Imperial Suite at the Ritz. The famed hotel became a magnet for many others in this gilded milieu. Maurice Chevalier helped to create this pretense of normality—another form of ostrichitis—by continuing to croon *"Paris sera toujours Paris!"* at the Casino; Greta Garbo's romantic comedy *Ninotchka* played to crowded cinemas; expensive shops in the Rue de la Paix did a roaring trade in patriotic silk scarves; and politics continued to play out its grubby game. Vincent Sheean went "to Cartier's to get a watch repaired and was told that the season had never been better. The well-to-do French, having no faith in their own government, army or currency, were putting their money into jewels."

And so it continued through winter and into spring. When Clare Boothe arrived in Paris in April 1940, the beauty of the place "brought a catch of pain and pleasure in your throat." It was as if the war did not exist. The roads were full of bustling traffic, sidewalks were thronged with people enjoying the first fruits of spring; cafés, restaurants, and shops were full. Cinemas were showing the latest American movies. Admittedly, there were many uniforms in sight, but they were all of the most elegant design. Whatever hiatus might have been caused at the onset of war the far distant September last, business was now booming. "There were art shows in the Palais de Elysee, racing at Auteuil, and Rugby games between the tommies and poilus in the suburbs. The fitting-rooms of the couturieres and modistes were comfortably filled with foreign buyers. The show windows of Van Cleef and Arpels and Mauboussin and Cartier sparkled with great jewels in the sunlight. And lots of people, too, bought them. The wide-windowed gilded corridors of the Ritz and its sunny restaurants were fairly well crowded with lovely ladies wearing simple dresses or the smart uniforms of the Union des Femmes de France services." The things that Abbott Liebling noticed when he arrived in the city at about the same time were the strips of paper pasted across shop windows to keep the glass from flying in case of aerial bombardment and the ancient jalopies that passed as taxis on the streets of the city now that all the half-decent motor vehicles had been requisitioned for the war effort. Otherwise, not much had changed since he had been here last, in 1927.

Twenty or thirty of the richest Americans banded together to help with the war effort in their adopted country. In October, Elsie Mendl organized a charity called Le Colis de Trianon-Versailles (Parcels from Trianon-Versailles) to send care packages to soldiers in the French army. The Duchess of Windsor accepted the role of honorary president of the group, which also included a clutch of those people whom Eric Sevareid so despised, the self-appointed cultural *célébrités* of the Parisian social scene. Within weeks, hundreds of individual boxes containing "one knitted sweater with roll collar and knitted hood, two pairs of socks, two large handkerchiefs, soap, woolen gloves, toilet paper, flea powder, aspirin, quinine, laxative, cigarettes" were on their way to soldiers at the front. Cynics claimed that all they wanted was a *Legion d'Honneur*, France's highest award for bravery, but Clare Boothe—who was a cynic at first—was pleasantly surprised to find herself changing her mind on the subject after watching some of these gilded butterflies roll up their sleeves in the blood and muck of the refugee crisis that threatened to overwhelm the city in the first days and weeks of the war.

The one thing that Parisians did was talk. On the subject of the war, the two primary sources of information were the daily official communiqués, which everyone ignored because of their simplicity, and rumors, which were always considered gospel truth. Seven million Frenchmen had been mobilized, yet this was a war like no other. The rumors, accordingly, were primarily about when this nonsense would be over so their menfolk could return home. The wishful thinking became elaborate. Hitler would recognize the impossible scale of his undertaking and blow his brains out. Both Boothe and Liebling reported on the extraordinary renaissance of Michel Nostradamus, the old astrologer, whose prognostications had become a best seller. *Les Boches* (a derogatory term for Germans, a legacy of the Great War) were hated to a greater extent than they had been in the last war, merely for bringing war to a Europe that was still recovering from the past conflict. What did they think they were doing? Some wondered whether the war was some kind of psychological joke, a gigantic bluff. Was Hitler merely attempting to frighten France into political acquiescence in his efforts to create a German-dominated European union? Maybe he had no real intention of fighting? Liebling told readers of the *New Yorker* of a popular cartoon character called Baju, who in one strip was shown cowering under yet another blast of vehemence by the German Führer. At each howl from the radio set ("I will destroy England before breakfast," "I will show the French what total war means") little Baju's hair stood on end, and at the close of the speech he turned to his radio, saying, "Oh, please, Adolf, don't stop; frighten me again."

—◊◊◊—

But beneath the calm and studied nonchalance of the Parisian streets France was failing fast. Sevareid watched in the Chamber of Deputies in the Palais-Bourbon with mounting dismay when, on March 21, 1940, Paul Reynaud—upright, principled, and intelligent—was appointed premier of the Third Republic after Daladier, the Marseillean leader of the Radical Party (which wasn't anywhere near as radical as the name suggested) and the man who signed the Munich agreement for France, went down. The cabinet Paul Reynaud thus formed was the 107th in the not yet seventy years of the Third Republic. It was clear from the moment Reynaud walked slowly to the podium that he was the wrong man for the moment. "He was terribly nervous," Sevareid thought, "he seemed to have lost all self-possession, he spoke in terms of cautious conciliation, not in terms of national duty." Reynaud had been appointed by one vote, most of his own party not supporting his candidacy. Where was the unifying national leader, the hard man of pragmatism who could bring the country together, stand up for and defend it against its threats and bring the people together at this time of crisis? The omens were not favorable, observed Vincent Sheean, when the members of the nineteen different political parties struggled even to understand the differences between them. "The rotating leaders of the Third Republic had been chosen and rechosen times without number by the French voters," observed Clare Boothe with some disdain. "It was with the full approval of the people that the French Parliament was largely a great Mad-Hatter's tea-party, at which its premiers moved from soiled portfolio to soiled portfolio, until each in turn sat again a little while at the head of the green baize table." In addition, significant factions in politics (like Pierre Laval, and even Reynaud's notorious 38-year-old mistress, Hélène, Comtesse des Portes), together with much of the print media, such as *Le Journal* and *Le Matin*, worked assiduously to seek an understanding with Hitler. The Communists, in hoc to Moscow, were a much more serious threat, sowing the servile philosophy of defeatism among the working classes and trade unions. Fifty Communist deputies in the Chamber of Deputies so repeatedly resisted—on Moscow's orders—the government's attempts to rearm that Daladier was forced to have them thrown in prison. To Sevareid it was clear that France was rudderless—a house divided against itself—in the face of the greatest storm it had confronted in its modern history. How could the government, in these circumstances, provoke the country to a spirit of combat and sacrifice?

The great tragedy, he thought, was that it had been France, despite its own painful domestic disunity, which had served as Europe's haven for the dispossessed of Europe as repression had grown during the decade, the "rivers of fear and hate" flowing into Paris from the discombobulated East. A small group of refugees from Czechoslovakia and Austria met regularly at his flat, and told stories of the repression they had experienced. Much of what they discussed, to the sensibilities of those brought up to believe the inalienable certainties of democratic liberalism, was unbelievable. This was the major problem with the stories of those who had escaped terror, a problem described by many at the time. Could one truly believe these stories of brutal repression, even murder? Surely this was mere propaganda, sown by disgruntled political adversaries? To those brought up to enjoy the trappings of democracy, the only limitations on individual freedom related to the civil law and the ability to pay for one's choices. To live otherwise was simply unimaginable. Now, the very thing the refugees from Germany, Austria, and Czechoslovakia had warned about was coming closer to France's door.

Journalists were expressly forbidden to visit the French fortifications and preparations along its eastern borders, but in time-honored tradition many attempted to do so. In the middle of September 1939, Sevareid, the New Zealander Geoffrey Cox, Walter Kerr of the *New York Herald Tribune*, and Charles Findley drove to Metz. They were stopped and had their papers examined several times by French military police, but no one turned them back. What they found at the front line, Sevareid related, was what he had always imagined of the Great War. It appeared that the "projector had stopped in 1918 and now was turning again." Ancient buses and trucks, many of which had probably served in the previous war, bustled around, lugging guns—the old 75s of fame—while blue-clad poilus, looking no different from their fathers and grandfathers, trudged wearily across the rolling countryside heavy with the late summer crops. Abandoned trenches from the previous war stretched across farmland, a few rusty tanks lay where they had been left a generation before, and the nonbelligerent attitude of many of the marching men he observed on the roads could be seen by the long-stemmed purple flowers they had stuck in the barrels of their rifles. Clare Boothe was spellbound by the beauty of the countryside of Alsace and Lorraine in April, until she realized that from each innocent haystack protruded the "ugly . . . snouts of field guns. Half-built cottages everywhere housed machine-gun nests. And on the little green brows of hundreds of tender hills nestled a vast nasty brood of camouflaged cement pill-boxes." Life seemed to carry on around all this bustle. Peasants went about their everyday business of staying alive, looking after their animals and harvesting the crops. No one had been evacuated from the battle zone. There was no noise of battle. They were just behind the front line, and yet no guns fired. The war was phony. It was inconceivable for most French people to consider the possibility of invading Germany just because the two countries were now at war. France certainly did not want to be blamed for precipitating military operations when politics in due course might be able to resolve the situation. In later months Sevareid watched the troops grow tired with inaction, beaten down by relentless propaganda from across the Rhine, the freezing winter, and poor conditions in the trenches. The few casualties to sniper fire and the like were depressing in their futility. Why did a young man have to lose his life in this meaningless way? It wasn't war, it was murder.

—⚹—

In Berlin, Bill Shirer noted that in a speech given at the Bürgerbräuke-ller in Munich on the anniversary of his 1923 beer-house putsch in November 1939, Hitler warned Germans to plan for five years of war. Most people Shirer saw on the streets were distinctly miserable at the prospect. Only minutes after Hitler had left, a bomb exploded, killing seven and wounding sixty-three. Wild rumors abounded. Could the whole affair have been staged, perhaps to kill off some old Munich enemies or for some other, nefarious Nazi purpose? As the days went by, Shirer observed that the German press seemed willing to publish news of the type of state violence that was unheard of in the democracies. The papers announced matter-of-factly, on November 12, that the Polish mayor of Blomberg had been shot. He had been court-martialed, apparently for leading a rebellion against the Germans. "That, I suppose, is a German peace," Shirer concluded. "I cannot recall that the Allies shot the mayors of German towns after the Rhineland occupation." In fact, the Nazi press had exercised considerable self-control, but what they reported was mere propaganda, an attempt to demonstrate their adherence to judicial process. The total number of people executed in Bromberg (Bydgoszcz)—most of them summarily—between September 4, 1939, and the end of the year is estimated to have been upward of three thousand. The mayor, Leon Barciszewski, was merely one victim among what would become millions as the Nazi project unfolded. (Shirer probably misquoted the town, which was likely to be that of Bromberg. Nazi propaganda described events there on September 3–4 as "Bloody Sunday," claiming that attacks were made by Poles on ethnic Germans. In fact, small groups of ethnic Germans fired on withdrawing Polish troops, and were killed in the fighting. The Nazis, as was their wont, took revenge on the Polish population and executed up to three thousand Poles during 1939, most of them summarily.) The press also seemed at liberty to report on subjects that the Nazi state might otherwise have preferred to keep quiet. On November 19, for instance, it was reported that Hans Frank, the gauleiter of occupied Poland, had ordered that the Warsaw Ghetto, into which thousands of Jews had been crammed, would from henceforth be closed, because Jews were "carriers of diseases and germs." Shirer reported that an American friend who had travelled to Warsaw believed that it was Nazi policy to exterminate the Polish Jews. At this stage there was no hint of a systematic program to kill off European Jewry, but the building blocks of persecution were clear to all who read the German newspapers. The foundations of extermination were being laid, in plain sight. State violence wasn't hidden, as it might have been in the West from shame or embarrassment. Instead, the Nazi press appeared to glory in this news of violence and repression. Shirer noticed that anti-Jewish propaganda was more in evidence just before Christmas that year. The war, the Nazis were preaching, was not merely one against the British and French "but a holy struggle against the Jews." Dr. Robert Ley, head of the *Deutsche Arbeitsfront* (German Labor Front), writing in *Der Angriff*, the Nazi Party newspaper, opined knowledgeably, "We know that this war is an ideological struggle against world Jewry. England is allied with the Jews against Germany . . . England is spiritually, politically, and economically at one with the Jews . . . For us England and the Jews remain the common foe . . ."

On Christmas Eve, 1939, before the evening curfew, and in a dusting of cold rain that would soon turn to snow, Shirer walked the streets of Berlin, a ritual he had undertaken for many years. But this time was different. This time of celebration was anything but, as the reality of a long, hard war beckoned. The clothes rationing regime, instituted on November 12, was now beginning to bite. Each person was given one hundred points to use up within a year, divided into three seasons. "Socks or stockings take five points, but you can buy only five pair per year," he noted. "A pair of pyjamas costs thirty points, almost a third of your card, but you can save five points if you buy a nightgown instead. A new overcoat or suit takes sixty points." The clothes rationing amidst one of the coldest winters in living memory, accompanied by the strict food and alcohol rationing, the absence of many of the men at war, and the threat of air attack, which blacked out the city, not even allowing the twinkle of a child's candle to illuminate the mean streets, made this year's Christmas festivities much more miserable than the last one, when at least the world was enjoying a precarious peace. In wartime it was much harder to live in Berlin than London, considered George Keenan. The winter of 1939 in Germany was vicious. Canals froze. Fuel was in desperately short supply, as was food. Life was miserable for lots of people. There wasn't enough fuel to heat the huge Berlin apartment blocks, which ended up with coal for an hour or so each day. There was no gasoline for private motoring, and the blackout was strict. Keenan would leave the embassy in the dark on the long winter evenings, and grope through the darkness to the bus stop, followed by a long, slow journey for five and a half miles over a snow-covered road with only dim blue headlights to show the way. At the other end he would stumble home through the darkness, wary of curbstones and other silent pedestrians making their own uncertain way through the darkness. The war had made the very business of living very difficult.

—⁂—

From the moment war was declared Bill Bullitt urged Roosevelt to help rearm the European democracies. Germany had been rearming on a massive scale for many years, in flagrant contravention of Versailles. Because of its now-failed policy of appeasement, both Britain and France found themselves militarily weak, and efforts to rebuild emasculated armed forces would take time that would almost certainly not be available to them if Germany decided to strike west. If Hitler was to be defeated, he argued, it could only be because of American arms and American industry. To do this, however, would mean overturning the Neutrality Act. Such a move would not be universally welcomed in isolationist America, but not to do so would be, he advised, insane. If the United States did not arm Western Europe, France and England would be unable to defeat Hitler, and "we shall have to fight him some day in the Americas . . ." On December 11, 1939, he quantified the number of modern airplanes that Daladier, the French premier, believed they would need to purchase from the United States in 1940: ten thousand.

Bullitt had never been busier. He saw his role to warm and cajole, not just the president in Washington but those of every hue who were struggling to provide leadership in France. Politicians of Left and Right, and leaders of the various branches of the armed forces, found their way to his welcoming salon at 2, Avenue d'Iéna. He had a difficult tightrope to walk, between encouraging French politicians to resist Nazism and allowing them to think that the United States would join them in the fight against Germany. In fact, he repeatedly warned that although most Americans of sound judgment recognized France's dire need in the face of the menace from Germany, America would not intervene in another European war.

On April 18, 1940, Bullitt told FDR that the spreading of the war across Europe was now inevitable. Ten days later he reported the German attacks on Denmark and Norway, as well as the subsequent recriminations between Britain and France about the ham-fisted approach that both countries took to the issue of Norwegian neutrality, which Germany used as the casus belli for invasion. On April 28, 1940, he reported that the danger of a botched intervention in Norway, if the fighting in Norway should go as badly as Reynaud and Daladier expected, was that "the neutrals of Central and Southern Europe will be so impressed by the superiority of the German Army that they will fall into the maw of Germany and Italy almost without resistance." Furthermore, both "Reynaud and Daladier expect defeat in Norway to produce most serious repercussions in France. Reynaud foresees his own fall and Daladier thinks that he as well as Reynaud will be completely discredited and that a defeatist government of Flandin, Laval and Bonnet will come in, with a program of peace at almost any price." At this stage he considered this "too gloomy a view," but anything was possible.

—m—

On April 25, Clare Boothe flew to London. Like Paris, the beauty of the city in late spring took her breath away. Carefully tended flowers bloomed in profusion around the city, and birdsong filled the air. "Sheep browsed in park enclosures, ducks splashed joyously in park pools, and hordes of pink-faced people lounged happily in tuppenny 'deck chairs' on the Hyde Park greens, feeding the pigeons." The war was as far away for Londoners as it was for Parisians. The signs were there, of course, such as the piles of sandbags heaped high against buildings in Westminster, barrage balloons in the air, and young men and women in well-fitting uniforms going about their business on the streets. But it wasn't *serious*. This was something she deduced from the fact that, unlike the start of the war the previous September, hardly anyone carried their regulation gas masks. People joked about Hitler's little mustache and his supposed lack of testicles. Children who had been dispatched to the safety of the countryside at the start of the war because of the threat of aerial bombardment had been flooding back to the sooty streets. Even the blackout had lost its terror, as the bright April moon allowed for relatively safe navigation of the streets at night. And one had to go out at night, to enjoy the wide range of entertainments available, everything from Shakespeare to musical comedy and burlesque, not to mention the quality and range of restaurants serving food that would satisfy the most sophisticated palate. The newspapers were full, and although talk was of the invasion of Norway, and of the looming threat to the Low Countries, somehow the war was still a theory rather than a reality.

London frustrated Liebling. Visiting for ten days at the same time as Boothe, he was shocked by the smugness of the place. Here was Hitler on the warpath, and nobody was taking it at all seriously. He was horrified that Chamberlain and his *Pax Umbrellica* remained in power. He raged at their complacency and, in light of the harm done to democracy by Munich, the almost "criminal tolerance of the ineptitudes and inadequacies of their government." Although he agreed with them, he was also irritated by the "open, smoothly stated criticisms of American isolationism, or what the *London Economist* called 'America's deliberate myopia.'" The rudeness of the British towards American neutrality was excused by them as the consequence of consanguinity. After all, they argued, Britain was America's elder brother. Part of Liebling's irritation, however, was his knowledge that the standard British assumption that Roosevelt would ride to their rescue, like the hackneyed cowboy-and-Indian stories that provided an entire genre for the American movie industry, was wrong. Like the French, the British always assumed that Roosevelt was on their side and, although hamstrung by the Neutrality Act, would do everything to support Britain in her hour of need. Boothe was never so sanguine, believing this to be an illusion. Roosevelt would offer nothing but honeyed words about "Nazi aggressions" and "the sanctities and beauties of liberty" without doing anything that might jeopardize his electoral chances. "If he really believes that we may also perish if the European democracies do," she observed, "why doesn't he say so in stentorian tones without waiting for a mandate from the people?" As Boothe watched, and listened, and worried about what the war might bring were it to explode into a new phase of violent activity, she felt "afraid for England, for France, afraid of that nameless, faceless, inhuman, unseen thing, *the enemy*."

CHAPTER SEVEN

The Offensive in the West

Eric Sevareid had been asleep for only an hour or so in his hotel bed in the Provençal town of Valence, halfway between Lyons in the north and Avignon to the south, when he was jerked awake by the onset of the town's air-raid siren. It was Friday, May 10, 1940. He had travelled on the overnight train from Paris and was in a deep sleep when the strangely unsettling wail brought him grudgingly to consciousness. Something else accompanied the rising tone of the alarm, a noise he could hear above the frantically undulating mechanical scream that all of Europe had now come to fear. It was the deep-throated rumble of aircraft engines. He lay there, confused. There was no airport at Valence, so what were low-flying aircraft doing here? Clambering from his bed, he made his way to the window and pulled open the curtains. In the dawn of the morning sky he saw above him, flying up the valley in the direction of Lyons, sixty miles to the north, two unmistakably German aircraft. With their twin engines they could have been passenger aircraft, but with Europe in a state of war they could only have been bombers, far behind French lines. Indeed, the black crosses emblazoned on the wings gave the game away. They must have made their way across Switzerland—possibly from as far away as Austria—to get there. But they had no sign of nefarious intent, lumbering leisurely into the distance as if they were on an early morning outing. In a short while they were merely a memory. Returning to bed Sevareid found himself, again, quickly asleep. But suddenly, as if in a moment, he was awake again. Another unusual sound had disturbed him. This time it was not from the air, however. He lay there, trying to understand what had brought him, once again, to consciousness. There it was, an unusual sound, in the otherwise dead stillness of the morning. Tripping across the cobblestones he heard the strange, uneven gait of a man in hob-nailed boots. A soldier. Getting up from his bed once more, Sevareid peered out his window. A man in uniform, struggling to get into his greatcoat as he ran, was making his way as fast as was practicable across the uneven street to the railway station. Somehow this man and the noise of his hasty, lopsided run seemed more alarming to Sevareid than the two enemy aircraft that had earlier flown overhead. Climbing quickly into his clothes, he went downstairs, and out into the street. A small knot of people had formed around the entrance to the station. As he got closer, he could see the local butcher, incongruously dressed—for this time in the morning—in his blood-spattered apron, chalking up a message on a blackboard. THE GERMANS THIS MORNING HAVE INVADED HOLLAND, LUXEMBOURG, BELGIUM. THEY BOMBED THE LYONS AIRPORT. The war had begun, in earnest. France was under direct attack.

Clare Boothe was asleep in Brussels that night in the residence of the American ambassador, John Cuddhy. She was sleeping so soundly that she failed to hear the air-raid sirens in the early dawn, until a maid frantically shook her with the news—"Wake up! The Germans are coming *again*!"—before running back down the corridor. Rushing to the window, Boothe looked up, and through the "lovely red-gold dawn" she saw a formation of about twenty planes approaching, at a great height:

> Then I heard a thin long, long whistle and a terrible round *bam!*
> The whistle was from the bomb that pierced the roof of a three
> storeyed house across the square, and the *bam* was the glut and

vomit of glass and wood and stone that was hurled into the little green park before me. For a long hour after that there was a terrible noise, of the great anti-aircraft guns . . .

From that point on, she recalled, there was no more talk of politics. All conversation now focused on defenses, airplanes, calibers, and the fabled Maginot Line. It was in Brussels that Boothe met for the first time one of the young Americans who had defied United States legislators to enlist in the RAF. His aircraft, a Wellington bomber, had crash-landed in neutral Belgium in February, and he and the remainder of the crew had been interned. Now they had been released, and were seeking a means of returning to Britain. Three other members of the crew joined Boothe on their journey back to Paris, crammed with their luggage into a small car. The journey via Ghent was uneventful. Life seemed normal, people wandering about on their everyday business. But within the hour they had come on the results of an air attack the previous night on the town of Aalst. Glass littered the streets, the railway bridge was little more than twisted metal, and buildings around it were still smoldering from the fires. As they left the town, they started coming across, first in ones and twos, and then in ever greater numbers, refugees attempting to flee the fighting zone. "Now we began to pass them on the roads, on foot with little bundles on their tired backs, in old carts, in high hay-wagons, on bicycles, in camions, and in broken-down jalopies of every sort." After struggling to get across the French customs post ("did they not realize there was a war on?") the tired little group arrived in Paris late that night. The first thing Boothe observed was that the Ritz had already thinned out its numbers of aged, bleach-haired, fur-lined, Pekinese-toting dowagers universally known in elevated circles as the "harpies" (some, she regretted, were American). They had evidently found a safer abode, most probably on the Riviera.

—◊—

In Paris, Abbott Liebling awoke to the sound of air-raid sirens wailing plaintively over the city. Rushing to his window above the little Square

Louvois, he saw that all the other residents were doing the same, peering out of their windows at the sky in various states of undress. The noise of far-off aircraft was barely discernable through the racket put up by the antiaircraft guns. The overwhelming attitude of the people was one of relief. Well, at last the *drôle de guerre* is finally over! Now we can get stuck into *Les Boches*, and show them what's what! One of his acquaintances, a Captain de Cholet, observed nonchalantly: "It's good that it's starting at last," he said. "We can beat the Boches and have it over with by autumn." At the races at Auteuil that afternoon (which he attended alone, as Cholet had to rejoin his regiment), Liebling observed no new concern that the war had somehow edged slightly closer, now that the German offensive had begun. German paratroops were landing across the Netherlands, Winston Churchill had replaced Chamberlain as prime minister of Great Britain that day, but the primary considerations in Paris remained the new three-year-old hurdlers and the new summer fashions. People were mentally settling down, like 1914 to 1918, to a long war. In any case, confidence in ultimate victory was a public duty. The greatest delusion of the time was that because the French army was the strongest in Europe, German defeat was inevitable. As all soldiers know, it's not the size of your army that counts but how you use it. It also helps if the army wants to fight.

Paul Reynaud was in high spirits, telling Bullitt as the French army advanced into Belgium to block the northern wheel of the expected Wehrmacht advance, "The battle which is now engaged is after all a fight for liberty in the world, and on the outcome of it will depend whether we in France and you in America as well can hold our heads a little higher or must hold them much lower." Bullitt wholeheartedly agreed. With isolated exceptions, however, America did not see that this was also her struggle.

That summer had been beautiful, the gentlest and prettiest in decades. The sun blessed everyone, young and old, rich and poor, native or *touriste*, with its soothing rays. The trees and plants in the wide avenues, open spaces, and public parks of Paris bloomed impressively with luxuriant growth. But to those like Jimmy Sheean and his wife, Dinah Forbes-Robertson, who were awaiting with trepidation a replication of the Teuton tsunami they had seen in Czechoslovakia, the balmy weather had a sting in its tail. They called it "Hitler Weather," perfectly arranged by the gods of war to offer the best opportunity for an invading army. The Sheeans were staying in the Hotel de Crillon, opposite the US embassy, which boasted a popular bar-restaurant on the Boissy d'Anglas side that, although frighteningly expensive, attracted an eclectic clientele, all prepared to proffer their views on every possible subject, including that of the strange state of war that existed with Germany. That night, however, the opening of the German offensive worried Parisians so much that, unlike Jimmy and Dinah, few ventured out.

For the week that followed, Paris seemed in limbo. The weather was hot, the sun shining strongly over all northern France. Not a drop of rain fell. Paris seemed full, even with the menfolk away at the front, because the weather brought people onto the streets. Families who had been drifting back from the countryside after being evacuated at the start of the war many months before went back to the country, but there seemed no slackening in enthusiasm for the cafés, theaters, and entertainments. The long-awaited invasion had begun, but there was no general expectation, at least among the mass of the population, that the war would follow any course different from the last one. The enemy would be held far to the east.

—m—

It was the first sight of carts laden with people and possessions meandering disconsolately through Le Perray, twenty-five miles southwest of Paris, where Philippe D'Albert Lake was now stationed, that first brought the realities of war to Virginia's kitchen window. It was a few days after May 10, 1940, the day that Sevareid had been so rudely awakened from his bed in Valence. The traffic trundling past Virginia's house was too slow to raise any dust from the hard-baked road, but with them came the first scent of defeat, something that seemed to permeate every particle of the atmosphere: fear. The German armies had invaded Holland and Belgium and were driving hard for France, just as they had done at the start of the Great War. In response, a large French and British force was pouring northwest to counter the German advance, just as they had done in 1914. History was repeating itself, she thought. The newspapers seemed to indicate that not all was well with the Allied defenses, something the presence of the refugees seemed to affirm. As the days went by, the numbers of tired evacuees multiplied, carts piled high with furniture, bedding, and children. Those unfortunate enough not to possess a cart made their way south pushing bicycles loaded down with bedding, or tiredly shuffling along on their feet.

By the time a week had gone by, Virginia was aware of a new feature of the exodus: nervousness. She could see it in the people around her, on the radio, even—if it were possible—suffused in the air. It was unsettling. Philippe was awakened at 5:00 A.M. one morning by an agitated and dusty officer who had travelled in haste from Paris, horrified to see, at this stage of the battle, that men were sleeping through the night in the rear areas. "It is complete hell up there," he blurted. "Nobody has any idea of what is going on." Soldiers began guarding important buildings, crossroads, and public utilities such as power plants, water and sewerage works, bayonets fixed determinedly to the ends of their rifles.

It was on Wednesday, May 15, that the first chink in France's fabled armor was suddenly observed. In the Ritz, Charles Mendl rushed into their suite and announced dramatically to Elsie that they must pack and leave. The Germans had broken through at Sedan, the lightly defended area between the end of the Maginot Line and the Belgian frontier opposite the great wooded forests of the Ardennes. Mendl recognized the Wehrmacht's breakthrough for what it was, and following some spirited debate, the following day a small caravan of three cars piled high with luggage, with the Mendls in their Rolls-Royce, headed south to Biarritz, far from the approaching storm of war. Abbott Liebling described May 15 as "the beginning of fear"; Jimmy Sheean, as the start of "the panic." For some days now Belgian refugees had been flooding into Paris, some to stay in the city and others to continue on, if they had the money and a place to stay. They came using every method. The rich came first in their large, American-built automobiles. Those who could afford train tickets flooded the emergency services put on by the Belgian and French railways. Every vehicular contrivance boasting a motor was pressed into service, as was anything with wheels and a harness, assuming horses could be found. The desperate even attached their protesting milk-cows to the traces. There were soon no bicycles left in the Low Countries, as all were being used to escape the advancing enemy. Those who had nothing, of course, had to walk. They did so pushing perambulators piled high with the pathetic moveable goods that desperate people believed might, in their panic, help them wherever they were going.

Sir Charles Mendl's prescience drew from the fact that he had been privy to secret information provided by the British embassy. This wasn't available to the ordinary population, for whom wartime censorship now prevented the rapid dissemination of accurate news. But from Thursday, May 16, people began to talk of the war in increasingly fearful tones. Did you know that the Germans were south of Soissons (actually, they didn't get there for another three weeks)? The stories carried by the refugees spoke of a living hell wherever the German armies had been. Bit by bit information was made public that indicated that not all was well with the state of the French defenses.

—⁂—

For Dorothy ("Drue") Tartière, the overriding emotion at this torrent of bad news was a mixture of astonishment that France was collapsing so quickly, and revulsion at the behavior of the country's political leaders. Tartière, a veteran of the prewar Charlie Chan capers, had only the year before given up Hollywood to become a proud Frenchwoman, through marriage into an old French family. In the first week of the war her new husband, Jacques Tartière, volunteered for the army, and she joined the new French shortwave radio station, Paris Mondial (Paris Global), run by the Ministry of Information, which, among other things, ran English-speaking programs about France into North America. Her manager was Jean Fraysse. The station did not hesitate in its broadcasts to be explicit to its international audiences about the threat that Nazi Germany posed to the peace of Europe, to the extent that Drue (announcing using her maiden name, Dorothy Leyton) received five separate threats from the Germans that should she ever be captured by them, she would be put to death.

Her first experience of Nazi cruelty came when, shortly after the German attack on the West on May 10, 1940, she and two fellow expatriate Americans, Louise Macy (the Paris correspondent for *Harper's Bazaar*) and Isabel Kemp, spent some of their spare time assisting the many hundreds of shell-shocked refugees who washed up, tired, hungry, ill, and sometimes injured, at the Gare Montparnasse:

> The large, grey, dismal railroad station was a mass of misery. I saw grandmothers holding dead babies in their arms, women with parts of their faces shot away, and insane women who had lost their children, their husbands, and all reason for living. Some of these Belgian peasants would suddenly remember the many things they had been forced to leave undone on their property, the cattle untended, the dogs unfed, and then they would let out screams of rage and despair, which resounded through the big bare station. Louise Macy and Isabel Kemp were kept busy day and night changing babies' diapers, bandaging the wounded, and tending the sick. The stench, the filth, and the grief that filled the Gare Montparnasse during those difficult weeks were almost unbearable.

On the day the Mendls fled, Paris saw the start of a mass migration, but this time into, rather than from, the city. Ordinary people, uprooted from their homes and livelihoods by the onrush of mechanized war, and with memories fresh in their minds of something similar that happened a mere quarter century before, turned the refugee movement into the largest ever seen in Europe. Initially, the railway stations were the first stop for those entering the city, although as the days went by every sort of perambulation could be seen making its slow, dusty way into the capital, either with smoking gas fumes or with four legs and plodding wearily in front of a cart, invariably piled high with every kind of personal belonging salvaged from a home standing in the pathway of a marauding army. With them came stories of real suffering, as well as the exaggerated fantasies of a panicked population. "Many refugees had seen German soldiers dressed as nuns," recorded Sheean, "the stories of parachutists and fifth columnists were wildly improbable—as improbable as the truth, but with less technical accuracy; many intelligent Frenchmen thought they had actually seen a German parachutist come down at the Etoile, in the heart of Paris." Drue Tartière heard many stories that shocked her. It was impossible to know what was true, false, or merely exaggerated by fear:

> One old woman told us that at a railroad station the Germans had ordered the frantic refugees to get into a waiting train. As some of them eagerly started for what they thought a means of escape, the Germans wantonly mowed them down with machine guns. En route their railroad cars had often been bombed by the Germans, though they were scarcely military objectives, and whole carloads of the dead bodies which were collected had been pushed off onto sidings, where the corpses lay unburied. I arranged for some of our radio writers to go to the Gare Montparnasse and take down accounts of some of these Belgian refugees for our broadcasts to America.

With this mass influx of humanity came the first stirrings of fear. There was always a lag between events on the battlefield and the people finding out about it at home, but from May 16 another terrible rumor was heard: the enemy was making staggering gains opposite the forest of the Ardennes at Sedan, and were in danger of entirely turning the French southern flank and making a run for Paris. It was clear to Drue that what the French had called the *drôle de guerre* had been nothing of the kind for the Germans, who had utilized every passing moment to prepare for war. They had attacked through the Low Countries, attracting to them the French and British armies, and deliberately generating group hysteria among these populations to create a destabilizing mass movement of people into France. At the same time, they were moving like a knife through butter through the weakly defended southern flank, opposite the Ardennes. The received wisdom from the Great War was that armies fought armies, strength on strength, trench on trench. Now it seemed as if the Wehrmacht was doing something different. They were deliberately avoiding the main Allied armies in the north to circumvent them in the south, and by so doing destabilizing the French defensive plan. The mighty Maginot Line was largely ignored. For the French, seeking to fight the new war on the same terms as the old, it was shockingly unexpected. For the Germans, seeking to secure both a moral and a tactical advantage over the defensive plans of their enemy, it was a stratagem of extraordinary brilliance. For the people of France, Belgium, and Holland, the entire experience was one of mental, physical, and emotional discombobulation. Millions were on the move. Nothing was settled or permanent. Would life ever be the same again? "One came to doubt the physical security of the universe," concluded Sheean, "the likelihood that there would be another day, and the possibility of personal survival, not for any exact reason, but because the whole question of life seemed to have lost its bearings in a general downfall of established structures." "Do you realize what's happening?" Hubert "Red" Knickerbocker demanded one day when he and Sheean were walking by the river and the Sunday afternoon crowds converged on Notre-Dame. "Do you realize it?" "Yes, I know," Sheean said. "It is the end of the world."

From May 16, events moved at an extraordinary pace. It appeared that all pretense by the government that the situation was in hand had been abandoned. Government ministries started burning files without bothering to hide their activities from the public gaze. Vincent Sheean could see truckloads of files being loaded in convoys at the Ministry of the Navy, next to the Hotel de Crillon in the Place de la Concorde. Walking past the Ministry of Foreign Affairs at the Quai d'Orsay after the news of the German breakthrough the night before had been understood, he could see, through the iron grille, the archives being binned in the courtyard. Reynaud assured the population that he would never leave the capital, but it was clear that the arms of government had different ideas. Rumors about what the government was doing, as well as the fantastical military powers now being attributed to the Germans, spread like wildfire in the confusion. When Virginia Cowles returned to the city on May 10, she saw little to demonstrate that the city was at war. The day was beautiful, Paris resplendent in all its glory, except for the fact that panic lay close beneath the surface. Fifth columnists were expected everywhere, and parachutists were routinely assumed to be dressed as priests and nuns. The Standard Oil Company, which owned large stocks of oil in dumps near Paris, began burning their supplies. One day in early June Robert Murphy recalled that for "days thereafter the city was covered with heavy black smoke, which provided a kind of Dante's Inferno background for the pitiful refugees from several countries who flowed in and through and out of Paris, most of them not knowing where they were going." Unfortunately, not everyone knew where the smoke was from: it was quite literally a fog of war. Some thought that it was a German smoke screen. Quentin Reynolds believed it was "a man-made fog, a smoke screen thrown over Paris to hide the railroad stations from the bombers." Walter Kerr told *Herald Tribune* readers in New York that at "9 A.M., from the Rond-Point on the Champs Elysees, it was so smoky that you could not see the obelisk on the Place de la Concorde or the Arc de Triomphe at the Place de l'Etoile."

Bizarre events impressed themselves on Sheean's mind. Driving in a taxi with his friend "Red" Knickerbocker down the Quai de Montebello during "the panic," he saw a crowd congregating outside Notre-Dame de Paris. The driver had no idea what the crowd was doing, as it did not represent any of the standard times for churchgoing. When he got to the US embassy, he was told that the ambassador and other members of staff had gone to the cathedral. A Canadian general was there, covered with decorations from the last war, who told them of this visit to Notre-Dame:

> *"What have they gone there for?" I asked.*
> *The Canadian general looked at us rather severely.*
> *"To pray," he said.*
> *"Do you mean to say," Knick inquired, "that that's the best we can do?"*

On May 15, 1940—a mere five days after the offensive began—Paul Reynaud told Bullitt that the "situation continued to be one of the utmost gravity. The greatest battle in history was in progress in the region of Sedan. The Germans had crossed the Meuse at many points north of Sedan." The French defenders were being overwhelmed, according to Reynaud, who pointed to the apparent disparity between the weight of German aircraft and the French forces available to counter them. Of course, this was because the German attack was concentrated at a single point, while French and British aircraft—of which there was at least a parity with Germany—were scattered across a wide territory. Nor too were Allied aircraft deployed in the same way as the Luftwaffe, for which doctrine expressly decreed that ground troops in the attack be supported by the coordinated use of specially designed ground attack aircraft, such as the infamous JU-88, or Stuka. Sedan marked the spot at which the Maginot Line ended: there were no fortifications between Sedan and Paris, and the French and British armies were deployed in the Low Countries of Belgium and Holland, far from the point of German breakthrough. Given previous concerns by Reynaud about aircraft numbers, he immediately asked Churchill to commit the remainder of the British-based RAF units to the battle. "In concluding our conversation," Bullitt commented, "Reynaud said that the French counterattacks against the German 'hernia' in the Sedan region had not been successful either in cutting it off or reducing it. On the contrary the 'hernia' was growing hour by hour. The situation could not be more grave."

As each day went by, the news got worse. Bullitt kept a running commentary going with Roosevelt. On May 16, he reported that the "Belgian army south of Namur had collapsed completely. The Germans had poured through this gap with fast moving, motorized units. These had now reached the region of Laon and Reims. . . ." On the same day, Bullitt sent the wives and children of the embassy staff to Bordeaux and agreed, at the request of the British ambassador, to take charge of Great Britain's interests in Paris. The British embassy was now burning its documents and the American embassy its codes.

From this point on, events rushed at a dizzying pace. On May 16, Paris was officially declared *la zone des armées*, an announcement that exacerbated the general panic and began the second great refugee crisis: that of Parisians loading up their belongings and heading to the country. If Paris was in the combat area, it would surely be a magnet for bombers. Clare Boothe noticed a sudden diminution of effort in support of the refugees arriving in the Parisian train stations when she next visited the Gare du Nord on May 18. At the start of the mass influx, a week before, Parisians and foreigners alike had thrown themselves into selfless endeavor in support of the poor, homeless masses who had suddenly descended on the capital. "Rich American expatriates (I saw now there were many good ones) rushed around saying to the nurses in loud and strident (and blessed) voices: 'What do you need? Bandages, alcohol, felt slippers? We'll buy them, we'll buy them!' And the nurses would say: 'Today we need nipples for bottles; we can't feed the little babies, they choke out of cups.' So the American women in their big long cars drove into the city to buy what the nurses wanted." Now those who had once provided succor realized that they themselves were in danger, and were in the process of flight.

The horror of Germany's rapid advance and its ruthless use of terror from the skies to cow the civilian population were widely reported. On May 20, Bullitt told of the wife of a government minister, "Madame Georges Monnet who had been at Soissons attempting to evacuate small children. They were walking on the road toward Paris since they had no means of transportation and she was trying to keep them singing to help their little feet to move. Two German airplanes came down and machine gunned them and the road was filled with little bodies." Wayne Chatfield Taylor of the Red Cross told him that stories of German barbarities were not exaggerated, and that "there were at least five million persons on the road and that a vast number of these would die of starvation and illness unless they could be cared for by American help." As much as a quarter of France's entire population of forty million was on the move. Dr. Charles Bove, one of the surgeons at the American Hospital at Neuilly, noted that many of the refugees' cars had bullet holes, courtesy of the Luftwaffe. Casualties from the fighting, soldiers and civilians, were brought back into the city's hospitals, and the American Hospital provided 240 beds (doubling its peacetime numbers) in Neuilly and at an outstation established for the purpose at Fontainebleau. The surgeons worked all the hours available to treat the wounded. Bove recalled operating "until late into the night, cutting away on jagged wounds like butchers in a slaughterhouse," feet becoming too sore to walk, and when attempting to "straighten up out of the bent position I had maintained for so many hours over the operating table caus[ing] excruciating pain." One of Bove's patients was a Mrs. LeClerq from Brussels:

> She and her husband had driven from Belgium with their six-months-old baby boy to escape the Nazis. A strafing plane had machine-gunned the auto. A bullet had gone through the mother's arm, which had been sheltering the baby against her breast, and it had penetrated the child's neck. Apparently, the baby's large blood vessel had been perforated, for the woman, when I first examined her, was covered with dried blood. The child had died instantly, but the mother had been forced to sit with its body on her lap for five hours until they neared Valenciennes. There they had pulled to the side of the road, and the father had dug a grave in a field. Wrapping the child in his overcoat, he had buried it. His face was ashen as he told me the story. He had soaked his handkerchief in a bottle of brandy that he had taken along and had tied it around his wife's wound. That was the only medication she had received until I saw her. I debrided the wound, put a splint on the arm and left the couple alone in their grief.

—m—

On May 21, the prime minister, Paul Reynaud, nervously warned his divided country that the nation was in danger as the Germans astonishingly seized Arras and Amiens, after repulsing a British armored counterattack the previous day. Pétain, the victor of Verdun, had been appointed military adviser on May 18. To anxious Parisians it seemed clear now that the brilliant German strategy was to drive hard for the

Channel ports, cutting off the French and British troops committed early to Belgium, before turning on an undefended Paris.

In the French capital Eric Sevareid did what he could to stay on top of the situation. It was difficult. As each day went by, it was increasingly hard to find out what was going on. France, of course, would never fall. That was obvious, and unquestioned. It was the most well-armed, best-defended country on the Continent, far stronger in terms of numbers of tanks, soldiers and aircraft, for instance, than the Germans arrayed against them. But what was going on? It was impossible to gain any real sense of the battle—where it would all end—from the official military spokesman. The journalists gathered each morning at the Ministry of War to hear Colonel Thomas wax eloquent about the latest events on the battlefield, far distant from his immaculately pressed uniform, care-fully brushed kepi, and sparkling black boots. According to the elegant staff officer, the Boches, each morning, had suffered massive losses in the previous day's fighting. Strangely, however, the line denoting their forward pocket in Flanders, at which Thomas waved airily with his bil-liard cue pointer, crept rapidly—and inexorably—towards the Channel coast. Nor could the truth be determined from the British and French newspapers. Each day fantastic claims of huge German losses in tanks, aircraft, and men seemed to do nothing to halt the relentless slide of the gray-green mass of helmeted German manhood towards the sea. Ambassador Bullitt swung from euphoria to despair, as Reynaud asked him repeatedly whether America could be persuaded to join the war alongside the Allies. For Bullitt, the calm passivity of the Parisian popu-lation as it awaited destruction from the air "did honor to the human race." He was quick to swallow some of the newly emerging prejudices of his hosts, one of which was an increasing hostility to the British, who to many Frenchmen were traditionally responsible for the country's woes, and who were now selfishly abandoning the country to its fate.

Who was telling the truth? Sevareid was not sure, but he was convinced nevertheless that actions in this instance spoke louder than words. Why did the German pocket grow every day if they were suffering the catastrophic losses claimed of them by their enemies? Something wasn't right. He began to suspect what it was. France was losing but had done nothing to prepare for the catastrophe that would engulf it if the French and British armies in Picardy were forced into the sea. Looking one morning at the couple of soldiers standing disconsolately on the road to Le Bourget Airport, he realized with a start that Paris was not defended. If the armies in the north were defeated—as all the evidence seemed to suggest they would be—Paris was entirely open to the invader. Everything the flailing government did seemed to be a reaction to a new crisis. On May 19, another ancient soldier—Weygand—was flown in with great fanfare from the Levantine colonies, to replace the clownish Maurice Gamelin, architect and exponent of the already redundant Maginot Line. But still onward the Germans marched. From Berlin, the strange nasal tones of William Joyce mocked the Allied defensive efforts and predicted the imminent fall of Paris and thus of the Third Republic. Sevareid tried to get some semblance of a story from the front, but no single tale he was told ever tallied with another. No one knew what was going on, except that the Germans were everywhere: ahead, behind, to the side. They seemed to be magicians. Certainly, witchcraft was afoot. Could it be that Joyce was right, and that the Wehrmacht was on the verge of a second—after Poland—astonishing victory?

Could the country truly be threatened? Many people now thought so, if the number of military cars, trucks, and other vehicles travelling away from Paris through Le Perray was anything to go by. Why, thought Virginia D'Albert Lake, was all this military traffic travelling southwest? Was it because they thought that Paris was no longer safe? Nearly every hour increased the number of people on the road. Refugees—military, political, and civilian—were all heading away from the advancing German armies and the threatened obliteration of Paris. Some cars, she observed, were full of exhausted French air force officers, who gave every impression of having just come from the front. Philippe reported breaking up a fight that broke out in a restaurant in Le Perray. Two hundred air force men had been abandoned by their officers, and morale and military discipline had collapsed. Their country and the army, they said, had let them down. Rudderless in a disorienting war, they did not know where to go, or what to do.

There was no food for them. They would have to sleep that night in the nearby forest. These men seemed to be a metaphor for a confused and collapsing country. They were followed the next day by large numbers of troops redeployed in the area after successfully making their escape from encirclement in Belgium. But it was at the cost of their cohesion. The French army was clearly in retreat, the Germans now advancing on every front in frighteningly focused thrusts.

The pattern was unfailingly similar. Artillery would batter a position before being swept aside by armored columns. The foot soldiers arrived in tandem with those damned flying artillery pieces, the Stukas, which could drop their bombs on a sous from a screaming dive. Each Stuka seemed to those at the receiving end to be diving directly at them, individually and personally. It was at best disconcerting; at worst, terrifying. The panzers would flood on through the fields while the truck-borne infantry would turn up to deal with the defenders. By this time, of course, the disoriented French and British would now consider themselves cut off, behind enemy lines, with no prospect of being relieved. Surrender would seem to be a more sensible option than the forlorn hope of continued resistance when the surrounding fields were dotted with the gray-green uniforms and coal-scuttle helmets of their enemy. This wasn't how their fathers had told them war was fought. How did the Germans manage to discomfort them on the battlefield so comprehensively? Were they inadequate soldiers, unable to meet the standards of campaigning set by the previous generation? Or was it that their tactics were simply not able to cope with the shock of a comprehensive assault by German infantry, armor, and air power all descending on them at once? Virginia could see from the exhausted, twisted faces of the soldiers who trudged in and around Le Perray that they had "seen hell let loose," many unable to comprehend what had happened to them. By Thursday, May 23, some three thousand soldiers milled around, to the consternation of the villagers, who did not understand why so many troops were so far to the rear. If the French army was here, where on earth were the Germans?

In Berlin, by contrast, the war seemed to be far away. No bombs had yet fallen on the city, and the sound of the guns was distant. The people wandered the streets window-shopping, chatting pleasantly, without seemingly a care in the world. It was as if they did not know of the cataclysms that were at that moment facing Holland, Belgium, France, and Britain at the hands of their husbands, fathers, and sons. On Sunday, June 3, even as the last of the British Expeditionary Force (BEF) were struggling off the beaches of Dunkirk, Shirer watched with astonishment the thousands of late-Sunday afternoon strollers meandering down the Kurfürstendamm and filling the Tiergarten, enjoying the warm summer Sabbath, "chatting quietly over their ersatz coffee or their ice-cream." Did they not know that there was a war on? Yes, certainly, but here in Berlin the war was an abstract concept, far from the experience of the ordinary person. Paris was being bombed, and London felt in danger, but in Berlin, all was at peace. Perhaps, the people thought, this war was not so bad after all. When, eleven days later, the news of the fall of Paris was announced, Keenan observed it "was received with the same inscrutable silence and reserve. I rode miles, that afternoon, on the enclosed upper deck of a bus, where practically everyone's conversation was audible. I heard no one as much as mention the event; the talk was all of food cards and the price of stockings."

—m—

Recognizing that her own evacuation might soon be required, Virginia filled her blue Simca 8 sedan with gasoline in preparation for a long drive. But still she waited, close to Philippe in the gathering confusion of Le Perray. On June 3, the BBC reported that the Luftwaffe had bombed Paris that afternoon. Every day the exodus from Paris grew, to the point that, on June 10, exactly a month after the German invasion, the A10 south to Orléans was a single stream of dusty humanity, military and civilian mixed haphazardly together. The British Expeditionary Force, along with many French and Belgian troops, had been evacuated from the Dunkirk beaches and taken out of the fight altogether. The Germans were reported as far east as Rouen. It was incredible.

Much of what Virginia saw was incongruous, even bizarre. Buses full of children were mixed with trucks full of troops; men, women, and children of all descriptions on foot, on bicycles, in ancient cars dating from the early days of motoring, together with ambulances driven by women—fancy that!—and hundreds if not thousands of horse-drawn carts. Whole kitchens went by on carts, as did every possible form of transport piled high with whatever the owners felt important. She saw an ancient car in which the calm black face of a sheep could be seen, looking out the open window. Elsewhere the Stukas had fallen on the refugees on the roads, causing havoc and terror as well as bloodshed, but so far, despite some air-raid alarms, no enemy planes had yet appeared over their village.

It was nerve-wracking, watching this sea of humanity wash past her door. But still Philippe had no orders to move, and Virginia was determined to stay. In any case, even as she heard that the government had evacuated its ministries from Paris, the thought of joining the wretches on the road horrified her. What if, as the newspapers were regularly reporting, the enemy machine-gunned the helpless mass of citizenry as they fled? It was no place to die. Clare Boothe recalled that time merged during this period. Nobody "ever knew what day it was or how many actual hours had elapsed since the last awful thing had happened. Let me see, you said, was that before or after the break-through at Sedan? Or was that the day the Bulge reached Arras? The daily habits which give us our sense of time were all brutally and irrevocably broken. You made no dates for the morrow. You followed no routine, or a skeleton one, had no plans, no plans at all for the future. You ate, you dressed, you walked, you did the chore or deed or duty the moment demanded. But pity, anger, frustration, uncertainty, the extraordinary feeling that tomorrow, tonight, an hour, might bring sudden death to those you loved, or to yourself, blurred all remembrance of place and people and occasion. You lived in a timeless world, punctuated at timeless intervals by sleepless nightmare nights. Only the progress of the battle out there, or the air-raids here, were matters for timing."

—ᴍ—

Fear crept up on people. Within a week of the German attack on May 10, the nonchalance of the early days had disappeared, replaced by grimaces of concern when people discussed the situation in the street. The nights were noisy with the racket produced by Paris's antiaircraft defenses shooting at high-flying reconnaissance planes, although there were few bombing attacks. Was this the lull before the storm? News of the destruction of Rotterdam was combined with the horror stories from Warsaw the previous year. Was this to be Paris's fate? These worries preyed on all, and were exploited skillfully by the Germans, who dropped propaganda leaflets warning of imminent destruction from the air. On May 12, Clare Boothe was returning to the city from a dinner party in Versailles when a gendarme stopped them in the Rue Suchet, warning them of an air-raid alert, and ushering them into a nearby cellar. Looking up, she could see the antiaircraft shells bursting like fireworks among the "pale, thin, greedy fingers of the searchlights," giving carnival-like gloss to the horror of aerial bombardment. The cellar was full. One of the women said to her, "I am very tired of this. I wish it would end. This is not a life for ordinary people to lead. Why can't the Germans let our soldiers fight this war? *Tout de meme c'est insupportable.*" This was a war in which the Germans deliberately targeted civilians, not just the enemy armed forces. This was total war. The whole country was at war, and the people suddenly knew it.

Abbott Liebling admitted to what he described as a funk, when, on the night of May 21, after Paul Reynaud had acknowledged that the Germans were at Arras and that France was in mortal danger, he thought of the ceiling falling in as a result of the bombing. People began grasping at straws. General Weygand was reported to be optimistic about the military situation. Rumors swirled around that negotiations were underway to secure a peace deal. Then more bad news would flood in from the front, and the Germans would be reported to be a few miles from Paris. In these circumstances people asked themselves who had betrayed them. Were the masses of refugees in the city fifth columnists sent by the Nazis as the vanguard of the attack? How could this calamity have occurred? Information was hard to obtain. What was actually going on? Did anyone know? The battle front was so fluid, and movements by one side or the other appeared so unstable, that it was hard to comprehend the exact situation. In the absence of hard facts, rumor abounded. In the circumstances, the wild yo-yoing of expectation about the outcome was hardly unexpected. The government was conflicted by the desire not to be the instrument of panic, which meant that the official communiqués remained hopelessly optimistic. On Monday, May 27, Liebling attended a press conference where the official spokesman, Pierre Comert, told the assembled journalists that things were "proceeding normally." Comert, a well-known anti-Nazi, had found himself duped by the attitude that although things seemed bad, it was simply inconceivable that France might lose. Comert had told Quentin Reynolds, who had arrived in the city on May 9, that it might "take three weeks or a month" to organize his press credentials. He shouldn't worry: he had plenty of time. The following day, however, Paris awoke to the devastating news that Belgium had capitulated. With Belgium gone, the entire northern strategy had been undermined, with the French and British armies deployed to a country that was no longer in the fight. In these circumstances the Luftwaffe did not need to undertake a mass bombardment of Paris: a mere demonstration was required to induce mass terror. An attack on the suburb of Passy reduced a block of apartments to rubble, and glass lay shattered across the streets. The exodus from the city accelerated. Liebling found his hotel emptying rapidly. Taxis had become a thing of the past, and the telephone system was permanently out of order.

Clare Boothe was a passionate interventionist, believing that the United States remained criminally indifferent to France's plight. She observed that the few Americans in Paris at the end of May were journalists, destined to write nothing more than "Baedekers to Armageddon" because there was no longer any point in attempting to persuade the American public—or politicians—that there was any significant principle at stake by supporting France in its hour of need. It was painful to be an American in Paris, too, because one was forced to make excuses for the inaction or indecision of those at home. Does America recognize and appreciate freedom and democracy enough to warrant helping to defend France? It appeared not. Most Americans who were so asked in those days gave evasive replies. Of course America was on France's side! Of course it would come to France's aid! Would America provide airplanes and financial credits? Of course! "Knowing how little the United States was likely to do," thought Abbott Liebling, "I wondered whether we should ever be able to go back to Paris with our heads up." It drove some mad with frustration. "Why don't people in America please stop being 'sorry for refugees' and 'ninety-eight per cent sympathetic to the Allies,' and answer that question God-damn quick?" "Red" Knickerbocker asked rhetorically of Boothe. "You think it is our war?" Boothe asked. "Hell, yes," Knick replied. She agreed.

CHAPTER EIGHT

Escape from Paris

There had been no thought in Drue Tartière's mind that Paris, let alone France, would ever fall to *les Boches*. A long and ugly war would no doubt follow the German invasion, but France had experienced this twice before in living memory, and had survived. She was surprised, however, by the speed with which her new world collapsed. By early June it was clear that an evacuation of the Paris Mondial staff might be required, to follow any government withdrawal from the capital. The news became ever more alarming, but no instructions were given to leave. Indeed, the Ministry of Information insisted that they remain. Then on June 10, the staff discovered that the government had fled to Tours. The Germans were at the gates. Wandering around that afternoon to the Ministry of Information, they discovered that the Ministry, too, had departed the capital, forgetting all about the forty-two-member staff of Paris Mondial. The following morning, June 11, it was a sad group who jammed themselves into the few cars they had pulled together, to slowly make their way out of the city. "As we passed the Gare Montparnasse," Drue recalled, "I noticed that as far as the eye could see, the streets around the station were one mass of people with their belongings, trying to get on trains going anywhere out of Paris. The day was stifling, and there were panic, misery, and anxiety wherever one looked. On the road out of the city people were pushing baby carriages or pulling small carts, others were on loaded bicycles, and some were walking, carrying their children and their valises. Some were moving their families and possessions in wagons drawn by oxen."

It did not take long for them to see the doleful effects of German barbarity, proof to Drue that terror was one the German stratagems in its war on the French people. Dead bodies—so far as she could see of men, women, and children—littered the sides of the roads where the vast columns of refugees had been struck by bombs and bullets. Memories of Guernica and Warsaw, together with more recent news reports from the cities of Belgium and the Netherlands, filled people with panic that the Germans would mete out death from the sky over Paris. This was the primary motivation for flight. As the fields, rich with red poppies, blue cornflowers, and yellow wheat waved gently and incongruously in the warm summer breeze, still-smoking vehicles lay overturned in ditches, people stood weeping, and blood stained the ground where broken bodies lay.

On that first night, the motley caravan of radio staff created a camp-site amidst a grove of trees outside Orléans, surrounded by hundreds of scattered vehicles belonging to other exhausted refugees. The rain fell throughout the night, adding to the misery of thousands lying out in the open without any form of shelter. A hasty breakfast the following dawn took the convoy down the Loire towards Tours, the involuntary tourists already feeling grimy and exhausted. The only accommodation they could find that night was a brothel: the local police threw out the working girls and requisitioned the building for them. That night they broadcast to America, describing something of their journey from Paris, the terror lurking in the air that deliberately hunted out the columns of refugees, and the misery of the millions of men, women, and children on the road. Back at the brothel that night, Drue's Alsatian maid, Nadine, refused to sleep in one of the "unchaste" beds so recently vacated. Drue, too tired to care, fell asleep immediately.

During the day Tours had been a scene of extraordinary confusion. Would the government stay, or go on to Bordeaux? No one knew. At least one answer came the following morning, when, once more, the Paris Mondial team discovered that they had been left behind. The entire apparatus of government had vacated Tours during the night of June 12–13, having only lingered in the town for a handful of days. Wearily, the Paris Mondial group packed up and joined the armada heading southwest at little more than walking pace. "Some of our French secretaries who had never before been outside of Paris enjoyed the variety of this trip," Tartière recalled, "but for the rest of us it was a heartbreaking, pitiful journey in defeat."

As soon as they reached Bordeaux they set themselves up in the government radio station and began broadcasting to the English-speaking world. Journalistic balance was now a thing of the past. In increasingly urgent tones they described the terror of war, the fearsomeness of the Nazi military machine, the wanton brutality of the German approach to war, which included the indiscriminate terrorizing of the population by such means as machine-gunning columns of refugees from the air. One night soon after their arrival in Bordeaux she recalled an air raid at about 1:30 A.M. The announcer at the time, a man she recalled as Smitty, screamed into the microphone, "Hear that, America, the God-damned sons of bitches are bombing us now!" It was an appropriate swan song for Paris Mondial, as the following morning the station went off the air.

—◊◊◊—

Abbott Liebling joined forces with other journalists, Waverley Root, the Paris correspondent for the *Chicago Tribune* and then the *Washington Post*, and John Elliott of the *Herald Tribune*, to flee Paris on Monday, June 10, when the government declared that it would not defend the city. Making their way first to Tours in the wake of the departing French government, they travelled in an ancient Citroën "with a motor that made a noise like antiaircraft fire and was responsible for a few minor panics during our journey . . . ," Liebling quipped. By the time they left Paris, the streets were empty but the railway stations remained a sea of helpless humanity, great, swirling crowds trying to secure passage out of the city.

The road was crowded with soldiers and civilians in every possible conveyance, some even on horseback. Progress was painfully slow, the roadside littered with the abandoned cars of a month of flight. Government departments had requisitioned the remaining city buses, each full to the gunwales. "Some of the girl stenographers and clerks," Liebling noted, "appeared to be enjoying the excursion." Everyone kept their eyes nervously peeled at the sky, but on this day the Luftwaffe were busy elsewhere, and the only planes overhead had French roundels. At Orléans they, too, attempted to find a place to sleep in a local house of ill repute, but had no luck. They were all full. "They are so tired," the *sous-mattresse* of one place told Liebling compassionately, "that some of them are actually sleeping." The little group slept in the car.

It was clear to all that as an alternative site of government, Tours was a mistake. It was too close to Paris, and it was undefended. There was insufficient accommodation for each of the departments of state, let alone the wives and "flustered and indignant" mistresses. Bordeaux or Biarritz were the obvious options. Four days later—the day the Germans unfurled gigantic Nazi flags atop the Arc de Triomphe, the Eiffel Tower, and the Quai d'Orsay—the massive cavalcade packed up and headed south, for Bordeaux. They stayed the night en route in the delightful walled village of Barbezieux, where a local teacher and garage owner assured them that France would carry on fighting. There was no notion in the minds of ordinary French men and women that their government would ever surrender to barbarism and leave them to fight the Germans alone. It was inconceivable. The remainder of the army and fleet would go to Britain and North Africa, and continue the fight from there.

—⚏—

Etta Shiber took too long to make good her escape from Paris. A 62-year-old widow, she had lived with British-born Catherine "Kitty" Bonnefous at 2, rue Balny d'Avricourt, a quiet residential area a mile north of the Arc de Triomphe, since 1936. Etta, the widow of William Noyes Shiber, the wire chief of the *New York American* and *New York Evening Journal*, had always loved France, and had spent three months of every year in Paris since 1925. With the loss first of her brother, Irving, in France, and then of her husband in 1936, she decided to make her home in Paris. The two women, while not wealthy, were sufficiently well off not to have to worry about work. Kitty lived apart from her husband, Henri, a wine merchant, an arrangement that seemed to suit them both, although they remained close. When war came, Kitty tried to persuade Etta to return home to the United States, concerned, as were most people, about the prospect of German bombing, but Etta refused. Her home was now in France, along with her most valued friends. So long as Kitty stayed, so would Etta. Wanting to contribute to the war effort, the day after Germany invaded Poland they both joined Le Foyer du Soldat Aveugle (Blind Soldiers' Home), one of three volunteer organizations recognized by the French government (the others were the Red Cross and the YMCA) that supported wounded and disabled soldiers with comforts and attention to alleviate their suffering.

As the Germans advanced, both women scorned the idea of fleeing the city. It was not possible, they reasoned, that the French would give up Paris without a fight. As the city rapidly emptied, however, they wondered at the choice they had made. The Germans were suddenly and unexpectedly close, and the awful possibility of aerial attack like that inflicted on Warsaw and Rotterdam—terror events widely publicized in the French press—loomed. On Thursday, June 13, Etta called the US embassy, and was warned that the government had fled, and that the Germans were expected in the city within hours. It appeared that the threat of aerial bombardment had now reduced, but the prospect of life under German rule decided it for them: they, too, would flee.

Doing so, however, was easier said than done. Their little car, crammed with what necessities they could jam into it, together with Etta's three small dogs, was immediately locked into a massive stream of frightened people, in vehicles of every description, on bicycles and on foot, attempting to depart the city through the Porte d'Orléans on the Route Nationale 20. It was an exodus driven by terror—a clear stratagem of the Wehrmacht to bring the country to a standstill, thus to make the country's defeat and occupation much easier—but the evacuation of Paris was not planned or controlled in any way. Their attempt to escape went at such a slow pace that it seemed clear that the Germans would reach Paris long before they could make a successful exit. Inch by inch they moved forward, along with thousands of others with the same thoughts in mind, in a queue that stretched east, southeast, and south for hundreds of miles. At 5:00 P.M. they had crawled a mere twelve miles, amidst a noisy, exhausting, dispiriting crush. The journey continued, stop-start, through the night. They dozed fitfully when the slow procession halted, awoken by a cacophony of hooting when the crawl began again, the cars behind them urging them forwards. Every time they stopped they could hear but not see the weary trudge of tired feet as people passed their car on either side. Gradually they saw the dawn rise on the horizon on June 14, the slowly awakening sky revealing a landscape on the outskirts of their beloved city littered with scenes they had never thought they would see: the roads around them clogged with people in the hundreds of thousands. The government, inept and broken, had fled before them, leaving the people to fend for themselves. A roadside restaurant offered the tired party a breakfast of Camembert and bread, which Etta and Kitty shared with the dogs, Etta observing that they "were obviously hungrier than we were, and less worried."

The day went from bad to worse. From a noisy crowd a little way forward at another roadside tavern they heard the terrible news that the radio had announced that German troops had reached Paris. The lives that they had once known—comfortable, ordered, and happy— were now behind them, their apartment under German control. *What will happen to us now?* Etta thought to herself as they edged slowly along the road, to somewhere they knew not. They could see the road reaching far into the distance, jammed with vehicles and people moving at less than walking pace. They weren't going to go very far in this state, and the thought of German air attack—for which there had been much comment in recent weeks as refugees had flowed into Paris from the northeast—made them urgently seek an alternative means of finding safety. After a hurried look at a Michelin map they decided to turn off at the next crossroads. For a while they found the freedom of the road and scooted along dusty country lanes unbothered by any other traffic, but these roads weren't leading them south, to safety. After a while they connected again with another heavily congested line of traffic heading towards them, with frightened people shouting, "Turn back! Turn back! The Germans are behind us!" The day became one of unutterable confusion. Every direction they took seemed to get them no closer to safety or away from the maelstrom of stricken humanity that assailed them on the main roads. At the end of another exhausting day, and after consulting the map, they determined that although the speedometer indicated that they had travelled two hundred miles, they were a mere twelve miles from the point at which they had left the main road many hours before. As the day ended the two women reluctantly decided to seek again the main road. At least they knew where it went, even if it was crowded to near impassability. They would just have to take their chances with everyone else.

It was already dark by the time the main road was reached, the route easily marked by the lights of cars and the endless honking of horns. Then, just as they reached the road, they heard it. The noise was inescapable. The Luftwaffe had arrived. At one level they could not comprehend how the Germans could attack obviously innocent refugees, but they knew, at another level and with absolute certainty, that wanton brutality to noncombatants was a deliberate tool of German strategy. A faint hum in the distance in the dark sky above quickly converted to a fierce roar directly overhead. In a moment Kitty had stopped the car and both women—and the dogs—were rushing into the nearby ditch. The noise above was now accompanied by the unmistakable roar of machine guns as the aircraft began to work their way down the now stationary column. Looking up from where they lay, they could see the dark bulk of the aircraft as they swept by and the muzzle flashes from the machine guns as they emptied death and destruction on the hopeless hordes below. In panic, drivers toppled their vehicles into the ditches alongside the road and screaming figures ran to the safety of the fields. Some cars, their occupants dead, stayed silent and smoking on the now empty road. The terror from the skies subsided almost as quickly as it came, but no one moved in the silence that then followed. A woman groaned in a nearby field. She must have been wounded, Etta surmised, but no one went to her aid. When they had read in the Paris newspapers that the Germans, in Poland, Belgium, and the Netherlands, had turned their guns on streams of innocent refugees, they hadn't believed it. It must be propaganda, they'd thought. How could civilized German officers order the deliberate massacre of innocent people? It wasn't possible. Now they knew. They had seen with their own eyes the extent of the barbarism Europe was having to deal with. It was shocking, almost incomprehensible. Had not the world only just finished the "war to end all wars," and yet here we had German aircraft deliberately attacking civilians? Etta heard Kitty say, almost to herself: "How does a young German flier feel, I wonder, when he opens fire on terror-stricken women and children—like us?"

Kitty and Etta lay in the ditch, holding hands to comfort each other, anxiously scanning the darkened skies in case the aircraft returned. They did. Twenty minutes later the skies were once again full of the sound of death, machine-gun bullets ripping up the road around them in an awful cacophony of death. When that attack, too, was over, it took a further half hour for people to begin getting up again, shocked to silence by what they had seen. Then, suddenly, another sound was quickly upon them. Racing down the road, headlights on full beam, came the German army, motorcycle outriders of the legions of gray-uniformed, steel-helmeted army following behind. Etta stood in awe of the purposefulness of their passing:

> Without slowing up, they swung around the few stalled cars still standing motionless in the road. There was something inhuman about those riders in their dark grey uniforms. They seemed like part of the machines they rode, as cold and as unfeeling. They looked neither to the right nor to the left as they roared by. I don't know what we had expected from the Germans, but certainly not this, certainly not that they would ignore our very presence. It was more fearsome than if they had dismounted from their

motorcycles and arrested us, almost more fearsome than if they had fired on us. This passage of mounted automatons who seemed not to see us at all imbued us with a chill far greater than any we had felt even during the confused panic of the airplane attack. I thought I had been frightened then. It was nothing to the deep-buried fear that clutched at the pit of my stomach, and twisted and turned in my flesh.

But there was nothing we could do. We could only wait. We stood by our car, just before the point where the crossroad entered the highway, and watched.

They spent the night anxiously watching the Wehrmacht columns race south. Light armored cars were followed by trucks full of steel-helmeted troops, stiffly upright in their vehicles and studiously ignoring the human detritus strewn around them. The road was theirs; its previous human population dispersed in the face of overwhelming military power. Then the tanks rumbled through, this time from the direction that Etta and Kitty had just come from, plowing through the fields and roads indiscriminately. Huddled together in their ditch, to where they had retreated, they felt useless, abandoned. It took the entire night and the rest of the following day—June 15—for the German army to complete its march south, and for the road suddenly to become clear. A German motorcyclist drove up. "You will go back to Paris," he ordered them, in excellent French. When they replied and said that they wanted to go south, to Nice, he responded contemptuously, "That, Madame, is the way we are going. You will go back to Paris." Wearily, they obeyed, and began the long tiresome journey back to 2, rue Balny d'Avricourt.

—⁂—

While Etta and Kitty were attempting to travel south, Paris had emptied, some estimates placing the population that remained in the city the day the Germans arrived at a mere seven hundred thousand (out of an original five million). Perhaps as many as fourteen million French men, women, and children were on the move in anything that could carry them, their lives torn asunder by the unexpected destruction of the country's defenses by the triumphant Wehrmacht. Robert Murphy, together with Bill Bullitt and a skeleton team from the US embassy, awaited the arrival of the conquerors. "There never has been anything like the eerie atmosphere in Paris during the two days between the departure of the French Government and the arrival of the German troops," Murphy recalled. The contrast between the busy days of peace and the empty days of war was an extraordinary one. On June 13, instead of "one of the world's greatest traffic hazards" on the broad expanse of the Champs-Élysées towards the Arc de Triomphe, Murphy saw only "three abandoned dogs cavorting beneath the large French flags which still hung at each corner of the great concourse."

At midnight that night, when he and the naval attaché, Commander Roscoe Hillenkoetter, came out of the guarded embassy door to have a look around the empty streets, they were immediately apprehended by Chief Rabbi Julien Weill, his wife, and two friends. Weill had determined to remain in the city, but at this late hour he had discovered that the government had fled and realized that he now had no protection. Would the United States help them get to Bordeaux? It was with a heavy heart that Murphy had to tell him that the time to escape had passed, as the Germans now surrounded the city. "I never saw the Grand [sic] Rabbi again but learned afterwards that he died in Paris," he recorded. (Murphy was mistaken. Weill survived the war in Paris, avoided deportation to the gas chambers, and died in 1950.)

—⁓—

The order for Virginia D'Albert Lake to evacuate Le Perray eventually came on June 13, Philippe's commanding officer instructing her to find a place of safety, away from the impending battle. She—together with Philippe's mother—had decided to drive northwest to her parents' home in Cancaval, near St. Malo. It was a distance, via Rennes, of 235 miles. Loading their Simca 8 with baggage in the back, a mattress, blankets plus a bicycle on top, and, on the trunk rack, fourteen rabbits, five chickens, and a canary, together with two additional lady passengers and their dog, they joined the long exodus west late that afternoon. A hug sufficed as a farewell to Philippe. The route was crowded all the way past Chartres with two lines of cars, a distance they covered only very slowly, in first and second gear. As they skirted the ancient city a mere five miles away they could see the dust rising from bombs dropped by enemy planes flying too high to be seen. A bed of straw in a field a short distance from Chartres that night had to suffice, although a steady drizzle of cold rain that began at about 1:00 A.M. forced the refugees back into the sanctuary of their tiny car. They set off again by 4:00 A.M., far before any of the others had emerged from the wet dawn. Successfully finding gas at Le Mans, and again at Rennes, the exhausted party reached Cancaval at 7:00 P.M. A journey that ordinarily took six hours had taken twenty-seven. But they were safe. The Luftwaffe were never far away, however, and every village they passed had thrown up barriers across all the roads in and out, adding to the congestion. At Le Mans they saw their first British soldiers, a startling contrast to the French soldiers Virginia had seen in Le Perray. These men seemed happy, smiling and flirting, raising thumbs in greetings to get past the language barrier. Virginia was surprised. Did they not know that there was a war on, and that there were few, if any, indications of a successful outcome for the Allies? Perhaps they knew differently? Did their gaiety indicate that the British had a plan to reverse French fortunes? This would be strange—the whole world knew that the main part of the British Expeditionary Force had been defeated along the beaches of the Pas-de-Calais at the start of the month, two weeks before. Were those who had been evacuated from the beaches on their way back, through Cherbourg or St. Nazaire, perhaps? The following morning, awaking from an exhausted sleep, they read in the local newspaper that any remaining British optimism was sorely misplaced. The Germans were making their move on Paris, with fighting taking place along the lower Oise. Nothing seemed to be able to stop them.

It was now that Sevareid and his friend Walter Kerr of the *New York Herald Tribune* decided it was their turn to flee. Both had found themselves forced to the unhappy conclusion that the braying voice from Berlin was closer to the truth than the elegant but ignorant Colonel Thomas. All the portents were clear: the Germans would soon be masters of Paris. Throwing their possessions into their Citröen, they joined the long, slow cavalcade driving south late one evening, joining the many Parisians who no longer believed that their armies could hold back the Teutonic deluge they had successfully resisted in both 1870 and 1914. Huge crowds had congregated with their suitcases around the train stations, desperate to flee. Where? Anywhere! Flight seemed the only action to take in the face of the impending battle. "We nosed into the silent, ghostly caravan on the Avenue de Versailles," Sevareid recalled, "and inched forward at torturously slow pace, our front bumper tucked under the van of an army ambulance, our rear one under the darkened headlights of a truck." They drove through the night, creeping forward in the darkness, until the gray dawn threw up the sight of Chartres ahead, as behind them, "Paris lay inert, her breathing scarcely audible, her limbs relaxed, and the blood flowed remorselessly from her manifold veins. Paris was dying, like a beautiful woman in coma, not knowing nor asking why." The vast stream of desperate people crawled through rural France, an endless flow of broken, molten humanity. The sight shocked them both. On the sides of the road lay hundreds of abandoned cars—some on their sides after being driven off the road by exhausted drivers during the night; dead horses by the score littering the ditches, interspersed with families huddled in rug-covered groups as they slept through the dampness of the early dawn. The bakeries of the little towns and villages they passed had long run out of food to feed the starving thousands, and there would be no miracles of loaves and fishes here. In the shadow of the spires of Chartres Cathedral, it was clear that God had forsaken them.

—m—

Bill Shirer, accompanying General Walther von Reichenau's 6th Army into Belgium—part of General Fedor von Bock's Army Group B—was shocked from the outset of the advance with the utter inadequacy of the Allied riposte to the Wehrmacht's "Plan Yellow." The British and French generals had obviously paid no attention to the devastating all-arms tactics the Germans had deployed in Poland. From the very start of the offensive the Germans had seemed to have held the initiative. German and Belgian roads were stuffed with endless columns of tanks, guns, and trucks hurrying west bumper-to-bumper at an amazing twenty-five miles per hour. Long mechanized columns growled relentlessly in the direction of France, fueled by a logistical miracle that provided gasoline bowsers along the main routes of the advance. Someone had thought the whole operation out to the smallest detail. Indeed, the slick professionalism of the gray-green war machine made a significant impression on Shirer, who favorably compared it to the industrial efficiency of Detroit. But where was the French and British interdiction of the arteries pumping forward the blood of the German advance? Why had the roads not been made impassable? He saw destroyed bridges, but these had been admirably bypassed with floating replacements put in place by combat engineers. He had expected the French to launch massive counterattacks into Germany at the onset of war; bombardment from the air; attacks on the German roads and railway lines heading west to the front; smashing of the road junctions, canals, and railway junctions upon which the Wehrmacht's offensive depended. Why were the Belgians not counterattacking these relentless columns? He saw nothing. The Luftwaffe appeared to enjoy complete control of the skies, too, their reconnaissance planes darting deep into enemy territory seemingly unimpeded. Was it a lack of aircraft that prevented the Allies from striking back? Could it be a lack of coordination, or intelligence? Worse, was their strategy to hunker down behind their defenses, waiting to receive the German onslaught? But what if this onslaught went elsewhere and left the frightened poilus in their bunkers? Or had they run away already? Wallace Deuel of the *Chicago Daily News* thought that he had spotted the Wehrmacht's secret weapon—psychology:

> The purpose of all war is to force the enemy to capitulate by breaking his will to resist. In the past wars have been fought on the theory that you have to destroy the enemy's ships and guns and cities and manpower—or deprive him of them—by military

means, and that then, when the enemy simply no longer has the implements and the means to go on fighting, he surrenders.

The Nazis have adopted a different theory. They are fighting this war by trying by nonmilitary means to paralyze the will of the enemy to resist before the actual fighting even begins, so that when the military operations commence the enemy collapses as much from his own weakness as from the superior power of the German armed forces.

And the principal nonmilitary weapon the Nazis are using is the psychological weapon. The Germans have set out to create a nightmare state of mind among their enemies, to cause nothing less than a collective nervous breakdown on an international scale, to bring about a paralysis of will on the part of all Western European civilization, including the United States. And they have succeeded, thus far, to an amazing degree.

From his position as an observer Shirer was impressed by what he saw. The German soldiers were clearly extremely disciplined, determined, and well trained, exuding calm professionalism, undertaking their dangerous tasks with cool nonchalance. Morale was fantastically high, the noise of aircraft swooping overhead was relentless, as was the constant thud and bang of artillery. Tanks, infantry, artillery, and logistical support—such as the ubiquitous fuel bowsers—appeared to be seamlessly integrated. It was obvious that nothing would stop this juggernaut. The extraordinarily high morale of the men was reflective, Shirer believed, of a new concord between enlisted man and officer. There was a distinct sense of egalitarianism in the German army that did not exist in the British or American armies of the time, or in the Imperial German Army of the Great War for that matter. It was something, he confessed, that he had not expected to see, and it had taken him by surprise. Lothrop Stoddard observed the same phenomenon, and proffered two reasons for it:

In the first place, it is part of the Nazi philosophy to break down class and caste distinctions, and weld the whole nation into a conscious Gemeinschaft—an almost mystical communion, as contrasted with the rest of the world. In such a socialized nationhood, the traditional caste barriers, first between officers and soldiers, secondly between army and civilians, are obviously out of line. The present German army is undoubtedly more of a Volksheer—a People's Army, than it ever was before. This new tendency is also furthered by the fact that with better education, specialization, and technical training of the rank-and-file, officers and men are more nearly on the same plane. The old Imperial Army, unmechanized and made up so largely of peasant lads commanded by Junker squires, was a vastly different institution.

The officers ate with their men, and were solicitous of their welfare in a way that the enlisted men regarded as genuine rather than patronizing. They had a free post office with which to communicate with their loved ones at home, and from what they knew of conditions in Germany—from petty restrictions to food shortages—the men recognized that they were given the best of what could be had. With such attention it is hardly any wonder that the men considered themselves invincible, members of the Master Race. Had they not smashed Poland in record time? Nothing was going to stop them now.

George Keenan likewise followed in the wake of the advancing German armies to check on the members of American Legations caught in the war zone. "I saw the bombed-out area of Rotterdam while it was still smoking," he recalled. "I saw the eerily deserted Paris of June 1940 after the panicky flight of almost its entire population, surely one of the strangest and most unreal spectacles of modern times." He admitted that these journeys were depressing affairs, not so much because of the destruction he witnessed but because of any lack of evidence that the German war machine might be defeated, and the fruits of Nazi aggression in Europe be reversed. The European powers had collapsed when confronted by the Wehrmacht's onslaught; there was no evidence that Britain would survive a cross-Channel invasion, and the United States remained committed to a policy of neutrality. His diary caught something of this pessimism:

The Hague, Friday, June 15, 1940

Rain—a misty English rain, smelling of spongy meadows and of the nearby sea—sifted down through the great lime trees onto the cobblestone streets of The Hague . . . It took me nearly an hour to find my way back to the legation. The search led through miles of sober streets, across bridges, along quiet canals, through shady little squares. I watched the sturdy, impassive, stubborn people trundling their bicycles and pushing their barges. Their fidelity to habit and tradition was so strong that it seemed as though nothing could ever change them. But try as I might, I could see little but ruin and decline ahead for most of them.

One could only expect that to the spiritual misery attendant upon the destruction of a great culture and a great tradition there would be added the misery of foreign exploitation and economic decline, and that someday large parts of these Dutch cities, sinking back into the swamps from which they had been so proudly and so competently erected, would become merely a curiosity for the edification of future generations of German tourists and would perhaps help to give the latter a sense of appreciation—tardy and helpless appreciation—for the values their forefathers had so lightheartedly destroyed.

The Hague, Saturday, June 16, 1940

I took another long walk this morning, only to hear a German military band playing on a square to a sizable audience of placid, politely applauding Dutchmen, and to see a place, only a block or two from the legation, where bombs had wiped out most of the inside of a city block.

[In] . . . Rotterdam [I . . .] came into town along a normal city street, with shops open, trams running, crowds of busy people on the sidewalks. Suddenly, with as little transition as though someone had performed the operation with a gigantic knife, the houses stopped and there began a wide open field of tumbled bricks and rubbish. Here and there a wall or even the gutted framework of a house remained, but in most places there was only a gray plain of devastation. The main streets leading through this great ruined area were left untouched. Trams and motor cars ran on them as usual, and the unfathomable Dutch wheeled along on their bicycles as though nothing unusual had occurred. At one of the main corners of the city, traffic was still fairly thick, but not a building was left standing anywhere near, and the impression gained was that it was a crossing out somewhere in the country, between fields that had been used as dumping grounds for debris and refuse.

—⚊—

On May 27, 1940, Bullitt told FDR that the war would soon be over, and that Paris would fall in about ten days. At the time, there was no clear view about what would happen to the city. On May 31, Daladier told Bullitt that he believed the German plan was to force the French government to evacuate Paris and then hand it over to the mob, to ravish and destroy. He wanted, therefore, the government to stay in the city even if it resulted in their capture.

Even if they now knew the extent of the crisis, few in government understood what to do about it. Most still had their heads firmly in the sand. When, on May 31, 1940, Winston Churchill flew to Paris to attend a meeting of the Supreme War Council, Paul Reynaud told Bullitt later that day the news was encouraging. The evacuation from Dunkirk was successfully saving scores of thousands of British and French troops, Bullitt reporting from the conversation that the "French with their customary spirit are holding the lines to enable the British to leave first." Reynaud was convinced that this would stem the tide of the German advance. New British planes had swept the Germans from the air; the fighting on the Somme had been going well, and the French had captured the German bridgehead at Abbeville.

But five days later, when Pétain had lunch with Bullitt, the message he passed on was very different. The French had been outgunned by Germany's vast superiority in manpower, tanks, and airplanes. They had also been let down—again—by *perfidious Albion*. The British had failed to support France with the aircraft it needed, and at a time of the "greatest attack in human history the British were pretending that they could send no reserves [of troops] from England." The British, he complained, were once more fighting to the last drop of French blood.

The Germans were drawing nearer. Unsure whether his greatest enemy would be members of the Wehrmacht attacking the embassy, or the communistic bands Pétain had warned would attempt to sack the place in the dangerous interregnum before the Germans arrived, Bullitt cabled the president on June 8, 1940: WILL YOU PLEASE HAVE PUT ON THE NEXT CLIPPER TWELVE THOMPSON SUBMACHINE GUNS WITH AMMUNITION, ADDRESSED TO ME FOR THE USE OF THIS EMBASSY. I AM FULLY PREPARED TO PAY FOR THEM MYSELF.

The following day Reynaud told Bullitt that he was planning to evacuate most of the government ministries from Paris to Tours. He asked Bullitt to accompany him. Bullitt decided, as had his predecessors in 1916 and 1870, not to leave Paris. This decision created enormous tension with Roosevelt, who believed that his ambassador's place was alongside the French government. In the weeks that followed, Bullitt's presence might have helped persuade the French government to escape to North Africa, there to continue the fight. And yet, Murphy believed that Bullitt's presence in Paris helped save the French capital from becoming a battlefield. Reynaud had urged the city to fight to the last paving stone, as had Winston Churchill and General Charles de Gaulle. "It was only at the very last moment that Reynaud asked the American Embassy's intervention in making Paris an open city," records Murphy, and, following representations to the Germans, the invaders began occupation on June 14 without any mass shedding of blood.

In the meantime, Bullitt provided increasingly dramatic messages to Washington about the French collapse, and the plight of the "six million persons in southwestern France who will die unless American aid for them is organized immediately with the utmost efficiency."

Unfortunately, most French people labored under the delusion in 1939 and 1940 that, if the chips were down, the United States would rush to France's aid. Nothing could persuade them otherwise. Boothe observed:

in those last awful days of early June it was a bitter, bitter shock to the French people and to tiny, desperate Monsieur Reynaud not only that Mr. Roosevelt couldn't bring America into war, or even repeal the Neutrality Act, but that he could not send what it turned out rather suddenly we didn't have, and which apparently nobody with a big voice had told them (or us) before that we didn't have, 'masses of matériel' and 'clouds of aeroplanes.' But the bitterest shock of all to them was that Mr. Roosevelt did not honestly tell the American people what they believed in their hearts he believed—that this war was America's war. 'What can he lose?' they asked, anguished. Obviously he could lose the third term [i.e., the presidential election, in November 1940] but that tragic loss was hard for them to understand when the fate of France hung in the balance. Then in the hideous confusion of retreat and surrender the politicians and the people alike cursed Mr. Roosevelt, cursed America, and might have done worse to poor Mr. Bullitt had he not been in the one safe spot in overrun France—German-occupied Paris."

Considering the problem on June 4, 1940, Brigadier General Raymond Lee, American military attaché to Britain, understood Roosevelt's quandary only too clearly. While Roosevelt was alarmed by a possible German victory, he was unconvinced that American voters or politicians would support him in choosing sides. Thus, the best that Britain or France could expect now publicly was anti-Nazi rhetoric from the White House, but little more.

—m—

In Paris, Dr. Sumner Jackson was one of the last surgeons left in the American Hospital during the first weeks of June. He had decided not to leave his patients, although all the other surgeons had gone, many of them three hundred miles south to a hospital established in Angoulême. Sumner's Swiss-born wife, Charlotte ("Toquette"), and son, Phillip, left the city on June 10, the day that Paris was declared an "open city," but Jackson remained in an apartment at the hospital. They were both determined to stay in France, but because they could not predict whether there would be a battle for Paris, Toquette and Phillip temporarily left their home at 11, avenue Foch in the 16th arrondissement and headed for the safety of Clermont-Ferrand. Jackson's friend and colleague Charles Bove had headed south, fearing that the Germans would round up all the Americans in the city. Their good friend Dr. Thierry Martell (incidentally, Drue Tartière's uncle-in-law) committed suicide on the morning of the German occupation of the city on June 14, and Dr. Gros, an American colleague who had worked in France since the start of the Great War, suffered a stroke and was evacuated home.

Dr. Bove had set off south for the Riviera, but he was caught up in the nightmare of the exodus from Paris. The entire route was pock-marked by burned-out motor vehicles and lonely wooden crosses in fields lining the roads. Most of those making the journey were women, children, and old men. All quickly ran out of food and pushed, pulled, or carried meager clumps of personal possessions. When exhaustion set in, most of this extraneous luggage was dumped by the roadside. When fuel ran out for those who had started the journey in cars, the vehicles were unceremoniously dumped, their occupants continuing their journey on foot. As he made his way south, Bove was repeatedly called on to help the sick and injured, and assist in childbirth. But by far the worst experience was being caught up in deliberate air attacks on the defenseless, bewildered columns. Thirty miles south of Paris, he was driving slowly through the town of Étampes when he heard the unmistakable scream of aircraft engines over the sound of his car. Looking up, he saw a dozen Messerschmitts flying low in formation and heading for the heart of the city. It was clear that an attack was about to start:

> I drew up at the kerb to wait until it was over. Just ahead of me was
> a car with two women in it, one young one who sat at the wheel,
> the other, very old, beside her. Presently, the younger woman
> leaped terrified from her car and fled into the open doorway of
> a nearby harness shop. Meanwhile the old lady was struggling

frantically to open the door on her side of the vehicle. Rushing to assist her, I wrenched the door open and she fell whimpering into my arms. Almost simultaneously the Nazi planes swooped low directly above us, spraying the road with their machine guns. The old lady slumped dead in my arms, blood spouting from a bullet wound in her head. Her granddaughter rushed hysterically from the shop. Together we carried the body to the sidewalk. There was nothing I could say to the girl in consolation. I returned to my car, regretting that I had gone to the grandmother's aid. Had she remained inside the car, she probably would not have been killed.

A few miles farther on, at Mereville, the enemy planes reappeared. Attempting to take shelter, he was horrified to find himself in a melee in the street, with people running riot, robbing buildings—and each other—of food and gas. An old man was knocked over by the rushing crowd and had his shoulder broken. He died in Bove's arms. "Screams, blows, curses filled the air; and, getting into my car, I drove away to escape the sights and sounds of people reduced to savagery." Back on the road, moving at a walking pace due to congestion, he came across a group of people huddled around a stationary cart. It had been struck by strafing planes. Stopping, he set to work. There were five wounded: four women and a young girl with a crushed and broken leg:

A stout woman with huge, pendulous breasts lay in a pool of warm blood, her clothing soaked by it. I found a large tear of the shoulder blade and back. Although haemorrhaging had stopped, even a slight movement would start it again. Her skin was hot and dry; already the loss of blood had been excessive.

Another woman, dark and middle-aged, had a bullet hole through her breast. The bullet had entered through the nipple, and the wound of exit lay in the fold beneath, next to the chest wall. The breast was swollen and tender, but the woman's condition was not too serious. A third woman's elbow had been fractured by a bullet, and beside her lay a young woman with a bullet in her shoulder.

Scenes from September 1939 on the outbreak of hostilities and the announcement of war, London and Washington DC. (Library of Congress)

Above: Ambassadors emerge from a secretive conference with President Roosevelt, December 1938. Left to right: William C. Bullitt, envoy to France; Acting Secretary of State Sumner Welles; U.S. Ambassador to Germany Hugh R. Wilson, and William Phillips, Ambassador to Italy. (Library of Congress)

Left: Joseph P. Kennedy leaves a conference at the Whitehouse with the President regarding an embargo on the transportation of arms to Japan and China, 1937. (Library of Congress)

The strength of the fervent support for Nazism among the German populace, young and old, could hardly be missed.

Dr Charles F. Bove, chief surgeon at the American hospital at Neuilly-sur-Seine. (Library of Congress)

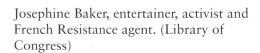

Josephine Baker, entertainer, activist and French Resistance agent. (Library of Congress)

Clare Boothe Luce, who wrote *Europe in the Spring* about her time travelling Europe in 1939–40. She went on to have a long career in the Republican party. (Library of Congress)

Fighter pilot Art Donahue flew with the RAF until he was killed in action in September 1942.

Prominent socialite and resident of Paris Elsie de Wolfe, also known as Lady Mendl. (Library of Congress)

Journalist and broadcaster Dorothy Thompson. In 1934 she became the first American journalist to be expelled from Nazi Germany, and in 1939 she was recognised as the second most influential woman in America after Eleanor Roosevelt by *TIME* magazine. (Library of Congress)

John Gilbert Winant, US Ambassador to the UK from 1941 for the duration of the Second World War. (Library of Congress)

Historian, eugenecist and klansman Lothrop Stoddard. A journalist in Germany on the outbreak of war, he was treated warmly by the Nazis.

American relief worker Tracy Strong Jr, who helped organize Prisoners' Aid and escort Jewish prisoners to Switzerland. (Mémorial de la Shoah)

Journalist William 'Bill' Shirer in Compiègne, France, on 22 June 1940 for the signing of the armistice. The first of 'Murrow's Boys', he wrote the hugely influential *The Rise and Fall of the Third Reich*.

Another of 'Murrow's Boys', Eric Sevareid was the first to report the Fall of Paris in summer 1940. He went on to have a successful career in journalism; he is pictured centre interviewing President Nixon in the 1970s. (National Archives and Records Administration)

Left: The Blitz.

Below: Four years later, photographer Toni Frissell entertains children with her camera in France. (Library of Congress)

Thus was Bove's journey punctuated, through the blood and misery of this terror-induced mass exodus from Paris, all the way to the Mediterranean.

—m—

Eric Sevareid likewise experienced the agony of a collapsing France as he travelled from Paris to Tours, then Bordeaux, following the remnants of the French government as it fled from the advancing enemy in the bitter hot summer of 1940. He compared the collapse of France to a cancer that spread rapidly to the brain of both body politic and military, disabling them entirely. Neither politician nor general appeared to know what to do. The people were largely left to themselves, and to the rumors that flooded the country in the absence of strong, visible, articulate leadership. The chaos that had descended so rapidly left people rudderless, unable to react intelligently. At Bordeaux on June 15, where he had managed to find rooms in the old Hotel Univers, Sevareid watched as a filthy, exhausted, working-class family who had seemingly walked all the way from their tenements in Paris stretched on the velour-covered sofas in the hotel lobby, "removing the shoes from their stinking, bleeding feet." The hotel manager "ran about wringing his hands in despair, not for the sufferings of his fellow countrymen, but for the injury to the name of his bourgeois establishment." Now was the time for someone to stand up for France, to provide leadership, defiance, hope. None came.

Sevareid had hunkered up in his hotel room with Michael Handler of United Press when one of Handler's informants ran in, gasping for breath. As he blurted out his news, Sevareid knew instantly that France had thrown in the towel. Reynaud had resigned as premier, Philippe Pétain had been appointed president of the Supreme War Council, and a number of those considered "wets"—Weygand, Darlan, and Colson among the military—had been appointed to the cabinet. It meant only one thing: capitulation. None of these men were fighters. Sevareid knew of a radio transmitter in the town and rushed to it with Handler. As he reached the station, he was met by his main competitor, an

English-speaking Frenchman who worked for another American company, walking smugly down the steps from the broadcast studio. He had gotten the scoop first. Deflated and angry, Sevareid questioned him about the news. "Why, I told America, of course," the man replied, "that this is a war cabinet, to carry on the fight. Look at all the generals and admirals." Ecstatic that the man had entirely missed the critical nuance of the reshuffle, Sevareid sent a second message to the United States, warning Americans not to believe that this new government was designed to fight but rather would immediately seek an armistice with Germany.

Bordeaux was a funeral parlor, considered Liebling, looking around him, with "a climate of death . . . heavy and unhealthy like the smell of tuberoses. The famous restaurants like the Chapon Fin had never known such business. Men of wealth, heavy-jowled, waxy-faced, wearing an odd expression of relief from fear, waited for a couple of hours for tables and then spent all afternoon over their meals, ordering sequences of famous claret vintages as if they were on a *tour gastronomique* instead of being parties to a catastrophe." Then, on June 17, 1940, it was all over. In the radio studios in Bordeaux, Drue Tartière was told that the new head of government, the famous Maréchal Pétain, the Lion of Verdun, was going to come into the studio to speak to the nation. It didn't start well. She watched in horror as an arrogant Philippe Pétain strode into the studio at 10:00 A.M., kicked aside the sound technician, and—without first negotiating a truce with the invaders—told Frenchmen everywhere that they should stop fighting. But don't worry, he told them, I, Pétain, will sacrifice my life for you, by offering myself to the Germans:

> At the call of the President of the Republic I assumed, beginning today, the direction of the government of France. I say that by the affection of our admirable army, which is fighting with a heroism worthy of its long military traditions against an enemy superior in numbers and arms, by the magnificent resistance with which it has fulfilled our duties to our allies, by the aid of the war veterans whom I am proud to command, by the confidence of all the people, I give to France my person to assuage her misfortune.

In these painful hours I think of the unhappy refugees who, in extreme misery, clog up our roads. I express to them my compassion and my solicitude.

It is with a broken heart that I tell you today it is necessary to stop fighting.

I addressed myself last night to the adversary to ask him if he is ready to seek with me, as soldier to soldier, after the actual fighting is over, and with honor, the means of putting an end to hostilities. May all Frenchmen group themselves about the government which I head during these trying days and control their anguish in order to be led only by their faith in the destiny of the fatherland.

Watching the old man closely, Drue could see no sign of the broken heart of which he spoke. His swagger, confidence, and self-assuredness told her something different. Astonishingly, he seemed pleased that the old regime of the reviled Third Republic had now gone, even if it had taken the Nazi bulldozer to do it. With a start, she realized that whatever he had previously stood for, he now wanted this situation. Perhaps he even reveled in France's humiliation. It was as if he preferred defeat to the fascists than France succumbing to some bogey of bolshevism. She could see that he believed that the Germans would breathe new life, order, and discipline back into a corrupted France, and rebuild it, not on the frivolous concepts of liberty, equality, and fraternity but on his own conservative principles of work, family, church, country, and tradition. Pétain had unilaterally decided not to fight on from Britain or France's North African colonies but to quit. Hearing him was a profound shock. All that she had come to love and trust in her adopted country was collapsing around her. From that moment on, for Tartière, her seven Ministry of Information colleagues occupying the tiny Bordeaux studio, and millions of French men and women elsewhere, there was only one prevailing emotion: despair. It would last four long, bitter years.

"When Pétain finished speaking," remembered Sevareid, "the sky exploded in a violent thunderstorm, sheets of water lashed the windows, and sparks crackled out of the radio control panels," as if nature itself was demonstrating its anger. He knew immediately that he was watching one of the great events in history unfold, in which the world was changed forever. Silence descended on Bordeaux, except for the sound of weeping. The people had heard Pétain, "the high priest, intoning the confessional of France and pleading the shameful supplication." Sevareid made his mind up. The Germans were only a few miles away, and he knew in his heart-of-hearts that he did not want to continue reporting in the kind of France that was soon to come: a servile, vassal state. "Somehow we all knew," he wrote after the war, "that England would continue to fight." This was no time to flee to Spain, or to attempt a passage back to America. He would go to England. The idea of England now "seemed intimate, understandable, and terribly important."

In Berlin, as Howard Smith observed, there was a noticeable lack of celebration for the enormous victories won for the German people by their extraordinarily successful armed forces. Indeed, he even noted a drop in public confidence. Why? The main reason was that people thought of this war in terms of the last, and the idea of more slaughter on that scale was enough to dampen even the most martial of spirits. It was only when the armistice was signed in the forest of Compiègne that morale began to surge upwards again. Before then, however, despite the fact that the Wehrmacht had secured one of the most astonishing "military triumphs of all time, there were no demonstrations on the streets, no open signs of elation anywhere in Berlin." Wallace Deuel attested to the same experience:

> I was on two of the principal streets of Berlin for the first half hour after the news became known that France had asked for terms. At last, I thought, I would see some normal, human reaction. It was, after all, one of the greatest military triumphs of all times.
>
> But there was no reaction to be seen—none at all. The Berliners looked neither jubilant nor happy nor even relieved. They looked just the same as they had looked for more than six years. They just looked tired.

At La Bourboule on July l, 1940, after Bullitt had left Paris for the new seat of government at Vichy, he came headlong against the defeatism of the French government. It was not merely an acceptance of defeat but a positive reveling in the ignominy of failure. He wrote to FDR:

> I had long conversations today with Lebrun, Petain, Darlan, and Chautemps; and also spoke briefly with Weygand. The impression which emerges from these conversations is the extraordinary one that the French leaders desire to cut loose from all that France has represented during the past two generations, that their physical and moral defeat has been so absolute that they have accepted completely for France the fate of becoming a province of Nazi Germany. Moreover, in order that they may have as many companions in misery as possible they hope that England will be rapidly and completely defeated by Germany and that the Italians will suffer the same fate. Their hope is that France may become Germany's favorite province—a new Gau which will develop into a new Gaul. . . . The truth is that the French are so completely crushed and so without hope for the future that they are likely to say or do almost anything.

"Never before had the balance of power in Europe been shifted so completely in so short a time," recalled Robert Murphy, looking back over the tumultuous three weeks of June 1940. When, after many weeks, the dazed French government reassembled at Vichy, it struggled to comprehend how the new France would manage to "live with the Nazi war machine which so suddenly had blasted its path through the entire continent." It appeared to them, and to many in America, that the war was over. Germany had won. Britain only had weeks—months at the most—before it, too, fell simpering into the Nazi camp.

CHAPTER NINE

Eagles at Dawn

Art "Donny" Donahue couldn't quite believe it when he clambered into his green-brown Spitfire on the grass strip at RAF Kenley in Surrey on the morning of August 5, 1940. Only five weeks earlier he had been cultivating corn on his father's farm in faraway St. Charles, Minnesota. Now he was about to go into combat against the waves of black-crossed bombers flying across England's clear summer skies, trying to attack the RAF's airfields. It was all very surreal. An experienced pilot, Donahue had taken easily to the superb Southampton-built fighter, even though the fastest plane he had flown back home had ambled along at 110 miles per hour. The Spitfire—on which he had just finished his meager eighteen days of advanced fighter training—made nearly four hundred miles per hour when on its full twelve hundred horsepower supercharge. He was excited. He had never seen France before and was eager to catch his first view of what was now enemy-occupied country. But he still couldn't imagine that all this was serious, and not something from a dream or Marvel comic. He was going to war.

He had made his way to Canada and thence to Britain, "drawn into the struggle like a moth to a candle," as he described it—a devout Roman Catholic driven by a deep anger against the "hate-crazed, power-maddened little man in Berlin who wanted to take the place of God." Those Nazis and their black-crossed machines, which had been so much a part of his youthful imaginings plucked from the pages of the *Winona Daily News* and *Minneapolis Journal*, would now be swooping and swirling the skies around him, trying to kill him, just as he was trying to do to them. It was something he found hard to comprehend, but he didn't dwell on it too long. "Stick together!" his squadron leader had instructed as the twelve raw pilots left to climb into their waiting aircraft. "Fly wide enough apart from your leader so that you won't be in danger of colliding with him, but don't lag behind if you can help it. If you see a Hun, don't go after him until I give you the OK. And if we sight a bunch of them, stay in formation until I call out the battle cry 'Tally-Ho!'"

The twelve sleek, round-winged beauties roared into the air behind the deep drone of their twelve-cylinder, 1050-horsepower Rolls-Royce engines, with orders to head southeast to patrol above Dover at a height of ten thousand feet. Not waiting to line up to take off, or bothering to calculate the direction or speed of the wind, the planes had simply pointed down the grass strip and taken off "like a stampeding herd of buffalo." Better a bad takeoff than a late one. Every second counted when they were hastening to repel the invader. Donahue could never quite believe the power of that amazing engine as it pulled him skywards at a speed he could only dream of a month or two before. Sitting embedded in the wings aside him were eight belt-fed Browning 0.303-inch machine guns, fired in pulsating unison and to devastating effect at the push of the red firing button atop the control column between the pilot's legs. The radio crackled in his ear. The squadron's radio call sign was "Tiger." He heard the instructions from the calm, clipped tones of his squadron leader, something that gave him deep confidence in the Englishman, and turned his aircraft in unison with the remainder of the squadron. The fighter controllers back at RAF Kenley were guided by the new top-secret radar. Did the instructions to rendezvous above the major port of Dover mean that the enemy was in the vicinity? Perhaps the controller was making sure that patches of sky across the whole of southern England had protective clumps of fighters above them just in case, and that their move to Dover was merely precautionary, rather than based on specific intelligence. Whatever, he was enjoying his first operational sortie with his squadron. The sky was beautiful and clear, with scattered clumps of woolly clouds decorating the heavens far above. Would he see the enemy close up on this, his first operational sortie? He was soon to find out, as a few moments later the controller's voice came over the radio: "There are bandits approaching from the north!"

"My pulses pounded, and my thoughts raced," Donahue recalled. "This was it!" The squadron leader then called out, "All Tiger aircraft, full throttle! Full throttle!" Pushing in his emergency throttle, Donahue felt the Spitfire surge ahead. He had never used all the horsepower in his engine before, and the effect was exhilarating. As he powered steeply upward, Donahue pulled the guard from his firing button. He was about to go into combat; kill or be killed. War was no longer a product of his imaginings but hard, cold reality. He turned the safety ring on the firing button from Safe to Fire and switched on the electric gun sight, which was instantly projected onto his windscreen. Where he turned the aircraft, the sight—and the eight Browning machine guns—would follow.

Upwards they pelted, at speeds that continued to amaze him, before the twelve aircraft leveled out at fifteen thousand feet. The controller on the ground was receiving information from the radar stations that ran along England's southern coast, and he ordered them to turn in direction "130 degrees"—southeast—and climb a further five thousand feet, taking them out over the English Channel. Rising to twenty thousand feet provided Donahue with his first panoramic view of southern England and northern France, the eager though nervous flock of Spitfires keeping anxious lookout on every side for the intruders they were being guided to intercept. At this height they were all forced to turn on their oxygen, without which it was impossible to operate. At the back of the squadron, the rear guards wheeled left and right, sweeping the skies for attack from above or behind.

The controllers passed information only when it was available. Otherwise the radio was silent. There was no need to give away their presence. Personal discipline was critical to their safety, though once contact with the enemy had been made, the proscription on talking was lifted. Half an hour went by as the squadron wheeled and watched from its great height for the telltale black spots indicating an incoming enemy.

Then, with no warning, battle was upon them. A sudden bright flash far in his rearview mirror alerted Donahue to something amiss behind him. He couldn't fathom what it was, and kept up his frenetic searching of the skies around. Staring down to his right, Donahue saw a light blue plane making its way far below towards France. Was it one of theirs? Before he could alert the squadron leader, a flock of enemy was spotted below and to Donahue's left. Without a moment's hesitation the squadron leader called out the RAF's battle cry: "Ta-al-ly-ho o!" Once the command was given, every pilot was on his own, responsible for finding and attacking his own targets.

To a man the eager pilots swung steeply to the left, aiming themselves in near-vertical dives towards the black dots approaching the English coast far below. "There weren't very many of them," Donahue recalled, "and the entire squadron was breaking formation and wheeling toward them like a bunch of wild Indians." From the staggering speed he'd attained while climbing into the skies, Donahue now shocked himself with the speed at which he was hurtling towards the ground. In vertical dives the Spitfire would reach speeds of nearly seven hundred miles per hour. The wind shrieked against his windscreen, drowning out the deep bellow of the Rolls-Royce engine. The airspeed indicator needle swung rapidly clockwise. He felt the Spitfire aircraft stiffen—at great speeds the controls lost their responsiveness and it took longer than usual for the aircraft to respond to the pilot's instructions. Considerable care was required for a pilot to bring his aircraft out of violent dives, because sudden moves could induce blackouts in the pilot.

As he leveled out, Donahue kept his eyes focused on his chosen target, noticing that as he reached his enemy's level he had gained on him fast. Heart thumping in his chest, he was nevertheless able to keep his rapidly ongoing enemy in his sights, thumb over the firing button while he occasionally glanced in his rearview mirror to make sure that he was not himself being "bounced."

> The other machine grew steadily larger in the circle of my gun-sight as I drew closer. I could tell its distance by the amount of space it covered in the sight: six hundred yards, five hundred, four hundred—my speed was dying down a little, and I wasn't gaining quite as fast. He apparently was going wide open too.
>
> Now I was only three hundred yards behind—close enough to open fire, but something made me hesitate. From directly behind, where I was now, it was hard to identify its type. Suppose it was a British machine after all?
>
> To make sure I eased my machine upward just a little so I could look down on the other and see the upper side of it. The old feeling that airplanes with black crosses and swastikas on their wings and sides couldn't exist in reality still had hold of me; but it was banished forever by what I now saw.
>
> For I could see that the other machine's wings were not curved, with nicely rounded tips, like a Spitfire's; and it was not camou-flaged green and tan; and there were no red and blue circles near the tips. Instead, the wings were narrow, stiff-looking, with blunt, square-cut tips. They were pale blue-gray in color, and near each tip, very vivid, was painted a simple black "plus" sign!

It was a Messerschmitt Me109. Donahue dropped back into firing position behind it. When his gun sights settled on the center of the enemy aircraft, he squeezed the firing button with his thumb, holding it down for a full second, pouring about one hundred and sixty bullets into his target. The extraordinary sound of the eight Brownings firing came through his helmet, and he felt his aircraft judder and slow from the recoil. In firing, Donahue became the first American to engage enemy aircraft in combat in the Second World War.

But his enemy had disappeared, and it took what seemed an age for Donahue to spot him, far below. There was no way of knowing if he'd scored any strikes, but his failure to follow through as the Me109 had turned had lost him precious time. Cursing himself, he flipped the Spitfire into a violent, diving turn and gave chase. Every ounce of his concentration was now focused on destroying his enemy, but in the intensity he forgot about the battle raging around him. This was a duel, one-on-one combat to the death. Gaining ground, he finally caught up with his prey just above Cape Gris Nez on the French coast, at which point the German turned to confront him. But however much the Luftwaffe pilot tried, he could not succeed in shaking Donahue from his tail as the distance between them closed rapidly. With his thumb sitting on the firing button, Donahue knew that he was successfully outmaneuvering his foe, now almost in the circle of his yellow electric gun sight.

Suddenly Donahue heard a loud bang and felt the Spitfire shudder. He had been hit—an enemy aircraft had bounced him while he'd concentrated on his own kill. In his desperation to destroy his own target, he'd forgotten the most elementary principles of air combat and had neglected his rear. He immediately guessed that the noise had been an exploding cannon shell fired from the nose of another Me109. Pulling with all his strength, he moved into a fast, tight turn. Attempting to stop himself from blacking out, Donahue saw his attacker sweep past him before climbing steeply to renew the attack. The sinister black crosses seemed to dance on his enemy's wings as he appeared spread-eagled in a vertical turn. Seeing it from this angle, Donahue remembered thinking that the Messerschmitt's square-cut wingtips seemed crude, but from that point on his memory of the combat between himself and the two Luftwaffe adversaries was hazy. It was a wild melee, a classic dogfight in which the three aircraft climbed, dived, rolled, wheeled, and pirouetted in vertical turns to get the enemy in their gun sights. He was conscious throughout of being a novice at this dangerous game. "One moment I would be maneuvering for my life to get away from one who was almost on my tail, and in the next moment I would have one of them in the same kind of spot and would be trying just as desperately to hold him long enough to get a shot." Fighting for his life, Donahue forgot the wider battle swirling around them. What seemed to be an age probably took only a few minutes. Suddenly finding himself on the tail of one of the Me109s, he looked to place the enemy in his gun sight but was horrified to discover that nothing could get the crosshairs onto his windscreen. The German threw his plane violently to shake the Spitfire from his tail. Donahue was then shocked by four long, vibrating, snaky white fingers reaching across his right wing and stretching far ahead. He was being fired on by the second German. He turned his aircraft violently to escape, frustrated that his first kill had been denied because his equipment no longer worked.

The maneuver managed to shake off his attacker, but Donahue didn't want to let on that he had a problem, so the melee continued. He was now aware that he was sweating profusely, and was terribly tired. The sun burned into the cockpit, and his clothes seemed heavy, his parachute straps and seat belt holding him in and limiting his ability to twist and turn in his seat to see what was going on around him. He started taking risks, accepting the blackouts that came on him rapidly as he turned tighter and faster than he had ever done before, trying to gain split-second advantages over his enemy. He now wanted to flee, but he couldn't do so without accepting that he would immediately have two Me109s on his tail. He had to stay and fight, and wear one or both down in this fast, furious game. During one maneuver, he saw a long strip of white in the distance, and realized they must be the famous white cliffs of Dover. He grabbed his chance as one of the enemy aircraft hurtled away from him to turn out to sea and race for home. "It was an ignominious way to end a fight which had begun with such promise, but I thought it was the wisest," Donahue recalled. "My enemies took after me, but when they drew close I turned around as if to go after them and they turned back. They were apparently willing to call it a draw, and I didn't feel quite so badly after that."

As he began the approach to land at RAF Kenley, he realized that his aircraft trimming controls were not responding. When he was safely on the ground he saw why: a cannon shell had blown a large hole in one side of the fuselage just behind the cockpit. A fraction of a second either way would have seen the end of his life. The control cables had been broken, the main elevator and rudder cables were hanging by a thread, and the battery connection had been destroyed—which explained the sudden loss of his gun sight. It was incredible that the Spitfire had managed to sustain such battle performance after the first strike. It felt strange to be walking on firm earth when only a few moments before, he'd been hurtling haphazardly through the sky pursued by enemies determined to destroy him. Donahue felt a wave of exhaustion come over him and he lay on the grass, utterly bereft of energy. It was a feeling that he came to recognize as a classic physiological response to the extreme mental, emotional, and physical energy fighter pilots expended as they fought for their lives in those bright blue, late-summer skies above the southern coast of England in 1940.

Over a period of seven days Donahue would fly a total of eight missions. He scored a "probable" destruction of an Me109 on his second sortie, and was in turn hit and damaged on his seventh. The life expectancy of pilots was very low during the Battle of Britain, a mere four weeks. During his second sortie he lost a friend, Peter, with whom he had completed advanced fighter training. Peter survived the destruction of his aircraft, but died in hospital from savage burns two days later. Of the 2,927 RAF pilots who fought during this period (a figure that included 574 non-British fliers, including Donahue), 19 percent were killed in action. A further 791 were killed later in the war. A pilot flying in 1940 only had about a 50 percent chance of surviving the six long years of war.

The joy of flying a Spitfire Mark 1 in the clear, summer skies sometimes allowed Donahue to forget the war. Flying on Thursday, August 8, to an advanced grass landing strip close to the Channel was:

> [u]nforgettably beautiful . . . it was just getting light when we took off, and the countryside was dim below us. Wicked blue flames flared back from the exhausts of all the engines as I looked at the planes in formation about me. We seemed to hover motionless except for the slight upward or downward drift of one machine or another in relation to the rest, which seemed to lend a sort of pulsating life to the whole formation; and the dark carpet of the earth below steadily slid backward beneath us. The sun, just rising and very red and big and beautiful, made weird lights over the tops of our camouflaged wings. . . .

It was never long before the pilots met the brutal reality of war. At 11:00 A.M. on August 6, the telephone rang in the operations room of the forward base. Heavy German activity had been spotted around the Pas de Calais, and moments later came the call to scramble: "Squadron into your aircraft, and patrol base at ten thousand feet!" The twelve pilots raced to their aircraft, where ground crew helped them into parachutes before they clambered into the cockpits. After strapping themselves in, they pressed their starter buttons and listened to the huge roar of the Rolls-Royce engines as they burst into life. The pilots took a quick look around to make sure they were clear of each other, and the planes ambled forward, slowly gathering speed as they began to take off in groups of three or four. It was a mad race to get into the air and climb as fast as possible to rendezvous at ten thousand feet. On this occasion, it proved to be a rush to wait.

The squadron loitered above Dover for an hour or more with no sign of the expected enemy. Half of the squadron returned to refuel. A gradual lethargy was allowed to encroach on the remaining flight of six as they waited their turn to circle down to refuel. Then, suddenly, the earphones in Donahue's radio came alive and a voice shouted, "Bandits astern!" From the skies above and behind them a mass of gray Messerschmitts screamed down from the sun, taking them by surprise. Only by violent, evading turns were they saved from the hurtling swarm, frantically wheeling to escape the deluge of bullets and cannon fire, before coming back—chastened—to engage the enemy, one on one, and to recover their position. In an instant the sky had filled with enemy aircraft, a group of about thirty, Donahue estimated. Their role was evidently to clear the RAF defensive patrols from the skies across the doorway to southern England so that the waiting bombers would then have unimpeded access to RAF bases and infrastructure (such as radar towers) across Britain. The suddenness of the attack was blood-chilling, but the calm, reassuring voice of the squadron leader immediately repaired their shattered nerves and enabled them to recover their wits. They were heavily outnumbered, but he led them directly into the thick of the swarm.

Completing his first urgent turn, Donahue caught sight of an Me109 directly in front of him and loosed off a burst of fire just ahead of the enemy's nose. He had no time to see whether his bullets had struck home, as at that instant he saw another Me109 heading directly at him, the aircraft spitting angry white tracer. In his excitement, the enemy was firing too high. This was hardly surprising. Terror and confusion washed together in equal proportions, as individual pilots tried to make sense of what was happening while pushing home their attacks. "We seemed to be milling about like a swarm of great gnats in this giant eerie amphitheater above the clouds," Donahue recalled. "Sets of long white tracers crisscrossed the air and hung all about, like Christmas decorations! They stay visible for several seconds after they're fired." Then, with no letup, a third Me109 came careering at him from the side, the cannon firing through the center of its propeller, the smoke this time blue-tinged. Again, the attack failed. The melee continued for several minutes, Donahue unable to determine whether any of the aircraft he caught fleetingly in his sights and loosed off at with his machine guns had been hit.

Suddenly another German latched onto his tail and fired a burst. Hauling his Spitfire upwards into a vertical turn, Donahue tried desperately to reverse roles and get onto his pursuer's tail. "We were going fast and I had to lean forward and hold my breath and fight to keep from blacking out, and I turned this way for several seconds. Then I eased my turn so that I could straighten up and look out of my cockpit, and I spotted the other in front of me." His stratagem worked. The enemy pilot now made an error, and instead of continuing an evasive turn attempted to flee, leveling out in front of Donahue. It was a target too good to miss, and the young American made the most of it, pumping three- or four-second-long bursts into the wildly twisting enemy before the aircraft stopped jerking and Donahue could get in a prolonged three-second burst directly into the body of the Me109. He concluded that the twisting had stopped for a reason, and although he was unable to see this opponent crash, the Me109 was last seen heading to earth at a steep angle, trailing smoke. "The powder smoke from my guns smelled strong, and I felt good," he recalled, as he turned to head for home, his ammunition exhausted. It took sixteen seconds for a Spitfire to expend its entire load of bullets, and, being no further use in this battle, Donahue hightailed it for the welcoming grass strip at RAF Kenley.

One week after his first sortie, Art Donahue prepared for his eighth combat patrol. Monday, August 12, was to be "a pretty busy day." The first patrol that afternoon had provided no sight or sound of the enemy, but while refueling they heard that a firestorm was going to break—a "450-plus" raid was reportedly gathering over the French coast, a phenomenal number of enemy aircraft heading for Britain. There wouldn't be many more than a squadron of Spitfires—twelve aircraft—to counter them. It was clear that the Luftwaffe were throwing in everything they had in an attempt to break the Royal Air Force and Britain's will to resist. Back on patrol they immediately encountered and engaged a group of perhaps thirty aircraft. Donahue spotted a group of three fighters among this number who all seemed to be following their tails in an endless spiral, so he turned in to the attack. As he did so, he caught a glimpse of the immense raid above the Channel: "I wasn't very high, perhaps seven thousand feet, and above me and to the southeast at very high altitude the sky seemed to be filled with fighters. I could see their wings flashing high above, almost everywhere I looked. Farther southeast, not far off the French coast yet, the bombers were coming. I mistook them at first for an enormous black cloud."

Spotting one of the enemy fighters, Donahue gave chase, failing to see two additional planes concealed by cloud. Closer and closer he edged, with emergency throttle on full to bring him up behind the enemy. Once more he began aligning the sights. The sound of exploding cannon shells striking his aircraft was one with which he was now frighteningly familiar. He had been bounced again from behind! Eardrums hammering, he desperately tried to turn, but his Spitfire was unresponsive, slowly gaining height in a straight line, an easy target for the three enemy fighters who turned the tables on him. He could now smell powder, and smoke from a burning incendiary bullet curled up against his leg. "My heart pounded and my mouth tasted salty, and I wondered if this was the end of the line. This was very bad." With limited options open to him, he opened his cockpit cover, just in case he had to bail out. He had never practiced doing so, it being one of those things pilots were expected to pick up on the job. He estimated that he was about seven thousand feet above the ground.

The Luftwaffe fighters closed in for the coup de grace, and a salvo of bullets hit him from behind. The noise and confusion in the cockpit was intense. As if in slow motion, Donahue could see bullets smashing his instrument panel, holes peppering the fuel tank in front, smoke trails from tracer bullets going between his legs. Moments from death, Art Donahue later recalled "being surprised that I wasn't scared anymore. I suppose I was too dazed. There was a finality about the salvo, and it lasted at least two or three seconds. Then there was a kind of silence."

He saw a light glowing in the bottom of the fuselage and tongues of flame licking out from under the fuel tank. Unlocking the pin securing his seat straps, Donahue hauled himself out of the Spitfire just as the cockpit turned into a blazing furnace. "There was a fraction of a second of searing heat just as I was getting my head and shoulders out, then I was jerked and dragged the rest of the way out with terrible roughness and flung down the side of the fuselage and away all in a fraction of a second by the force of the two-hundred-mile-an-hour wind that caught me. Then I was falling and reaching for my rip cord and pulling it. A moment of suspense, and then a heavy pull that stopped my fall and there I hung, quite safe if not sound." As he floated serenely under his white silk canopy, the sound of battle disappeared. Looking down, he saw that the fire had burned off one of his trouser legs, and burned skin hung off in folds. He was heavily bruised from escaping the burning Spitfire, but he had no bullet wounds. "Well, Art," he said to himself, "this is what you asked for. How do you like it?"

The first American to engage the enemy in battle, Art Donahue was now the first to have been shot down. He later discovered that sixty-one enemy aircraft had been destroyed in the battle. The official communiqué went on to state, "Thirteen of our fighters were lost, but the pilot of one of them was saved."

CHAPTER TEN

Blitz

As the Wehrmacht swept over northern France, Brigadier General Raymond Lee watched preparations for war in London take on a new urgency. He had recently returned to the British capital, reappointed to the role of military attaché by General George C. Marshall, a position he had held between 1935 and 1939 because of his close personal acquaintance with the senior British military hierarchy. Public parks were converted into areas for antiaircraft guns, great swathes were transformed into trenches, and mounds of earth were dug up for filling the millions of sandbags that adorned the outside of every public building. The Luftwaffe were regular visitors to Britain's skies, trying, as Art Donahue knew from personal experience, to destroy the RAF. By so doing they confidently predicted that they would secure air superiority over the British Isles prior to undertaking an invasion across the English Channel. London was a very different place from the city Lee had left the previous summer. In a letter to his wife, Jeanette, on July 10, he made a list of the things that were now different because of the war:

There is much less traffic in town and very few cars on the country roads. Policemen and LDV's [Local Defence Volunteers, known colloquially—and famously—as "Dads' Army"] are much more inquisitive and one is scrutinized by everyone more carefully.

The clubs have waitresses instead of men.

No one dresses any more [for dinner]. Most of the men are in uniform.

Most people carry gas masks and everyone must have identification and ration cards.

One gets only a lump of sugar and a thin little flake of butter.

No more iced cakes. Fewer kinds of cheese.

Only six pages in the newspapers. All paper is saved. Iron railings are being torn down and all metal junk salvaged.

Many women are in uniform, driving cars and ambulances. Others are bus conductors, land workers, munitions workers.

Lights are all cut off or shaded after dusk on pain of heavy fines or even a month's imprisonment.

Theaters are mostly closed and the hotels have only the merest handful of guests. Claridge's is like a lamb except at luncheon.

At every road junction or bend there is some sort of pillbox and there are barriers of concrete at frequent intervals along them.

Lee repeatedly expressed his admiration for the British. He was taken by their stoical indifference to the enormity of the threat that faced them, and for refusing to be bowed by the disasters in previous months like Dunkirk and the destruction of the British Expeditionary Force in France. The army had few rifles; internal security was now reinforced by an army of pensioners from the Great War, and everything—from tanks to trucks to artillery—was either in short supply or nonexistent. Much of the British army's equipment was now in German hands. Nevertheless, across the country morale remained high. "What a wonderful thing it will be if these blokes do win the war!" Lee wrote in his diary on July 25, 1940. "They will be bankrupt but entitled to almost unlimited respect. They are not quitters."

At night, searchlights played over London's skies. They were quite beautiful, Lee thought, if one did not think of the reason for their existence. In mid-June 1940, Illinois-born Member of Parliament Henry "Chips" Channon walked home through darkened streets. "London was astonishingly beautiful in the moonlight," he confided to his diary. "I adore the blackout at this time of year." Lee dined one evening with some friends. After a simple dinner they went onto the rooftop to watch the nightly show as the searchlights attempted to find any German raiders, illuminating them for the gun batteries scattered across London's parks. "We hadn't long to wait before the sirens began to wail and we searched the heavens expectantly. What an occupation on such a lovely summer's evening. And what weather there has been this summer. Day follows day with cloudless skies, brilliant sunshine and no rain, but as matters are, the Germans are the only ones who are getting any good out of it. It was some little time before the all-clear sounded. No planes appeared. The attack which had crossed the coast somewhere had been either diverted or driven back. Berlin is catching hell now, night after night, but London itself is still undamaged save for some stray bombs."

Being forced into cellars and basements when the air-raid sirens sounded had some unexpected effects. Channon found himself sharing his basement with his servants, giving him the opportunity to observe them at close hand for the first time. It was an education. On June 25, he observed:

> I had hardly got to sleep last night when the sirens sounded, and I went to the cellar where I was soon joined by 4 female servants in various stages of dishabille. The scullery-maid read the financial section of "The Times"!

Lee wasn't impressed with the failure of the civil authorities to provide adequate space for bomb shelters for all who needed it, a problem that would have its greatest impact among the poor:

> It is now one month since the heavy attacks on London started. For that length of time the people, particularly the poorer classes, have

resorted to all kinds of improvisation for safety. Unused subways, public building basements and railroad freight warehouses are crowded every night with uncomfortable refugees, men, women and children. This was all very well for a temporary expedient in warm weather, but now that the nights are growing colder and it becomes evident that these conditions may obtain for the whole winter, the Government are being confronted with the problem of safe and sanitary accommodations for millions of people. For two years past they have shied off the provision of deep, well-constructed shelters on account of the expense, but something now must be done. There will not only be deep resentment among the working classes but, more serious still, epidemics will be sure to rear their ugly heads.

On September 7, 1940, everything changed both for Lee and the eight million people who lived in Greater London, and for the millions who lived in Britain's other cities, as the German strategy changed from attacks on the RAF to direct bombing of London and Britain's major port and industrial cities. On the afternoon of Saturday, September 7, a huge, surprise attack was made on the Port of London by 348 Luftwaffe bombers supported by 617 fighters, causing extensive damage, killing about 400 and injuring 1,200. An additional 247 bombers renewed the attack that night, guided to the fires started by the bombardment earlier that day. These attacks began an aerial bombing campaign—nicknamed the Blitz by the public—that continued for fifty-six of the following fifty-seven days and nights.

Londoners had of course expected bombing from the beginning of the war, and had been fascinated observers of the fighter duels fought that summer over England's bright blue skies, complex vapor trails leaving long white tangled fingers charting where fighters—British and German—were chasing each other across the sky. But this time it was different, as a large-scale aerial campaign was launched against Britain's war economy and the workers who sustained it. Much of the fear of war during the 1930s had been fueled by what turned out subsequently to be grossly inflated estimates suggesting that many hundreds of thousands of civilians would be killed by mass aerial attacks. This fear was reflected in popular literature, such as that provided by H. G. Wells's *The Shape of Things to Come*, reinforced by newsreels of aerial bombing in Spain during the civil war.* Americans living in Britain were not immune to these worries. Despite expectations, the Germans had not yet launched any offensive against Britain's civilian population, even though at the outset of war, arrangements had been put in place to evacuate hundreds of thousands of people from the capital. On August 13, Channon confided his fears to his diary: "Another big day along the Channel, with many planes down; shall we be invaded tomorrow? As I write, I hear the buzzing of planes on high, and think that London will certainly be raided soon. I feel that at long last we are entering upon a decisive phase of the war." On September 5, Lee recorded in his diary the standard response to the shrieks of the air-raid warning alarm:

> They are really an alarming sound till you get used to them. They don't necessarily mean that a bomb is going to fall on 42 Half Moon Street but only that aircraft have crossed the coast headed thither. As a rule they are intercepted or beaten down to a considerable degree before they reach London although a few get through and the peculiar grinding noise of their unsynchronized motors can be heard in the sky. The weather still favors Hitler and is really remarkable. (Bang—bang—bang—I can hear the antiaircraft guns going off, not so far away either—sounds about like Hyde Park.)

The next time he wrote about air attack—only two days later—the situation had suddenly become much worse. On September 7, a hot Saturday afternoon, Lee was working, clearing paperwork in his office in Grosvenor Square. At about 5:45 P.M. he heard some ack-ack

---

* During September and October 1940, about 13,000 civilians across Britain were killed and 20,000 injured. Horrific in itself, it was nowhere near the prewar predictions, which talked of many multiples of these numbers. Civilian casualties in London during the Blitz amounted to 28,556 killed, and 25,578 wounded.

guns barking in the distance and the crash of heavy explosions. After ignoring the noise for a while, he was suddenly aware that this attack was much bigger than anything he had experienced before. The drone of seemingly vast numbers of aircraft overhead forced him to leave his work and walk up to the roof. The aircraft were so high that he could only make out a mass of tiny specks, but the effects of their visit could be clearly seen. He could hear the occasional burst of distant machine-gun fire. "Over beyond the Houses of Parliament, a huge mushroom of billowing smoke had risen so high as to blot out the sky and the barrage balloons, which float at about five thousand feet. In the heart of it, fierce red glows showed that immense fires were raging."

When news of the attack that day broke, Eric Sevareid and Larry LeSueur of CBS rushed down to the docks to see for themselves. They were immediately struck by the hundreds of disheveled civilians, many of them women and children, fleeing from the great pillars of black smoke rising high in the sky behind them. The streets were covered in shattered glass. That night, near the docks at Tilbury, Sevareid decided to stay overnight in an old wooden hotel situated about three hundred yards from the waterfront. Intending initially to stay in his room during that night's raid, it was when the building began to move and shake soon after the bombardment began that he decided discretion to be the better part of valor. Realizing that he was the only person left in the building, he rushed downstairs and ran headfirst into the temporary air-raid shelter in the garden, where all the other guests had taken cover. It was the experience of this single night that enabled him to comprehend, for the first time, the true nature of terror. As the long, slow night went on, German bombs fell all around the lonely Anderson Shelter and its huddled, terrified occupants. A lone candle lit the earth-floored shelter, flickering with every explosion. A woman wept, rocking back and forth as dust eddies were propelled with every new detonation. Every explosion shook the corrugated tin, covering those inside with dust. When, many hours later, dawn came, he stepped outside, tired and disheveled, to see, through the early morning fog, a disordered world. A tree in the garden lay splintered and smoke rose from the nearby docks, but by some miracle, the old inn, for the time being at least, remained standing.

On the afternoon of the following day, September 8, Lee—hearing of the extent of the damage and news that Victoria Station had been struck by a bomb—decided to walk down to have a look for himself. The station was closed, with the roof severely damaged. He was amused to see a sign that said, with what he considered British understatement, CLOSED ON ACCOUNT OF OBSTRUCTIONS. He kept walking, the bright dahlias in St. James's Park offering a bizarre contrast to the sights and sounds of war around him. By the time he reached the Houses of Parliament in the early evening, the streets had cleared except for an occasional bus, and a distant rumbling from the docks indicated that another attack had begun where slowly spiraling clouds of smoke still drifted up from the attacks the previous day and night. He walked up to Trafalgar Square with the sound of bombs in the distance—sounding like "blows on tremendous kettledrums"—before slipping into a movie theater to watch a newsreel. After an hour he emerged onto Jermyn Street, by then shrouded in darkness. The sky over the distant docks glowed red. In Piccadilly, the blackout meant that the few passing pedestrians came upon one another suddenly out of the darkness, and passed quickly like shadows. The ack-ack guns in Hyde Park barked and cracked, and the sound of falling bombs could be distinctly heard through the noise. Some made an unsettling, screaming sound, as though deliberately designed to sow even more fear in the listening population far below. "These screaming bombs make me a little more angry than the high explosive," he wrote in his diary later that night. "They seem to indicate that Hitler believes he can scare people into defeat." On that day, the second of the long-awaited Blitz, a further 412 civilians were killed and 747 wounded.

Within a matter of days London had become pockmarked by bomb damage. Craters marked where bombs had fallen; glass littered streets damaged by explosions, and in places entire houses had been obliterated. In a letter to his wife, Rose, on September 10, Joe Kennedy confided that "the last three nights in London have been simply hell. Last night I put on my steel helmet and went up on the roof of the Chancery and stayed up there until two o'clock in the morning watching the Germans come over in relays every ten minutes and drop bombs, setting terrific fires. You could see the dome of St. Paul's silhouetted against a blazing inferno that the Germans kept adding to from time to time by flying over and dropping more bombs." On a guided tour of inspection on September 11, only four days after the onslaught had begun, Lee observed the crater damage firsthand, but was nevertheless struck by how much of the city had not been damaged. Even in streets where sticks of bombs had fallen, most buildings remained habitable. The only exceptions were the areas around the docks, where whole blocks of cheap houses for workmen had been comprehensively burned out. But no one seemed to be complaining. One workman he spoke to remarked phlegmatically, "All we want to know is whether we are bombing Berlin. If they are getting all or more than we are, we can stick it." Nevertheless, Lee was furious at those in the American press who exaggerated the extent of the damage, describing the bombing in terms that made one think that Londoners were forced to grope "from one street corner to another with shells and bombs falling like rain."

Some of these exaggerations were grotesquely sensationalized. On September 16, *Time* magazine reported, for instance: "on the first day and first night, as many as 1,500 planes . . . dropped a vaunted 4,400,000 pounds [2,200 tons] of bombs on London in eight terrible hours." In fact, 760 bombers were involved in the first day and night attacks on September 7, and for the two months between the start of the Blitz and mid-November, the Luftwaffe dropped 13,000 tons, an average of 216 tons per night. Photographs of Londoners amidst bombed-out buildings made it appear that the entire city of eight million was in ruins. Believing that this misinformation merely aided Nazi propaganda and spread defeatism in the United States, Lee added comments whenever he could in his cables to Washington describing the true state of affairs, stressing that morale was very high despite the very natural concerns, not to say lack of sleep, that people had when enemy bombers were overhead dropping bombs on their homes.

On September 12, Lee noted in his diary that while the previous night's raid had caused considerable damage, far fewer people were killed than previously. Air Raid Precautions (ARP) were having their effect, and the seriousness of the raids now had Londoners, especially in the East End, Westminster, and the City of London, running for their shelters or basements when the air-raid sirens began their distinctive, deadly wail. Antiaircraft artillery was in constant use, as was the RAF, but in the early weeks and months of the German campaign, the effectiveness of both was limited. It took some while for the RAF, for instance, to be able to track enemy aircraft at night, something they eventually managed to do by using early radar guidance sets: while it initially took about twenty thousand shells for an ack-ack gun to bring down a single bomber, this rate was to improve rapidly, to three thousand per destroyed aircraft, by February 1941. A few months later Ralph Ingersoll watched his first bombing raid from his room in the Dorchester Hotel, on Park Lane, initially with curiosity. A single German aircraft was making its way across the capital, apparently seeking out its target. The thing that alerted him to the approaching aircraft was the distant thud of an antiaircraft gun. As the enemy aircraft grew closer, the guns across the capital followed its path, getting progressively louder as the aircraft made its way towards Ingersoll's location, until one in nearby Hyde Park began thundering away, shocking him by the belligerence of its retort:

> It went off so suddenly and violently it almost literally threw me back from the window. The conception of a gun crash splitting the air is inadequate. It seems to fractionalize it. The curtains and I blew back together. Out of the centre of the all-enveloping noise came a high, thin whine, fading rapidly. A whine with a swoosh in it. When I first heard it I only knew it was there. Later I came to recognize it as the whistle of the shell going up. I knew the crash was a gun and it did not frighten me. I leaned out of the window again and started to count to see if I could tell when the shell was to explode. It came, a sharp white flash, this time not where I was looking in the dark, but off to the right. And then a second later the noise of the shell bursting, a hollow thump like someone knocking gently on heaven.

Fighter Command suffered heavily during the daylight raids, forcing the Germans after a month to switch exclusively to night attacks. Lee noted on September 12 that the RAF had claimed to have brought down eighty-three of the enemy raiders in as little as two hours, a third of the entire force. It wasn't true, but the Germans nevertheless suffered losses that they were unable in the long run to sustain. On the first day of the attack only 4 percent—fourteen—of the bombers were shot down, but this number rapidly increased. By Sunday, September 15, now commemorated in Britain as Battle of Britain Day, 18 percent of the raiders were destroyed.

London's ability to continue under this nightly bombardment perceptibly raised morale, even though the threat of invasion remained high. "Chips" Channon recorded a working day at the Foreign Office (where he was parliamentary private secretary to Richard "Rab" Butler) on September 12:

> I had not long been at the Foreign Office when the siren sounded, and we retreated to the cellar, where Rab sat surrounded by a body of B.B.C. journalists to whom he administered a heartening tonic. He is more optimistic about the war now, as is Harold [Nicolson], who is happier about our air defences and says that the new barrage over London ought to protect it, at least at night. Later Harold and I went to the Dorchester together for dinner, and found half London there. . . . The dining room was full of well-known people and friends waiting for the air raid which soon began. Somerset Maugham was nearby, and dozens more. . . . Later, the lobby was crowded, and people settled down for the night with rugs, etc. Just before midnight I left, and although warned not to do so, I walked home. It was inky dark and the incessant gun fire was alarming, like the battlefields. The invasion is expected any moment now, probably some time during the weekend. This island race is extraordinary: everyone I have seen today was in the highest spirits. They are all convinced that an English victory now lies just round the corner, and that our Air Force is actually superior, not only in quality but in numbers, to the Germans.

One problem for citizens of London and other British cities subjected to aerial attack was the noise. Droning bombers overhead were one thing, but the tremendous crescendo of the ack-ack guns, firing furiously through the night, not to mention the crump and crash of exploding bombs, was another. Lee estimated that Central London had some 450 ack-ack guns, all performing their noisy duty as soon as the enemy planes appeared overhead. On September 13, he managed to fall asleep in his room at the United Services Club on Waterloo Place but was awoken by two earth-shattering explosions. The bombs seemed awfully close. The next morning, he observed two large craters just across Piccadilly and only about 150 feet from his bedroom. His embassy driver arrived late for work at the embassy in Grosvenor Square that morning, looking "a little shaky. Ten houses in his row were blown down about 3 A.M. and he was pinching himself to see if he was all right. He moved his wife to the country just in time. He really had a narrow squeak as a bomb hit his chimney but kept going to explode next door."

On the night of September 14, again after dining with friends, Lee stood with them on their roof to watch the nightly fireworks. "It was a lovely dear night. One could see a tapestry of shell bursts all around the horizon at varying heights. Two fires began to glow as incendiary bombs came down from the heavens and fire apparatus went clanging by in the dark empty streets below."

On the following day, September 15, Channon drove back into London from his country home in Kelvedon, Essex. His journey took him directly through the East End on the East India Dock Road. He crawled through the debris caused by the bombing, stopping regularly to give people lifts in his car, this part of the city a "scene of desolation; house after house has been wrecked, debris falls from the remaining floors, windows are gone, heaps of rubbish lie in the pavements. A large hospital and a synagogue still stand, but they are windowless. Some streets are roped off because of time bombs. The damage is immense, yet the people, mostly Jewish, seemed courageous."

Ingersoll was in London to gain a firsthand view of how Britons were coping with the Blitz. Instinctively Anglophile, he was full of admiration for the apparent willingness of ordinary people to fight back against the threat to their lives and safety, despite the awful blows suffered by France and the loss of the BEF. He managed to interview one of Art Donahue's colleagues, a young American pilot who, originally from Los Angeles, had first travelled to Europe to fight with the French air force but had flown with the RAF since the fall of France. He told Ingersoll that on September 15 he had had only thirty hours in a Spitfire. That morning there hadn't been much enemy activity over southern England, so that the lunchtime return to the aerodrome made him think that there would be no further flying that day. The moment they landed, however, came an order to refuel and return. It was only at twenty thousand feet above London that he realized something big was up. The air was full of Spitfires and Hurricanes, wheeling high above the capital in anticipation of a mass attack. Cumulus clouds broke the sky and gave good cover to the enemy as they approached. The next minute the battle began. Smoke suddenly poured from his wingman's plane, the aircraft struck by a sudden, devastating fusillade. For what seemed like ages he sat there mesmerized by the sight of his friend being burned alive in the doomed aircraft as it slipped below and began its dive to earth. He was then startled from his reverie by a Heinkel bomber flying immediately beneath him. Kicking himself into a dive, he fell on the enemy from above and shot it down before it had the chance to escape into some beckoning clouds. After exhausting his ammunition, he returned to rearm and refuel, and then, like hundreds of his comrades, returned to the fray. And so it went on all day, hundreds of aircraft, friend and foe, diving, wheeling in confusion across London's deadly skies.

Following the exhausting air battles of the summer, and his wounding on August 8, Art Donahue decided to pick this moment to recuperate in London, and to enjoy some of his hospital leave sightseeing. He arrived by train on Monday, September 16, the day that followed the heaviest raid so far. It was immediately apparent that the city had taken a pounding:

> [The] sun was a red ball glowing feebly through the haze of brown smoke that covered the city. Fire fighters were working

everywhere; streets were roped off, littered with broken glass and scattered brick and masonry and other rubble; fire hoses lay all about. Piles of rubble marked where buildings had stood the day before. Other buildings still stood, burned out or burning out inside. Here and there was a great pit in the middle of a street, with dirt and rock scattered all about and water from broken mains flooding the street. Firemen were still working heroically against the flames of buildings struck by fire bombs; and A.R.P. workers toiled in the debris of buildings hit by high-explosive bombs, to rescue persons trapped inside.

He saw a young auxiliary fireman drinking a cup of tea, and felt nothing but admiration for these men.

He had assumed that he would be able to cope easily with the bombardment. He retired at the end of his first day in the capital to his lodging house, and the sirens began their doleful wail soon after dusk. To his surprise, everyone else immediately hurried downstairs to seek the sanctuary of the cellar. Donahue decided to ignore the alarm and wander out into the street to watch what he assumed would be some desultory fireworks:

> I could hear German planes droning overhead, and there was continuous barking from the anti-aircraft guns scattered about the city, echoed by the distant, eerie whoompf of the shells exploding high above. Far up among the stars the exploding shells appeared as little silent red flashes winking about first one point then another in space, where enemy planes were located. No searchlights were on.
>
> No bombs appeared to be dropping anywhere. From the sound there seemed to be at least a dozen Huns over the city, scattered about, but they just seemed to be droning around aimlessly. There were few people on the darkened streets and very few cars about. What people I met were mostly wearing helmets, and I began to feel a little self-conscious without mine. Once in a while I'd hear a little humming noise followed by the noise of something small

and metallic dropping near by. These were the little pieces of shrapnel falling, from shells that had exploded overhead. I knew the shrapnel wasn't likely to injure me, as the pieces are small and don't fall very fast; but one of them could give me a good bump if it hit me on the head when I didn't have a helmet, so I soon went back to my room and retired. Few noises bother me, and I got to sleep all right in spite of the gunfire.

About midnight I was suddenly awakened by a distant sound like steam escaping from a radiator. It was a ghostly sort of noise, like something slipping through the air in the distance at great speed, and it was rising in intensity. In perhaps four or five seconds it rose to a noise like that of a locomotive letting off steam close by, and then to a fiendish shriek, ending in a heavy explosion not far away, that shook the building. I had heard a big bomb falling for my first time! In the last second it had seemed to be coming straight for the house, and after it was over I found my heart pounding and my courage taking flight. That was the start. It kept up for about an hour, during which I alternately tried burying my head under the covers so that I couldn't hear the bombs so plainly, and then straightening out and calling myself a coward and trying to ignore them, so that I could sleep. Neither method worked. There was a bomb every two or three minutes on the average. They made various sounds. Sometimes they fell with a long wailing sound, like an American fire siren. Sometimes it was a whistle building to a crescendo; but when they were close it usually sounded like a locomotive passing overhead and letting off steam. Sometimes there would be a "stick" of four or five in a row—the entire load from one machine being dropped at once. None landed really close, but each sounded, before it hit, as if it were aimed for a point midway between the washbowl in one corner of my room and the suitcase under my bed.

In addition to the noise and terror of this encounter, the streets outside were also full of the racket that accompanied the raids. Fire engines and ambulances rushed by with their bells clanging, adding a little musical color to the dull bark and distant crack of the ack-ack guns firing relentlessly and without unison at the German engines growling in the heavens above. Occasionally an air-raid warden could be heard shouting, "Put that bloomin' light out!" to some unfortunate who had failed to comply with the strict blackout precautions, perhaps by momentarily opening their curtains to peep out. On this occasion the bombing lasted an hour. Donahue managed to fall asleep, only to be reawakened by a repeat performance at 4:00 A.M. When the all-clear siren sounded at dawn, he finally fell asleep, emotionally and physically exhausted. The only reason he stayed in London the next day was that he had some shopping to do on Oxford Street, which he found in a state of disarray, with many of the shops having suffered bomb damage. He spent a further sleepless night in the capital before buying a railway ticket the following day to Plymouth, hoping to spend a quiet few days as far away from the noise and terror of London as possible. When, after the period had passed, he returned to London, where he had left most of his belongings, he discovered that most of the street where he had stayed was covered in broken glass. A "stick" of four bombs had landed in a row on the buildings right across the street from his accommodation, and the windows in his room had been blown out. That was enough for him. It was safer living at a forward Spitfire base on Britain's southern coast than it was in London, and so he hurried "home" determined to spend the remainder of his precious leave with his squadron.

Eric Sevareid hated the feeling of not knowing where the bombs might fall as enemy bombers droned overhead. Those with things to do, such as air-raid wardens, ambulance drivers, and firefighters, were kept occupied during attacks, whereas people without jobs to do were left alone with their terrified imaginings. On one occasion the terror overcame him as he dashed downstairs from a shaking bedroom to a basement shelter, whereas he felt no fear at all when he helped extinguish a burning incendiary device on the roof of the building opposite. The noise of descending bombs, he observed, created differing reactions. If people were walking while they heard the bombs falling, they stopped. If people were standing still, they started walking or running.

Those sitting would rise, and vice versa. The worst place to be when the whistle of falling bombs could be heard was the bath. What to do? He observed that it was easier being brave when he was with another person than when he was alone with himself. "To be alone was sometimes awful," he recalled.

The real heroes, considered Raymond Lee, were the men and women who stayed out on their official duties during the raids. On September 16, amidst the drone of enemy planes overhead, he could hear the sounds of a city urgently dealing with the attack as it took place: the noise of ambulance and auxiliary fire crews; air-raid wardens who guided people to safety and watched for unexploded bombs so that the Bomb Disposal crews could dispose of them (as much as 20 percent of bombs never detonated), and the ordinary citizens who selflessly rushed to extinguish incendiary bombs with the now ubiquitous buckets of sand that sat in prominent places in all buildings. "And one can never forget the stout fellows who have dug [7] feet and exhumed an enormous bomb which has for several days past threatened St. Paul's Cathedral and the area round about," he recalled. "They hauled it away and exploded it in a marsh. How could they tell whether it was a dud or a delayed-action?" When he thought of the lives being lost nightly to this terror from the skies, Lee fumed against "the paranoiacs [in Berlin] who are behind it all."

The Luftwaffe bombing raid on September 15 was immense. Lee was not to know that it was to prove the climax of the weeklong daylight bombing raids that initiated the Blitz. Some 1,120 German aircraft took part in mass raids across London and other cities. The following day, Lee repeated gleefully the Air Ministry claim that between 175 and 185 enemy aircraft had been brought down. This was wishful thinking: the real number was closer to 65. Daylight raids were phased out in favor of night bombing, which had the advantage of hiding the Germans from the defenders but also made it more difficult for the crews to place their bombs accurately. A feature of the new approach was for lone bombers to scuttle in under cover of darkness and then fly around until they had identified a target, or thought they had, before dropping their bombload and scurrying for home like cockroaches fleeing the light.

As the battle continued, London's ancient landscape changed forever. On September 28, Raymond Lee wrote to his wife describing sites that would have been familiar to her from their life in prewar London:

> I went over to Myers, which is still open and had some good coffee (but no cream, which went out in October), and delicious rolls and pastry. The old man asked all about you and Jenifer. He still has plenty of chocolates and cakes and cream puffs, which rather give the lie to German claims of British starvation by blockade. Then I walked past Buckingham Palace, where the bomb damage is being repaired, and past Queen Anne's Mansions, hit four or five times, and Westminster and the House of Commons, both damaged. After this the War Office, which had a big bomb. From here past Trafalgar Square, where there are numerous sandbagged pillboxes and barbed wire entanglements and to Albemarle Street, where two buildings next [to] little Jon Arnat's are a heap of ruins. Dover Street has a dent in it where a bomb demolished two or three buildings next [to] Batt's Hotel. Piccadilly Arcade is blocked up completely at one end. Savile Row is fairly battered to pieces; all the glass is out in Bond Street and Regent Street. Not a shop in Conduit Street has any glass in it. Kenneth Durward's is an empty shell. And so on back along Oxford Street where John Lewis is a burnt-out ruin and Selfridge's huge plate-glass windows have been shattered. Nevertheless, I look at the ruin in the West End with satisfaction for it marks another of the famous German mistakes. Had they continued to batter the East End and kill and destroy among the slums, there would certainly have been great discontent. As it is, the only complaint the poor people have is that Government assistance to the homeless and the provision of deep shelters are not being attended to with the necessary promptness.

The bombing appeared endless. On March 5, six months after it had started, Channon recorded in his diary that the previous night's raid was particularly heavy, hitting Buckingham Palace and killing over eighty people in the Café de Paris. He had driven into London from

Kelvedon during the afternoon and regretted it, the city looking melancholy and life noisy, maddening, and nerve-wracking, with planes and bombs everywhere. On April 10, he recorded that the city looked "like a battered old war horse." During the intervening months, German strategy changed. Between September and November, the main raids had been against London, with harassing raids only against other cities, such as Birmingham, Coventry, Liverpool, Hull, and Glasgow. The plan now was to switch the mass raids to other British industrial centers while continuing to harass London at night. Birmingham and Coventry found themselves badly hit, while London continued to receive the attention of the bombers. Herbert Mason's famous photograph of St. Paul's Cathedral standing resolute and unscathed amidst the smoke of an attack was taken during a massive raid on December 29–30, 1940. The four-hour raid was the most devastating on the historic heart of the City of London since the Great Fire of London in 1666. Lee recorded:

> Seven churches have been burned out, including four of Sir Christopher Wren's which were the glory of London. The Guildhall is likewise gutted, and so disappears this ancient fifteenth-century building which, more than any other one, has been the cradle of individual liberty from which the citizens of London have defied all kings, from the Normans down, and forced the written acknowledgment of their rights even from William the Conqueror. The great and mysterious statues of Gog and Magog have been destroyed in the conflagration, together with many of the other ancient records and souvenirs of the history, running back to the days of the Conquest. There is no measure of the value of the carvings by Grinling Gibbons and others which have gone up in smoke. The grand library of the Guildhall, up the aisle of which Jeanette and I walked when we first came, to be received by the Lord Mayor in his robes and accompanied by all his retinue, is only a mass of smouldering ruins.

But Lee puzzled at the Luftwaffe's tactics. The mass attack on the medieval city center of Coventry, in England's Midlands on November 15, was devastating to the ancient city, and caused about a thousand deaths. A series of attacks by five hundred aircraft, blotting out targets one by one, would, he believed, have been far more effective in bringing Britain to her knees than the seemingly halfhearted attempts so far, in which bombs were dropped widely across the country. One of the answers to Lee's skepticism about German tactics was a reality that never became fully clear to protagonists on all sides during the war, which was that despite the exaggerated prognostications of the past, air bombardment alone had a limited material and moral effect in war. Despite the horror of bombing attacks, there were always enough people on the ground afterwards to continue resisting, and the Luftwaffe in 1940 and 1941 was a fraction of the size that the Allied air forces became in 1944 and 1945.

Ralph Ingersoll experienced firsthand the insouciance displayed by Londoners during the Blitz. Life was a strange coexistence between the ordinary and the occasionally terrifying. People went about their daily business as though they were living in a time of peace, although they always had half an eye cocked at the sky. If an aircraft was directly over-head, it might be sufficient for pedestrians to check their stride and look cautiously and momentarily into the sky, but otherwise life went on as normal. Soon after arriving in the capital, Ingersoll was standing one day in the queue for Alien Registration, where he had waited patiently for some time to be processed by the police:

> I was almost at the top of the line when the first air raid came. I did not hear the siren—most of the time when you are indoors you do not hear the siren. A policeman from the street simply stuck his head in the door and blew loudly on a police whistle. I jumped a mile. The room was suddenly still. The sergeant in the middle of the counter chanted in a monotonous voice without looking up: "An air-raid alarm has been sounded. There is a shelter underneath this building. The man at the door will show you the way to it. If you do not choose to go to the shelter we will carry on." Nobody went. The buzz of conversation resumed. I thought everyone was very brave, myself included. Later I found out that no one in London ever pays any attention to daylight raids unless

he is on the street and hears the plane directly overhead or sees it diving toward him.

Nevertheless, it was a mistake, he concluded, to confuse nonchalance with indifference. The British people he happened to observe were fighting for their lives, and while he noticed a daily sangfroid—or "stiff upper lip"—they were not indifferent to what was going on around them, or to their fate. It was clear that they—people from all classes, so far as he could judge—were prepared to fight, and matched Churchill's rhetoric. In fact, the only thing noticeably unusual about London for visitors during the early days of the Blitz, apart from the piles of rubble heaped here and there, and the periodic wail of air-raid sirens, was the nightly blackout. As dusk fell each night, "no cheerfully lighted city" emerged from the gloom. Kathleen Kennedy, the US ambassador's nineteen-year-old daughter, wrote of her experience of the early days of the blackout:

It is an eerie experience walking through a darkened London. You literally feel your way, and with groping finger make sudden contact with a lamppost against which leans a steel helmeted figure with his gas mask slung at his side. You cross the road in obedience to little green crosses winking in the murk above your head. You pause to watch the few cars, which with blackened lamps, move through the streets. With but a glimmer you trace their ghostly progress. You look, and see no more, the scintillating signs of Piccadilly and Leicester Square, the glittering announcements of smokes and soaps. Gone are the gaily-lit hotels and nightclubs; now in their place are sombre buildings surrounded by sandbags. You wander through Kensington Garden in search of beauty and solitude and find only trenches and groups of ghostly figures working sound machines and searchlights to locate the enemy. Gone from the parks are the soapbox orators and the nightly strollers. But yet the moon shines through and one can see new beauties in the silent, deserted city of London. It is a new London, a London that looks like Barcelona before the bombs fell.

Life continued, however, despite the bombing, even if normal service was somewhat disrupted. Lee went to the ballet one night at the New Theatre and was introduced to Margot Fonteyn, the principal ballerina. The ballet's existence was somewhat precarious, he observed. "There is no orchestra but two grand pianos played, accompanying the dancing. A great many of the people who were formerly in it have been called up and others have dropped out, so that they are badly crippled."

Ingersoll was impressed by the signs of purposeful activity he saw all around him among ordinary citizens:

> One cannot move around London more than a few days without being impressed by how busy a city is that is being bombed. People have written about how terrible bombs are, or how inconvenient or how exciting it is to be bombed. Nobody has written about how much work it is; but that is the most striking thing of all. It is twenty-four hours a day work for millions of people. Every morning the ruins of the night before must be cleaned up. Telephone and gas lines and water mains repaired. The business of bringing food and supplies into the city carries its load of inconvenience and added labour. The smallest white-collar clerk may have added work to do at home repairing his own house, helping his neighbours, chipping in his spare time as one of scores of volunteers. And the act of getting to and from his office may be more work to him. The work of putting out fires is multiplied ten or twentyfold. The sheer work of keeping a city in operation while it is being bombed is appalling.

Eric Sevareid likewise observed not panic in people but a society coming together under the shared burden of common trial. He also saw a new respect from Londoners for Americans who had stayed in the city to share the trials of war with the inhabitants.

Lee's diaries over the nine months from September 1940 are a catalogue of bombs falling and the damage and casualties they caused. The Blitz—and its attendant destruction of human life and property—angered him. "What a barbarous period this is we are living in!" he raged. "And there is no question at all about who is responsible for it. It is the Nazis who have turned the ordinary everyday life of the world into a promenade through the Valley of the Shadow of Death, so that every citizen has to live his life with a fortitude that no previous generation has been called upon to show. When I look at all the crowds going along the streets here, shopping and following their normal activities, and realize that out of them a certain number are going to be blasted into oblivion every night, it makes me wild with anger to think that a few scoundrels can put the world in such a fix." Ralph Ingersoll experienced the same anger. Hearing for the first time the explosion of an antiaircraft shell high above him, he felt a surge of fury at the intruder who was bringing death and destruction to the city. "I wanted the gun below me to shoot again and again. I wanted it to reach up and slap that bastard down."

Lee had several narrow escapes. On October 24, 1940, he went to watch the popular movie *Britain Can Take It*, narrated by Quentin Reynolds. Later, he wrote of walking home that night in the dark to Claridge's Hotel in Mayfair and hearing "the paralyzing swish of a bomb down the street. As it had gone off I pursued my way but was in a moment a little disturbed by myriads of shell fragments which came rattling down in the street and off the slates of the roofs. . . ."

It was clear to Lee from the moment he returned to London that, despite its sangfroid, Britain would require American intervention if it hoped to survive a long war against Germany. On October 16, 1940, he observed, "Most of the British to whom I talk are not anxious for us [i.e., the Americans] to come in at once—or so they say. They explain that the first thing they need is the fruit of our factories and that, should we start to war on our own account, we would have no weapons for them." However, in a long war, he concluded, Britain would run out of money, and need help. The fabled stiff upper lip would be of no avail if the cupboard was bare, when trying to defend herself from the Luftwaffe in the air and U-boats in the Atlantic. A week later he observed that the war that had swept Europe was an existential struggle for liberal democracy, for which the United States was "the final reserve force." Only time would tell whether it would gird its loins and join the fight to defend the freedoms it so enjoyed.

On May 12, 1941, Chips Channon returned to London from Kelvedon with what he described as regret: the weather was beautiful and he would much rather have remained in the comfort of his country home. London continued to burn under the attentions of the Luftwaffe. As Channon drove into the capital towards Westminster, "burnt bits of paper fluttering about in the street, and broken glass everywhere. The rubble and debris are heaped high in the streets. I tried to get to the House of Commons but the crowd was so large I could not fight my way through; but I could see the huge hole in the Westminster Hall roof. I met Jim Thomas who tells me that the Chamber is gutted: no more shall we hear fiery and futile speeches there . . . gone is that place, as I always foresaw. Itself the cradle, the protector of democracy, in the end it went a long way to kill what it created. . . ." The attacks on Westminster made Lee furious. They seemed to encapsulate the essence of Hitler's assault on the long traditions of democratic liberty in the Anglo-Saxon world:

> What wrung my withers and made me feel extremely angry was to see a large hole burned in the roof of Westminster Hall, which was built by William Rufus and is the only remaining part of Westminster Palace. The House of Commons is completely burned out by fire, so it will be a long time before Winston Churchill can stand pounding the despatch box in front of the Government bench, under the eye of the bewigged Speaker in his ancient chair. The Deanery in the yard of Westminster Abbey is completely wrecked by fire and a long tangle of hoses was running into the Abbey itself, where the lantern, just over the spot where the King and Queen were crowned, had been burned through. Some damage had also been done to the stonework of the Henry VII Chapel, but this is not irreparable. A much more modern structure, Thames House, on the Embankment, had had a large bomb on the top corner, and the huge blocks of stone which fell from the cornice were scattered thickly over the Embankment road and the side streets. One had landed on top of a taxi and completely demolished it.

From the start, the daily experience of Britain under the Blitz was presented to American radio and newspaper audiences by a handful of men and women, determined to break through the fog of confusion and propaganda in which Germany was mounting military operations and Britain was responding to them. Sevareid considered the most important journalist in London to be CBS's Ed Murrow, who quietly but effectively explained to the American people on the radio what Nazi brutality was doing to ordinary Britons, and how people were standing up to this violent bullying. Murrow did not advocate an unthinking intervention by America in Europe's war. Rather, in Sevareid's words, he "made the British and their behavior human and thus compelling to his countrymen at home." It was about connecting ordinary Americans with the harsh reality of a war imposed on ordinary people in Britain, who had had aggression forced on them. Murrow and others like him managed to capture in short daily broadcasts what it meant to be at the receiving end of sticks of bombs, and to continue to live day-by-day despite the horror of this new kind of warfare. Murrow was so successful, Sevareid observed, that he was of more importance to how the war was understood in millions of American homes than Kennedy or any of the formal arms of government or diplomacy. And it was Murrow and those like him who did more than any other to illuminate ordinary Americans about the holocaust of Nazi bombs being thrown against an ancient civilization by this new barbarism, and, in doing so, "awakening the American people to the issue before them."

In Sevareid's final broadcast from Britain in late 1940, he contrasted Paris's spirit, which had broken, with London's, which had not, and how the capital city, though it was not England, had become Britain, a city-state in its own right, populated by "a peaceable people who had gone to war in their aprons and bowlers, with their old fowling pieces, with their ketchup bottles filled with gasoline and standing ready on the pantry shelves." He finished, with his voice wavering with emotion, "When this is all over, in the days to come, men will speak of this war, and they will say: I was a soldier, or I was a sailor, or I was a pilot; and others will say with equal pride: I was a citizen of London."

CHAPTER ELEVEN

Occupation

I n Paris, Sylvia Beach and her lover, Adrienne Monnier, owner of a bookshop on the Rue de l'Odéon in the Latin Quarter opposite Beach's Shakespeare and Company, decided not to flee the city. They couldn't see any reason for leaving. Beach was one of only about five hundred Americans who stayed in the capital in June 1940. Instead, the two women wandered the chaotic streets during the early weeks of June, marveling at the misery of a city at war, watching the poor refugees trudging through, on their journey to who knew where. All that these people wanted to do was to put the war behind them. They thought that the armies following them would be far behind. Unfortunately, none of them realized until it was too late that 1940s Blitzkrieg moved much faster than they. On the morning of June 14, close behind the cattle-drawn carts piled with household goods, marched the Germans in uniformed arrogance, a deafening roar of tanks, armored cars, and stiffly seated, steel-helmeted soldiers in the back of trucks rumbling across the ancient stone cobbles of the capital. On that morning Walter Kerr of the *Herald Tribune* got up at 4:00 A.M., climbed onto his bicycle, and pedaled to the unusually quiet Place de la Concorde, in peacetime a place of riotous busyness in the heart of Paris, where he hoped to get a good view of the country's conquerors. Louis Lochner, one of nine war correspondents from neutral countries travelling with the Wehrmacht (along with Bill Shirer and Fred Oechsner), came with the first German troops who pulled up outside the Hotel de Crillon at dawn. It's not clear whether Lochner and Kerr managed to meet. Lochner told *Life* magazine:

> You who have been to Paris, just imagine this picture: at the Place de la Concorde no such merry-go-round of honking autos, screaming news vendors, gesticulating cops, gaily chatting pedestrians as usually characterizes this magnificent square. Instead, depressing silence broken only now and then by the purr of some German officer's motor as it made its way to the Hotel Crillon, headquarters of the hastily set up local German commandery. On the hotel's flagstaff, the swastika fluttered in the breeze where once the Stars and Stripes had been in the days of 1919 when Wilson received the cheers of French crowds from the balcony.

Commander Roscoe Hillenkoetter, the US naval attaché at the embassy in Paris, had heard artillery firing the night before northwest of the city, but the occupation the following morning went ahead without any resistance. At 10:00 A.M., seeing the swastika raised above the Hotel de Crillon, he, Robert Murphy, and Colonel Fuller, the military attaché, walked across Place de la Concorde to introduce themselves to the new German military commandant of the city, General von Studnitz. Hillenkoetter's account excludes the presence of Murphy, although it is clear from Murphy's account that the three men went together:

> Fuller and I went across the street to the Crillon, identified ourselves, and were immediately shown into the German general's office and sitting room. We were received most graciously and affably, and although it was only about 10:30 A.M., were offered

a glass of what the General said was the very best brandy in the Crillon. . . .

Before leaving the General, Fuller and I were invited by him to assist him in the review of the Green Heart Division which he had previously commanded, and which was to march through the Place de la Concorde at 3:30 that day. There being no easy way to decline, Fuller and I accepted.

The call on the Ambassador went off in the most "correct" fashion. The Ambassador was assured that all American interests would be respected, etc., etc., and after about ten minutes of correctness, the General left. Fuller and I accompanied the Ambassador on his return call to the General at about 2:30 which also lasted just about ten minutes.

Robert Murphy recalled that after announcing themselves to a German officer, the man exclaimed, "Murphy! What are you doing here?"

I looked at him in astonishment; his face was vaguely familiar. "I am Colonel Weber," he announced, and then I remembered that he was a Bavarian army officer whom I had known fifteen years before when I was vice consul at Munich.

Murphy recalled that during the hour-long meeting, Studnitz expressed complete confidence that "England" would fall soon. The preparations were in place. Operations in France would be complete within ten days, after which the focus would switch to Britain. A return visit by Studnitz to Bullitt took place in the early afternoon, after which Fuller and Murphy were invited to join the German commander in a review of his troops:

Both Colonel Fuller and I could easily see how that would look in newsreels, photos, etc.—two American officers taking a review with a German general. So we hastily, but firmly, declined, saying that we didn't feel worthy to share the General's honor; that it was his division and his glory; and that it would be a shame to deprive him of even a share of the glory. Colonel Fuller and I then moved back into the crowd of civilians watching the "march-past."

—⁊⁊⁊—

On the day that Pétain announced that he was throwing in the towel, Drue Tartière sat with a friend at a café in the Place de la Comedie, Bordeaux, the two holding each other's hands and weeping as they watched a few French airplanes making good their escape, in open defiance of Pétain's orders, pointing their aircraft northwards, in the direction of Britain. What could they, the employees of Paris Mondial, do? Jean Fraysse and the entire team remained full of fight. Indeed, most of the stunned people she saw and heard that day in Bordeaux repudiated the notion of surrender. *Their* France had not yet subjugated itself to the invader. Already there was talk of resistance. Plans to move Paris Mondial to Martinique, however, were short-lived.

Pétain's call to end the military resistance to Germany was followed by news—first provided by the BBC in London—of the terms for France's surrender. The ritual humiliation of the act of surrender at Compiègne Forest was followed by terms that instantly made France a slave state. "The Germans would occupy the most heavily populated part of France, where its main natural resources and industry were located. The cost of that occupation was to be paid for by the French people. All German refugees in France were to be handed over to the Nazis. All French prisoners of war in Germany were to remain there, and prisoners of war in German hands in France were to remain prisoners of war working for the Germans."

At this stage Drue had the opportunity to leave France. Indeed, both her father and father-in-law in the United States began making frantic efforts to persuade her to get to safety, especially with the threat of the death sentence over "Dorothy Leyton's" head. But she refused. Watching France collapse seemed to make her determined to stay. She would remain to help her adopted country in its hour of need in whatever way she could. A passionate anti-Nazi, Jean Fraysse was determined to find a way to resist and decided to leave Bordeaux—now a sea of confusion and recrimination—and make his way to Toulouse. Drue decided to attach her colors to Fraysse's mast. "Since I had now decided to remain in France and had already been working with Jean for some time," she recalled, "I determined to follow his example. I took Nadine, my maid, and my French poodle called 'Ondie' the French word for shortwave, and went with him in my car to Toulouse." On the way, staying overnight at a hotel in Cahuzac, they witnessed some of the emotions released at the destruction of their beloved country:

> Soldiers from the defeated French armies were wandering in hordes in this region. A group of them arrived at our inn, and they were so enraged that Nadine and I were frightened. We locked ourselves in our room that night and heard them in the dining room below, cursing the government and smashing wine bottles. "How could we fight?" they kept demanding. "The filthy government wouldn't support us! The Boches just mowed us down!"

Unable to find any way of actively opposing the new regime in Toulouse, they made their way to the Auvergne town of Vichy on July 12, the new seat of the post-armistice government, in an attempt to decide what to do. Vichy was, however, no better: a "scene of intrigue, suspicion, and confusion," Drue recalled. It was here that they experienced the first signs of the collaborationist imperative that was to define Pétain's new government, and immediately understood that anyone who resisted the Nazis would be no friend of Vichy. Woodruff Wallner of the US embassy, which had also moved to Vichy, warned her not to "expect any further exhibition of spirit in France," at least for the time being. The women decided to return to Drue's house on the Rue Vital in the 16th arrondissement in Paris, even though they had no idea what to expect when they got there.

The return journey gave them an insight into the new rulers of France. At Moulin they passed the German checkpoint between unoccupied and occupied France, and couldn't help observing how the conquerors deported themselves. "Tall, blond, impressive-looking

Germans stood guard," she recalled. "They strutted with an air of self-importance and seemed thoroughly conscious of their own strength in relation to the weakness of the people they believed they had just crushed for a thousand years. They were trying at the same time to be very 'correct'"—a term widely used by those who observed the first weeks and months of occupation. The women had to pass another checkpoint to get back into Paris, where the German sentries were much more intimidating. Long lines of vehicles queued at the roadblock at the Porte d'Italie, where passes and papers were examined in minute detail before people were allowed through. By the time the women did get through, the city was dark. Sandbags remained piled against buildings from the days when a German ground offensive against the city was expected. Roads had been blocked off, German guards manned the intersections, and a vast array of signposts provided directions for the German military vehicles that now dominated the city.

The house on the Rue Vital, protected by a seal on the doors declaring it to be the property of an American citizen, was undisturbed, and for the first time since June 11 Drue and Nadine slept in their own beds. In the days that followed they explored a city under occupation, noting the rapidly decreasing availability of food and the increasing ubiquity of the secret police and the apparatus of the totalitarian state. It seemed astonishing to them just how quickly the world had changed. It was no longer "Gay Paree" but a very different, frightened, and subdued place. Informers seemed to be everywhere, and as an American, Drue was warned by one of Jean Fraysse's friends—Revilliod, now secretary-general of the Paris Prefecture of Police—to keep a low profile, as all foreigners were under suspicion and observation. Telephone conversations were eavesdropped upon, listening to the BBC was forbidden, and saying anything in public that was derogatory to the occupiers could quickly land one in prison. One day in September Drue and Nadine had their first experience of how extensive the practice of informing had become. An English friend of Drue's husband's family rang one day to ask her some questions about Drue's experience in Vichy. The woman explained to Drue that she hadn't been interned along with all other Britons, as she was working for the French Red

Cross, but hinted that she was after information that she could feed back to the British intelligence service. Drue gave her some nondescript information and warned her not to call on the telephone. A few days later, however, the woman rang again. This time Nadine answered the phone, and, as Drue was busy, said that Drue would ring back later. Nadine and Drue were due that day to cycle out to the industrial area of Suresnes, at the edge of the Bois de Boulogne, where they understood that black market food was available. While waiting at a café, Drue used the opportunity to ring the English woman from a public telephone near their table. After a brief conversation, Drue returned to her seat next to Nadine to finish her coffee. Five minutes later the telephone rang. A waiter picked it up. Drue overhead him say, "Yes, they had accents." Looking worried, the man ran over to the café owner, and said, loud enough for her to hear, "I'll be right back. I have to go and get a gendarme." Immediately understanding what was going on, Drue and Nadine quickly made their exit, losing themselves in the local crowd. Drue attempted to disguise herself by taking off her hat and coat. Looking back at the café, they could see that before long the waiter had returned with three policemen, who searched the area for them but to no avail. A heavy rain was now falling, which allowed them the opportunity to make good their escape. But it had been a close shave. Nowhere was it safe from the listening ears of the state. The English woman's telephone was clearly under surveillance, and it was only a matter of luck that her earlier calls to Drue had not led to a visit from the French police working for their new masters, and that on this occasion Drue had kept her wits about her and had narrowly avoided arrest. The incident demonstrated just how dangerous Paris had become, and persuaded her to seek the sanctuary of the countryside. Accordingly, she began to make plans to move out to Barbizon, the small town southeast of Paris where she had spent the summer with Jacques, and where his father had once owned a house.

—◊—

The Melbourne *Argus* of July 23, 1940, carried a syndicated report from Lisbon reporting the adventures of Walter Kerr, shortly after he'd escaped from France using a doctored visa. Entitled GERMAN GRIP ON FRANCE, the report provided a graphic description of life in Paris following the surrender:

> German-occupied France is an economically twisted country with its millions of people broken in spirit and doped with propaganda. They are groping about in an effort to reorganise their lives as best they can. Thousands and thousands are out of work and many are living on credit. Families are scattered, transportation and communication are almost unavailable and food is poor and meagre. The German army rules. The army is working night and day for the coming attack against England. Everything is subordinated to this preparation—food for the masses, transportation for refugees and hospital care. The occupation is deadening and the sight of troops in grey is deadening. And yet there is an undercurrent of resistance. The penalty for defacing German posters is death but I do not know of one of them in Paris that has not been ripped or torn. Scores of people tell the German soldiers that their radios are unworkable so that they do not have to listen to German broadcasts. I know many Frenchmen who listen constantly to the London radio although the penalty for doing so is severe. Kerr says that there is virtually no fresh fish, meat, milk, butter, or eggs. Only frozen meat and few vegetables are available in Paris where the Germans buy everything with paper marks. Hotel prices for Germans are fixed at 10 francs a day in Left Bank hotels and 20 francs at the Ritz. What a city Paris has become, he adds. The Germans have their eyes everywhere. It ceased to be an open city on the day they arrived. Planes fly overhead constantly diving on the Arc de Triomphe and skimming rooftops.

Paris was forced to recognize from the very start of the occupation that the Germans were the masters now. In the months following the invasion the occupation forces stripped France bare. For Germany, the cornucopia they found in France constituted the legitimate spoils of war. Vast quantities of foodstuffs, domestic goods, and items of every description were "purchased" using occupation currency at fixed rates, then shipped to Germany. Equally vast quantities were simply expropriated from their owners on the quasi-legal pretext of "to the victor the spoils" and transported home. "It was thus, in Berlin," recorded Howard Smith, "that the first effects of war were not the traditional ones of decay and scarcity, but a sudden leap upwards in visible prosperity. Berlin charwomen and housemaids, whose legs had never been caressed by silk, began wearing silk stockings from the Boulevard Haussman as an everyday thing—'from my Hans at the front.'" Little street corner taverns began displaying rows of Armagnac, Martell and Courvoisier Cognac from the cellars of Maxim's and others. Every little bureaucrat in the capital could produce at dinner a fine, fat bottle of the best French champagne. The first winter after the Norwegian campaign, the streets were filled with luxurious silver-fox fur coats wrapped around gleeful servant girls. A soldier coming home on leave was a fine sight to see. He carried in addition to his war-kit, baskets, big cardboard boxes and cheap suitcases filled to overflowing with all kinds of goodies and luxuries from the "front."

Expropriation did not just extend to goods, of course. In accordance with Nazi ideology, the French were now occupants of a slave state, and French labor, both male and female, could be forcibly taken for the victor's use. The city was systematically looted, not just by individual soldiers taking what they wanted but by state-organized despoliation. A new occupation currency was imposed, with an exchange rate to the deutschmark that massively devalued the franc. Hordes of polite, uniformed, and "correct" Wehrmacht tourists stripped Parisian shops bare like locusts, to send back to their *hausfrauen* at home. The Germans, at least in the early days, behaved "correctly." This meant, the joke went, that they raped and stole from you politely, and thanked you afterwards. Politeness was a mechanism deliberately designed to humanize the occupiers, even when one's liberty, goods, freedoms, and future had been taken. "They are good fellows, really" was a common refrain about the Wehrmacht troops. "They had no say in their leader's political ambitions. Don't blame them for what their masters are doing!" Not everyone was polite. Sumner and Toquette Jackson found their weekend house eight miles north of Paris at Enghien-les-Bains, famous for its lake and thermal baths, stripped by German looters when they returned to it in August for the first time since the invasion. In a matter of a few weeks after the Germans' first triumphant arrival, Paris was emptied. If the humiliation of having one's goods and chattels stripped and piled into trucks by uniformed soldiers organizing vast convoys of goods back to Germany was bad enough, enforced starvation was far worse. Parisians, the occupation government decreed, would have to live on twelve hundred calories a day. For the elderly, it was even less. This was a surefire way of demonstrating to the French that they had been defeated: it would also take the sting—and energy—out of any residual impulses towards resistance.

Many changes became quickly apparent in the city. Sylvia Beach was helped in her shop by a young Jewish friend, a student at the Sorbonne, named Francoise Bemheim. In September 1940, the first formal restrictions were placed on Jews. A census was ordered, and Jews were banned from holding public office or any form of employment judged to "influence public opinion." Despite being denied permission to attend her classes, Bemheim, a student of Sanskrit, attempted to continue her studies with the help of her friends. The French authorities, however, obeying their new masters with enthusiasm, did everything they could to put barriers in her way. She was forced, along with all other Jews in the Occupied Zone, to wear a large yellow Star of David on her coat or dress when she ventured out in public. Beach, in a form of solidarity with Bemheim, determined to share many of these restrictions with her, but she was not unaware of the dangers she was running. "We went about on bicycles, the only form of transportation," Beach recorded. "We could not enter public places such as theatres, movies, cafes, concert halls, or sit down on park benches or even on those in the streets. Once, we tried taking our lunch to a shady square. Sitting on the ground *beside* a bench, we hurriedly ate our hard-boiled eggs and swallowed the tea in our thermos bottles, looking around furtively as we did so. It was not an experience that we cared to repeat."

Janet Flanner attempted to describe the state of Paris in those early months of occupation to her readers, using information sourced from refugees from France, as well as information that reached her from friends still in the city. The city was, she argued, in a dangerous state of limbo:

> First: Anybody who loved Paris and grieves at its plight is fortunate not to see it now, because Paris would seem hateful.
>
> Second: Parisians permit themselves exactly two words to describe their conquerors; Parisians say that the Germans are "corrects" and that they are "emmerdeurs." This superficial adjective and this scatological substantive, taken together, are probably important historically. By corrects, the French mean that physically, militarily, one might almost say socially, the Germans have up to now conducted themselves with disciplined decorum. By the second word (now used as practically political terminology by polite Parisians who never before used such a word for anything), Parisians mean that they find the German mentality, its shape, its principles, its whole Teutonic mentation, boring to a malodorous degree. These two curious words so far represent merely the intellectual periphery of a vocabulary not yet filled in with words for the despair and anguish which some of the conquered French are beginning to feel not with their brains but with their stomachs and hearts.
>
> Third: Owing to the Germans' mania for systematic looting— for collecting and carting away French bed linen, machinery, Gobelin tapestries, surgical instruments, milk, mutton, sweet champagne—the French will have to become a race of liars and cheats in order to survive physically. For example, milk is now sold only for babies, pregnant women, and people over seventy. Parisian housewives stand outside dairy shops for hours with rented babies in their arms, or with pillows stuffed under their apron fronts, or with borrowed grandparents hanging on their shoulders. In the old days, soldiers, Christian or pagan, looted with disorderly enthusiasm—raping, robbing, staggering down

roads with booty and with blood on their hands. In the new Aryan looting manner, Nazis ring the French front-door bell while an Army truck waits in the street, and soldiers do the job of fanatical moving men.

Fourth: The German passion for bureaucracy—for written and signed forms, for files, statistics, and lists, and for printed permissions to do this or that, to go here or there, to move about, to work, to exist—is like a steel pen pinning each French individual to a sheet of paper, the way an entomologist pins each specimen insect, past struggling, to his laboratory board. For years, Parisian liberals had suspected that their Republic's increasing tendency toward petty bureaucracy was weakening France. As totalitarians, the Germans seem sure that their bureaucracy, organized on the grand scale, is their strength. Even the suburban fisherman now must have written permission to fish in the Seine, though they haven't caught anything in generations worth writing a line about. As one old fisherman cried, "Soon even French minnows will have to learn to read and write German!"

Food very quickly became a major preoccupation. In rural Normandy, Virginia Lake felt the effect of the German occupation from the start. On Wednesday, June 26, she complained to her diary that they were being more "Nazified" every day. The German-controlled newspaper in St. Malo published a raft of new regulations on its front page. A curfew was in place from 10:00 P.M. each night. Listening to foreign (i.e., British) radio stations was forbidden, as was walking in the street (as opposed to on the sidewalks), driving private vehicles without permission, or making unnecessary journeys. The Germans, too, immediately reversed the Great Migration of refugees fleeing to the South by ordering everyone in the Occupied Zone who was not at their normal place of residence to make their way home. At the same time, Lake felt cut off from the world. News was now under the control of the Germans, and strictly regulated. There was no mail to the Unoccupied Zone.

Like that of many others, Victoria's experience of the Germans in those early days was that they were fastidiously "correct" in their dealings with people. But she was irritated by how calmly, even obsequiously, the locals regarded them. They displayed neither hatred nor hostility, merely sheeplike inquisitiveness about their Teutonic visitors. It was as if the Germans were tourists, or temporary guests, rather than conquerors, and the seeming lack of awareness of the humiliation and subjugation of their country annoyed her. It seemed as if the whole of German manhood was now in uniform, and in France. Even in rural Dinard, they were everywhere:

Went to Dinard yesterday and never once was out of sight of Germans! They are everywhere; many of them race about in high speed owned cars, sport types. Others were having tea at "Le Bras," the most famous pastry shop in town, and many, many were on the beach.

On Tuesday, July 9, she met her first Germans face-to-face. Five soldiers arrived at the gate to the farm at Cancaval, asking for stabling and accommodation for several men for several days. They were well mannered, but it was clear that this was an instruction, not a request. On a personal level, the Germans she encountered were simple and polite. But the German presence was accompanied by an onslaught of draconian orders. All farmers had to declare the extent of their property. Only German-authorized crops could be grown. All unmarried people between the ages of eighteen and thirty-five had to register for labor duties. They heard that German criminal law had been imposed on Holland. The Germans were serious. It meant the death sentence for crimes that before the war might have resulted in a clip around the ear by the local gendarme.

At the same time, the dramatic contraction of the supply of food became painfully apparent. The countryside now had to feed many more people, while at the same time large volumes of foodstuffs and other consumables had been removed, presumably to Germany. Within days of Virginia's returning to Normandy, food became increasingly hard to find, and coal deliveries ceased. The food situation grew rapidly worse. It was as if the tap had been turned off. Even in the countryside, where people had the opportunity to grow their own food, the pinch was soon felt. In February 1941, strict rationing had limited butter to 150 grams (a third of a pound) per month, together with the same amount of cooking fat, and 90 grams (two fifths of a cup) of oil. These were starvation levels. The only source of food—for a price—was the black market, where food seemed plentiful but out of the reach of poor rural folk. Meat was officially unavailable on restaurant menus, although customers could pay inflated prices for black-market-sourced meat if one was on good terms with the waiter. "No exciting desserts, only fruit," Lake recorded. "Pastries forbidden. It is also forbidden to serve sugar for coffee but it appears often all the same—otherwise it is a saccharine pill or the same thing in liquid form. It has a taste I dislike." Refined sugar became almost unobtainable, as did onions (a good source of vitamin C) and meat of any kind. Rabbits bred for eating could only be found in the countryside, and notices appeared across Paris warning of the dangers of eating cat meat. It became pointless declaring meatless days, as none was available in the shops. In March 1941 Virginia invested a small fortune—nearly a thousand francs—in the purchase of five hens, but then found that she couldn't find feed for them anywhere. Nor could farmers source fertilizer; glycerin had simply disappeared, as had other prewar staples, such as turpentine, kerosene, alcohol, sanitary pads, starch, thread, and knitting wool.

But it was food that drove every thought. "One thinks of nothing but food," Pauline Crawford wrote in Paris in the late fall of 1941. In Paris, the German restrictions placed poor people on a starvation diet, and there were times when she, too, even with the ability to buy black market food and to benefit from the generosity of friends who owned farms in the countryside, was hungry. People spent whole days in the search for food. Even bread was hard to find. The egg ration was two per month. When extra eggs could be found, they were priced extortionately. An illegal trade began in the import of foodstuffs from the countryside, small amounts being smuggled into the city in suitcases carried on trains and bicycles, but the volumes were small, prices high, and the penalties of discovery severe. Everyone lost weight. It wasn't long before people could see who was enjoying German or collaborationist or black market food: their faces were less pinched than those surviving on more meager fare. Pauline Crawford lost so much weight that she had to adjust all her clothes. She was fortunate in that an extensive network of friends with connections to the countryside kept her supplied with tiny but regular supplies of potatoes, butter, and cheese. She saw a piece of chicken once in six months, and, from a friendly gardener from the Luxembourg Gardens, where she had a little plot, some vegetables were forthcoming. She always regarded herself as one of the lucky ones.

At the American Hospital at Neuilly, Dr. Sumner Jackson and his depleted staff were faced with the challenge of feeding their 250 patients. The hospital was fortuitously placed under the care of the French Red Cross, which offered it some degree of protection from German interference, although this did not mean that the provision of food was somehow made any easier. They were forced to improvise. The hospital gardens were turned into vegetable plots, and a borehole was sunk for water. Everything became difficult, although the hospital had a range of powerful benefactors who could ensure a trickle of produce from the country. Heating fuel became difficult to obtain, the gas pressure was reduced, and both gas and electricity supply became intermittent. Coal supplies became infrequent, and many resorted to collecting firewood to keep their houses warm.

—◊—

Sylvia Beach observed that the initial correctness of the occupiers only went so far. Once the veneer of respectability had been pierced, the authoritarian Teuton emerged, angry, demanding, and possessive. She, the publisher of James Joyce, had a copy of *Finnegan's Wake* in her shop window. One day a German officer entered the building and asked politely if he could buy it. He had an affection for Joyce's writing. Every impulse and emotion in Beach prompted her to refuse.

"Why?" asked the man.

"Because it's the only one I have left," she lied.

He was shocked at her effrontery in refusing the polite request of an officer of the German Reich, and left unhappily. He returned two weeks later. Where was the copy of *Finnegan's Wake*? he asked.

It had been put away, she replied. At this point the mask of respectability dropped. Trembling with rage, he shouted that he would be back and would confiscate all her books. He turned on his heels and, slamming the door, marched away. There was only one thing to do. With the help of her friends, it took the work of a day to transfer all her stock to an attic room, tear down the shelves, repaint the shop, and remove the sign above the building. A day later it seemed as if the shop had never existed. If the German officer returned, it was not to a bookshop but to an innocent dwelling seemingly bereft of books of any kind.

CHAPTER TWELVE

Mesdames Pimpernels

D espite the obvious changes, such as the presence of Germans in the city, new rules and regulations, and a fast-diminishing supply of food, it didn't take long for Paris to get back to some form of superficial normality. People needed to live, to pick up where the recent six weeks of mind-boggling events had left them, and to make their peace with their country's conquerors. At least, that is what most people seemed to want to do. Occupation was the new reality, and few seemed to have the energy or moral purpose to challenge the status quo. Within a month, forced in part by the demands of the hordes of gray-green sightseers traipsing wide-eyed around the capital of the Reich's newest province, mouths agape at the somewhat subdued delights of the famed City of Light (few German soldiers had ever been to Berlin), and in part by a population desperate to return to normalcy, the vast bulk of businesses was back in operation, cinemas and theaters were in full swing (perhaps with something less of their prewar exuberance), and cafés were open, albeit with a largely new clientele, visitors splashing out with their occupation reichsmarks, trying awkwardly to behave as if they had come by tour bus rather than by panzer. Ominously, many of these newly reopened cafés already had signs on the doors forbidding entrance to Jews. Other restrictions and regulations, both small and large, were imposed on the citizenry. The Nazis had ways of making people understand that they had been defeated.

Between 1940 and 1944 there was such a thing as *la résistance française* only in the most general sense, at least until the formation of General de Gaulle's Forces Françaises Combattantes in 1943. Many in France who were naturally inclined towards resistance struggled at first to find expression for their opposition to the enemy occupation, lost as they were in a confusing world that had seen all its certainties removed with the invasion and the humiliating armistice that followed. The dramatic social and political divisions in France at the time, exacerbated by the confusion of defeat, meant that resistance, when it emerged, had many parents, and struggled for several years to find a single, coherent voice. De Gaulle's movement, based in London until 1943, provided one rallying cry, but his voice took a long time to be accepted as the genuine or primary expression of French liberation. For some people, especially on the Left in France, as well as policy makers in Washington, he never succeeded. A relatively junior officer in 1940, de Gaulle was virtually unknown at the time of France's surrender: his greatest challenge was to persuade a cowed and divided nation that he had the right to speak on their behalf. In 1940 the people of France needed to know that they could place their trust in something more than a phantom, when their existing political leadership—of all shades and hues—had so spectacularly failed them.

Very little of the resistance undertaken in occupied France in 1940 and 1941 could be described as organized or formal. The small amount that took place occurred as spontaneous reactions by individuals humiliated by German occupation and angered by the collaboration of their political masters, and exhibited itself first in a myriad of small and perhaps ostensibly insignificant ways. The most common involved individual acts of protest such as anonymous graffiti, vandalism of German and Vichy posters, the cutting of telephone and electricity lines, and the slashing of tires on unguarded military vehicles. It was the little things that excited rebellion in Pauline Crawford. She could not take up arms herself, but she nevertheless felt a compulsion to rebel against this monstrous subjugation. Britain's refusal to surrender in 1940 provided her and her friends with a glimmer of hope that Germany's much-vaunted thousand-year subjugation of France would last a little less than this. She and her friends scattered paper V (for "victory") cutouts on the sidewalks, for instance, and always spoke English in the presence of Germans. They were small things, but for Crawford it was still warfare. Others felt the same. Hiding Allied soldiers on the run, for instance, something Dr. Sumner Jackson at the American Hospital did routinely; quietly ignoring the prohibitions on Jewish citizens; trading in the black market; disobeying some of the multitude of new restrictive ordinances propagated by the occupation forces or the subservient Vichy authorities; distributing leaflets or underground newsletters; listening to London on the radio or scrawling the V sign on German posters: all served as legitimate measures of dissent. Where public protests did occasionally erupt, they were immediately and brutally suppressed. When Germans were shot, or injured, vicious reprisals were meted out indiscriminately, to cow the population and prevent wider rebellion.

On August 13, 1940, barely two months after the occupation had begun, a German sentry was shot dead outside the Hôtel Golf in Royan in Charente-Maritime. In reprisal, the German authorities rounded up several prominent citizens and imprisoned them indefinitely as hostages against the threat of further "terrorism." On August 22, in Bordeaux, a 32-year-old docker, Raoul Amat, allowed himself to be caught slashing the tires of a German truck and was sentenced by a military court to thirteen months' imprisonment. Others merely shook their fists—and lost their lives for it. On Saturday, August 24, Leizer Karp, a refugee Polish Jew, shouted abuse at German military musicians playing near the Saint-Jean railway station in Bordeaux. Taken into custody, he was transported to Sougez camp and sentenced to death. He was shot two days later. At the end of 1940 German posters around Paris celebrated the execution of Jacques Bonsergent, who had been executed for the offense of attacking a German officer. Unable to express their sentiments safely in any other way, Parisians resorted to placing bunches of flowers on the pavement under the posters.

Many Americans in France at the point at which the occupation began played their own role in resisting the tyranny that had been so dramatically forced on their adopted country. Josephine Baker, "the Black Venus," needed no urging to fight the Nazis, falling into the work first of espionage and then of resistance almost instinctively. France was her home. It was the place that had given her fame, and had embraced her to its egalitarian bosom in a manner that would have been impossible in the land of her birth. When, in 1939, 33-year-old Jacques Abtey, Paris chief of Le Deuxième Bureau, the military intelligence branch of the French General Staff, tentatively approached her to inquire as to whether she would be prepared to work for them as an unpaid "honorary correspondent," she accepted with alacrity. As a woman of color, married at the time to a young Jewish sugar entrepreneur, the Nazis were her natural enemies. It took no great leap at all in November 1938, following the Kristallnacht violence in Germany, for her to become a member of Bernard Lecache's Ligue Internationale Contre le Racisme et l'Antisémitisme, or LICRA (the International League Against Racism and Anti-Semitism). Here was a side to her character that she could hide easily beneath her theatrical veneer, and exploit for France. The link with the Deuxième Bureau came via her agent, Felix Marouani, whose brother Daniel worked for Jacques Abtey.

Abtey was at first reluctant to use such a well-known—if eccentric—theatrical performer, assuming that she would be fickle, demanding, and unintelligent. Daniel persuaded him to at least meet Joséphine, and Abtey agreed. He immediately fell under her spell, and she became an honorary member of the Secret Service. "France made me what I am," she told Abtey and Marouani. "I will be grateful forever. The people of Paris have given me everything. They have given me their hearts and I have given them mine. I am ready, Captain, to give them my life. You can use me as you wish."

Her first task was to use her charm and the broad social networks gained over many years of entertaining in Paris to pick up gossip from the expatriate population of Paris. The Italian embassy was, as Abtey described it, a source of "some extremely useful information." Refugees, too, were a rich source of intelligence. In her role as a helper at the Red Cross relief center on the Rue de Châteaudun, she kept a watch on the floods of refugees, to see if she could spot any who might also be Nazi spies. Despite her eagerness to examine some young blond Belgian men, she did not find any. Now that she was officially spying for France in secret, Baker filled her working life promoting France in public. During the phony war she sang for the troops, in hospital and on the radio, sent them signed photographs at Christmas and listened as hard as she could to spot any fifth columnists among the massive flows of refugees clogging the roads into Paris. Her recordings of "Mon Coeur Est un Oiseau des Lies," "Oh, Tommy," and "London Town" waft hauntingly at the touch of a keyboard from YouTube today.

The German invasion of France in May 1940 forced her to move to the relative safety of Les Milandes, a château she rented in the Dordogne. Her strident anti-Nazi and pro-French views made her vulnerable to German sanction if they managed to seize the country, and Jacques Abtey advised that for her, discretion would be the better part of valor. Loading up her Packard with extra gas (carried in champagne bottles) and accompanied by her Belgian maid, Paulette, two Belgian refugees, and three dogs, they made their slow way, over roads crowded with desperate refugees, the three hundred miles to Les Milandes.

—※—

Etta Shiber and Kitty Bonnefous fell into the resistance game by accident. During their depressing return to Paris on June 15 on the perfunctory orders of the German motorcyclist, they rejoined the subdued column of vehicles returning north. As darkness came they reached the tavern at which they had heard, the previous day, that the enemy had reached the outskirts of Paris. Exhausted, they pulled in to stop, but, even as the vehicle was still moving, they were urged away by the innkeeper. He had nothing to offer them, he said. But he had not reckoned on the single-minded Madame Bonnefous. "A cup of tea will be enough for us," she said, making her way into the building. Beaten, the innkeeper let them in and locked the door behind them. Etta was amused to see Kitty's winsome smile and disarming manners persuade the man to bring out a small piece of salami and a little cheese also. It was the first food they had tasted in thirty-six hours. It was then that the innkeeper asked the question: "You are English?" When they replied in the affirmative, the man said, with evident relief, "Then you can do something for me." He had a secret visitor, he said, who couldn't speak any French but, by the uniform he was wearing, was clearly a British flier. The innkeeper was terrified lest the Germans find that he had been sheltering one of their enemies. The two immediately agreed to talk to the man. Moments later he was brought out, a tall young man of no more than twenty years with reddish-blond hair wearing a leather coat over his RAF uniform. He was delighted to be able to speak English, to explain who he was and his circumstances. The pseudonym used by Etta Shiber in her 1943 account, *Paris Underground*, was William Gray. A pilot, he had been left behind at Dunkirk, and had been travelling south ever since, trying to stay ahead of the advancing Germans. As he talked, explaining how he wanted civilian clothes to enable his escape further south, a plan was hatching in Etta's mind. The young man didn't stand a chance on his own, and if he was wearing civilian clothes when caught, he could be shot as a spy. She touched Kitty's arm and suggested hiding him in the luggage compartment of their car, and smuggling him into Paris. They talked through the options, discussed and dismissed the obvious dangers, and determined to bring William Gray under their wing. They were sure that, once in Paris, they would be able to help him hide from the Germans and find a way of assisting his escape to Spain. So it was, as Etta wrote, that "we were launched upon an adventure which a week earlier we would have dismissed as impossibly fantastic. Yet it had come about so naturally that neither Kitty nor myself realized that we had projected ourselves into a new course from which we would not thereafter be able to escape. We had closed the door on our calm unruffled existence."

The luggage compartment in Kitty Bonnefous' car was unusual, in that it was accessed from the rear of the back seats and had no external door. Gray stowed himself away in his hiding place and they began the final part of their journey home. Germans seemed everywhere along the route, and they were stopped three times and asked to show their papers. Aside from perfunctory glances inside the car, no searches were demanded, to the women's relief. They reached the Porte d'Orléans in darkness. Here they had to wait many hours for the queue to slowly dissipate. When they eventually reached the sentry, dawn was breaking on a new day in Paris. Again, no request was made to open the trunk, where the long, thin William Gray lay ensconced. Showing their proof of residence, they were waved back into Paris by a German soldier. In the few days of their absence, Paris had already changed. German uniforms were everywhere. Driving towards the Eiffel Tower, Etta saw a massive swastika flying, and military transport filled the roads. At the Louvre, likewise, the Germans had wasted no time in hauling down the tricolor and replacing it with the Nazi flag. Then, a few moments after circling the Arc de Triomphe, they drew up outside their home—2, rue Balny d'Avricourt.

The next step was to safely extricate Gray from his cramped hiding place, where he had been for the best part of ten hours. As they were contemplating their next steps, they saw a French soldier being marched under guard by two Germans down the street. He had obviously been trying, unsuccessfully, to hide. The two women remained in the car, motionless. The extreme danger of the business in which they were now involved struck home: William Gray was not the only one who risked being shot, as they were quite clearly aiding and abetting an enemy of Germany. Quietly they waited until the street was empty, and then gave Gray his instructions. They were going to go into the building. He was to button up his leather coat and follow them, behaving as nonchalantly as he could, and follow them into the elevator, which they would have open for him. Kitty and Etta got out of the car, moved some luggage from the rear seat to allow Gray to get out, then made their way into the building. Fortunately, the hall was empty, and the elevator was also empty, waiting for them on the ground floor. The three of them got in, Kitty pressed the button for the sixth floor, and the door closed behind them, the machine taking them upstairs to the safety of their apartment. It seemed, to Etta at least, to take an age, but eventually they arrived.

Kitty got out and unlocked the door, and they all hurried in. Etta was, she confessed, in a state of near panic. "For a moment, I leaned against the door. My legs seemed too weak to support my weight. Then I tottered towards a chair and sat down. It was good to sit down, safe in my own apartment, surrounded by my own familiar belongings. Kitty's nerves must have been better than mine. She threw herself into an armchair and laughed happily." They had done it. Their first steps in their resistance to the German occupiers had begun. All they had to do now was work out what to do with William Gray, and how to get him to safety while preserving their own lives in the process.

So far Etta and Kitty had acted spontaneously, from their human instincts, to get William Gray to a place of safety. Of course, their apartment in Paris was not this. They now had to find a way of getting him across the demarcation line into that portion of the country that as yet remained unoccupied. But how could this be done? By chance, some days before, Kitty had bumped into M. Chancel, who was a member of a remarkable group of wounded Great War veterans with facial wounds who called themselves Les Gueules Cassées (The Broken Mugs). All three had worked together at Le Foyer du Soldat Aveugle before the fall of France. In the brief conversation they'd exchanged, Kitty had judged that he would be willing to help. She was right. Etta and Kitty arranged to meet him in his apartment near the Bastille some days later. They broached the question very gently, Kitty not daring to say that she had a British airman hidden in her house, but almost wondering whether such a thing might be possible, with help of course, in the future, to continue the fight against *the Germans*? After determining that both parties held the same views, Kitty let the cat out of the bag. Chancel whistled with surprise, but then agreed wholeheartedly to help. They relayed the whole story to him and immediately planned how to spirit him out of occupied France. By serendipity, Chancel already had a solution in hand. "Some very good friends of mine have transformed their home into a refuge for soldiers in hiding," he told them. "They're not rich, but they're fairly well off just the same. They've got a roomy house on the Left Bank in a secluded street, very well placed for the purpose. Both of them wanted to do something to help the soldiers of this war. The man is a veteran of the last war—he was wounded then, and still has a slight limp. He and his wife lost their only son in this war. Through some of his acquaintances, they got word around to soldiers in hiding, who were looking for a chance to escape to join the Free French, that they would take care of them until they could be smuggled out. They've got a secret room for them in the cellar, with comfortable beds and furniture, well heated, where they stay for two or three days until some of our other friends can get them across the demarcation line."

William's lack of French was the only major hurdle. The procedure was for the young French men to be provided with travel passes, after which they were placed on a train from Paris for the border. Other friends owned a farm that straddled the demarcation line, across which the men would be escorted at night. Without any knowledge of French, it would be impossible for him to get through the checkpoints. To complicate matters, Gray was so Anglo-Saxon in appearance, suggested Kitty, that he would be arrested the moment the Germans clapped eyes on him. After a moment's silence, Kitty came up with a solution. "Give us the address of the frontier estate," she said. "I'll undertake to get him there in our car." The problem with this suggestion was, of course, the complete unavailability of fuel. It was Chancel who came up with the solution.

"I have it!" he said. "You ladies belonged to the Foyer du Soldat, where we met. It's still operating, you know, even under the Germans. They're perfectly willing to have someone else take part of the job of feeding the prisoners of war off their hands. Among other things, they're collecting food and other necessities for prisoners, and visiting wounded men in hospitals. Offer your services, and the use of your car, for these purposes, and you can put the Red Cross emblem on the auto, get Red Cross armbands, and be allowed ten gallons of gasoline a week. Besides, you'll have an excuse for moving about the country, visiting hospitals and camps for prisoners of war. That's our solution! Just leave it to me. I'll make all the necessary arrangements."

"The actual escape of William Gray," Etta wrote in 1943, "was so uneventful as to be almost disappointing." William Gray was first taken to the house belonging to M. Chancel's friends. For several days Kitty begged and borrowed small amounts of gasoline for the journey. She persuaded an English-speaking officer to siphon gasoline from his own car into hers, and she even managed to cadge some from the Germans after driving up to the entrance to Les Invalides wearing the uniform of the American Hospital of Paris.

That night, with William Gray once more hidden in the boot of their little car, they headed south. The emblem of Le Foyer du Soldat Aveugle was painted on the car, and the rear filled with parcels and gifts for several military hospitals in different sections of the country. They found Chancel's friends without trouble and handed William over to them in what Etta described as "a sentimental farewell." A week later, at the end of July 1940, a postcard arrived from Marseille intimating William's safe arrival, and saying that he was hopeful that he would soon visit his parents. Of course, William Gray was merely the first in a considerable number of escaping and evading servicemen helped from France by this redoubtable pair. By the autumn, and their arrest by the Gestapo, they had managed to secret 150 men to safety.

—m—

For Americans caught up in the occupation, resistance against the Germans took many forms. For prominent art patron and collector Mary Hoyt Wiborg, for instance, it entailed using her network of wealthy friends across the country to help evaders escape captivity. She spent a year as a neutral American in Paris before managing to return to the United States in mid-1941. Speaking at a memorial event in East Hampton on July 8, 1943, she described one occasion when she got information about a downed British flier to his family in England. For Drue Tartière, resistance began by helping Jean Fraysse to write and distribute anti-German leaflets across Paris. This they did in conjunction with other writers, but also alongside a growing network of ordinary people—dentists, doctors, book-dealers, and others—who slowly and carefully came together to fan the flame of rebellion. Fraysee used booklets of poems by the poet Paul Eluard, which, according to Drue, "proved some of the most inspiring items of resistance literature, as well as the most beautiful." These early dabblings in resistance were to lead her, in 1942, into a full-blown operation to support the British Special Operations Executive (SOE) flying in weapons and supplies to resistance groups, before developing into an escape and evasion line for Allied aircrew on the run.

In Barbizon, southeast of Paris where she and Nadine had repaired late in 1940, Drue and Nadine rented a house that had previously belonged to her father-in-law. They planted vegetables and hunted rabbits with a ferret purchased from a local farmer, despite the Germans forbidding all hunting or trapping on pain of imprisonment. Jean Fraysee made frequent trips into Paris for consultations with the writers, publishers, merchants, and students who were gradually developing the nucleus of a resistance movement. He also made two trips across the line of demarcation into unoccupied France. Resistance on the French railroads had developed both more completely and more actively than in any other branch of endeavor, and Jean passed easily between occupied France and unoccupied territory, disguised as a mail sorter. He sorted the mail until the train got across the line and then returned the cap and costume to the railroad resistance worker who had been assigned to help him get through.

Tartière found that keeping up the fight against the occupiers was hard, relentless and exhausting work. With no signs that the Germans would ever be beaten, it was easy to slip into unconscious forms of collaboration, not least of all by meekly acquiescing in the subjugation of one's country, and not even doing the small things to fight back. "The BBC broadcasts did their best to keep up hope, but it was difficult to carry conviction when there were so few tangible evidences of action. But, although collaboration with the Germans became a habit and in some cases was a faith, there always remained a hard core of resistance. Propaganda circulated widely against the Germans and their Vichyite satellites within occupied territory, and it was easy to get false traveling papers." The initial failures of the Soviets to resist the German invasion when it started in June 1941 also led to a fall in morale across France. For Tartière, the resistance habit built up slowly over time:

> During the remainder of 1941 I lived quietly in Barbizon and scarcely ever went into Paris. I raised my plants and animals and stored up food for ourselves and the friends in Paris who would need it. I continued to assist Jean by typing his resistance literature, but there was little I could do that was more active in direct resistance work. Even Jean was more concerned now with formulating resistance ideas on paper rather than taking action, for action was still premature. The contacts were slowly being built up within France with the resistance forces in England, who were not yet ready for any armed action in France itself and were merely preparing to store up the arms and ammunition which would be needed when action was to come. It was painful to wait for action, but there was nothing else to do. My own previous experience did not make me fit for any particular tasks in this preliminary work, but through Jean I was known to some active resistance men and was ready for any tasks I could do when the proper time came. Meanwhile, organizations were being set up in Paris for distributing literature within France and for receiving arms and ammunition from England. Resistance people were in constant touch with England by short-wave radios which had to be moved constantly from apartment to apartment to avoid detection by the Nazis. Sabotage was being planned and carried out by the railroad resistance organization particularly, which was the most highly organized of all the resistance groups. Frenchmen in factories producing for the Nazis were being instructed how to destroy their products and how to put the machinery out of commission. Resistance was still feeling its way cautiously at this time, learning to work in an atmosphere of terror and acceptance. It was progressing slowly and fumblingly from infancy to a growth that was to make it a sturdy fighting front within the Nazi lines.

—m—

From the point at which Jacques Abtey heard the voice of resistance speaking across the crackly radio waves from London, he determined to support the man uttering defiance against the Germans, and against the French government that so cowardly collapsed in the face of the aggressor. Josephine Baker, when she heard Abtey tell her his plans, immediately joined the small circle of friends who agreed to give their allegiance to General de Gaulle rather than Pétain. But how? The answer came in an unexpected way. With the fall of France, the French security apparatus collapsed, and its old relationships with, among others, the British Secret Intelligence Service (MI6) were fractured. Nevertheless, elements of the official French security service were slowly reestablished from the ruins by the new Vichy government. Many officers who resumed their jobs in the revived Deuxième Bureau, although invariably right-wing, were strongly opposed to Germany. Many of them worked assiduously against German interests in the Zone Libre (Unoccupied Zone) until the French occupation of this remaining part of France following Operation Torch on November 11, 1942.

The British Secret Intelligence Service quickly reestablished communications with the Deuxième Bureau, as well as building, in London, an organization to support de Gaulle's intelligence apparatus. MI6 thus became an important link between Vichy and de Gaulle. It was to an old colleague, Captain Paul Paillole, that Jacques Abtey now turned. Paillole, working for Vichy but secretly supporting de Gaulle, described the extent of the revived networks in his memoirs, especially the problem of connecting parties using the few radio transmitters (TR) that had survived the invasion:

> In Marseille the problem was resolved through Captain Garrow of British intelligence, and Toulouse was in contact with the British consulate and the Intelligence Service in Barcelona. In Lyon, TR 114 had established with Major Lombard of the neighboring SR station a way to get our military intelligence out through Switzerland. In Clermont-Ferrand TR 113 was in contact with our honorable correspondent, van den Branden, a Belgian, who had been close to many U.S. diplomats in Brussels before the war. He

had succeeded in reestablishing those connections in Vichy. In Limoges TR 112 and its Paris branch TR 112 *bis*, were both connected to British intelligence agents and the first Gaullist agents, to whom they passed on (directly or through others) operational information.

Paillole was delighted to receive the commitment of Abtey and Baker, when they met in Marseille in September 1940. Abtey described how Paillole was initially skeptical about using Baker, but her record of assisting the Deuxième Bureau through thick and thin spoke for itself, and Paillole accepted her into his network. Their first task, Paillole recorded, was to travel via Spain to Lisbon to contact Commander Wilfred ("Bitty") Dunderdale, the MI6 officer who had been responsible for relationships between London and the Deuxième Bureau. Dunderdale was a career MI6 agent and talented mid-European linguist, who, until 1940, had been its station chief in Paris. Abtey's task was to explain to the British the difficulties they were having with establishing radio communication with London, and to propose a solution. Abtey's cover (using the pseudynom Jacques-François Hébert) was as an actor in Josephine Baker's travelling show, which was purportedly on the first stage of a journey to South America. Paillole recorded that "she diligently accepted the kind of risks she had to take with youthful enthusiasm and agreed to a tour of the theaters in Portugal." The intelligence he entrusted to the two for transmission to London was significant:

> Just before he left I gave Hébert intelligence we had gathered on the German army in western France, the air fields, the ports, the landing barges and other preparations for a coming attack on Gibraltar. I also gave him some items we had received from our Ws about the Abwehr's intentions to infiltrate into England: Russell, the head of the Irish Republican Army, and two Frenchmen from Brittany, were to be dropped off by submarine on the southwest coast of Ireland. [Seán Russell never made it. He died at sea of natural causes, in U65, on August 14, 1940, and the U-boat returned to Germany.] A group of Abwehr II agents was to land

in Wales, on the coast west of Swansea in November 1940. The mission was to take over the Welsh nationalist movement and Scottish separatist groups.

I also drew our friend's attention to the fact that spies were being sent to Great Britain via Yugoslavia and that the Abwehr III was planning to infiltrate provocateurs into the intelligence networks operating in France. Abtey-Hébert transcribed part of this information in disappearing ink on the song partitions used by Josephine and memorized the rest.

Their time in Lisbon, a hotbed of intrigue, swarming with secret agents from across Europe and full of gossip, was fruitful. Abtey managed to deliver his precious intelligence to MI6 through the British embassy, and to make contact for the first time with de Gaulle's organization in London. From this point on they were officially members of the Free French intelligence organization, the Bureau Central de Renseignements et d'Action (Central Bureau of Intelligence and Operations), or BCRA, which had its headquarters at 10 Duke Street, London, and was run by de Gaulle's intelligence chief, André Dewavrin. Their first instructions were to make their way back to Marseille. Baker's occupation as a well-known chanteuse gave them the perfect cover—as they had just demonstrated—for spiriting secret intelligence out of France. Arriving back in Marseille on December 6 after an exhausting journey across Spain, Josephine booked herself into the Hotel de Noailles (Abtey remained for the time being in Lisbon) and contacted Captain Paillole, who was understandably very pleased with the success of her mission. During that desperately cold winter of 1940—it was so cold even in Marseille that she slept in her overcoat—she put on a revival of her famous *La Creole* show for the Christmas season at the Theatre de l'Opera. It provided useful income and was the ideal cover for her presence in the city.

Their sojourn back in Marseille, however, was not to last long. Fear in early 1941 that the Germans were about to forcibly occupy the Unoccupied Zone (in fact, they didn't do so until November 1942, following the Allied invasion of North Africa) prompted the BCRA to order Baker and Abtey to move permanently to Casablanca. They successfully arranged, courtesy of Paul Paillole and the Deuxième Bureau, to fly to Algiers, taking with them, at Josephine's insistence, several refugees from Nazism. One of these was Rodolphe Solmsen, a German Jewish film producer who had escaped to France in 1933. He had no apparent means of escape. The world had largely closed its eyes and ears to the plight of refugees from Nazism, refusing to acknowledge that those whom the German state had declared its enemies could lose their lives as a result. Solmsen had no exit papers from France, and without these he had no hope of securing a visa for a third party willing to take him in. How could he escape? Josephine's insistence that she wouldn't leave without him prompted the Deuxième Bureau to achieve the impossible in the Vichy bureaucracy. To Solmsen's amazement one morning the required exit papers and visas for North Africa arrived at his hotel. "Josephine and Jacques had kept their word," he later wrote. "When I almost did not believe in it anymore, they had opened the door to liberty and life. I do not know if I could have managed this escape by some other means and I do not even want to know. For me, it was Josephine and Jacques who saved my life."

CHAPTER THIRTEEN

Berlin

At a time when most Americans were leaving Europe, fleeing the onset of war, Leonard Kenworthy, a 28-year-old Quaker from Philadelphia, accepted a request to represent the interests of the Society of Friends in the German capital. At the time, in early 1940, there were only 275 registered Quakers in Berlin, but the organization was well regarded by the Nazis, who remembered the self-sacrificial work of the Society of Friends in feeding starving children in the dark days at the end of the Great War. Kenworthy's predecessor, Howard Elkinton, was returning to the United States after two years in charge of the Quaker International Center, coordinating the international and domestic (German) support of the Society of Friends for those mistreated minorities, such as Jews, who sought their help. "Here was a rare opportunity to live in a nation at war," he reasoned, "and to have a front-row seat for an important event in world history." He wrote that he was "convinced that there were many people in Germany who believed in democracy, in everyday Christianity, and in tolerance and understanding of all religious groups. Such people were in trouble, and if my presence there as a representative of men and women of good will would help, then I should go."

A drawn-out journey by aircraft through Bermuda, the Azores to Portugal, and thence from Rome to Vienna, allowed him to reach the city in June 1940, just as the dust was settling on the ruin of the French Third Republic. On the outside, Berlin looked to be a normally functioning city. People continued to carry out the everyday business of life, with little apparent signs of disruption. But there was some evidence of the New Order. A derelict synagogue, for instance, warned Kenworthy of the persecution of the Jews. Earnest members of the Hitler Jugend practicing their military skills in the public parks, and the plethora of men in uniform marching purposefully across the city, pointed to the fact that the country was now at war, even if Berlin was far from the scene of battle and had not yet experienced the whistle of falling bombs. He quickly noticed signs that the Gestapo were interested in him: the telltale clicks on the telephone that indicated recording apparatus; returned, opened letters to the United States that had failed the censor; and at least one 5:00 A.M. knock on the door by felt-hatted members of the secret police, asking questions about his activities. Amusingly, on one occasion they confused the Society of Friends with the Quaker Oats Company, an error he was not minded to correct.

He observed that Nazi ideology was far reaching. Textbooks in use in German schools decried American individualism as selfish and greedy, and far inferior to the family-centered Nazi creed of *ein volk, ein reich, ein führer* (*one people, one country, one leader*). He was shocked to see one textbook, for instance, assert:

> The young, capable American quickly selects a vocation in which he can make a lot of money. He works and rushes around not always in the same tempo as in New York City, but on the average much more rapidly than in Europe. The American doesn't work in order to live, but he lives in order to work. Someone has also said that the American "thinks economically." He doesn't see the landscape, but the plot of land; not the fields, but the crops; not the forests, but the wood; not the

waterfalls, but the waterpower. The object of all work is to make money. In this way one also explains the struggle for wealth and the admiration of the rich—the millionaires Ford, Rockefeller, Vanderbilt and others.

On the surface, the things he noticed were those that would have struck any American tourist visiting the German capital for the first time: outdoor public telephone cubicles; automatic vending machines dispensing everything from tickets for the public transit system to the many newspapers on sale; streetcars with separate facilities for dogs, bags, and babies. The newspapers—and the radio, for that matter—he quickly learned to ignore, or at least challenge, as programs were heavily propagandized. At increasing risk to himself he relied on listening to the broadcasts from London, or the daily news bulletins he could digest during his frequent visits to the US embassy.

The many bookstores, flower shops, and specialist shops selling a single type of product—vegetables, groceries, fruit and so on—contrasted strikingly with the supermarkets that dominated shopping in American towns, although the absence of food to sell, and the long queues for whatever food was available, was immediately striking. Food was severely rationed, although the people, at this early stage of the war, were not starving. "Accustomed to living on a [simpler] diet than Americans, they were able to survive, largely on potatoes, cabbage, and bread," he observed. In the cities, meat was scarce, adults were allowed only one egg per week, fruit was nonexistent, and proper tea and coffee had long been replaced by ersatz varieties of both, while milk was reserved for babies. In the countryside, where people could grow their own food, not all of it under the scrutiny of Nazi officialdom, they fared somewhat better. Rationing for many everyday household items began soon after the invasion of Poland. These new restrictions came as something of a shock to most Germans, who by now were used to food rationing, but who were now being told that virtually every other aspect of domestic life would also be placed under the control of the state. By the time that Kenworthy arrived, rationing for all major foodstuffs and most domestic commodities was a part of life for all

Germans not able to escape the ration card by special Nazi Party status or membership in the Wehrmacht.

With no threat at this point from the air, Berliners had not yet developed a fear of the night that was to become an overwhelming obsession from late 1943, when the RAF's Bomber Offensive was launched. Kenworthy saw that the theaters appeared to be flourishing, at least four presenting plays of William Shakespeare at the time of his arrival to no obvious official opprobrium. Indeed, as Howard Smith observed, there was little if no popular hatred of Britain or Britons. The Nazi propaganda machine spouted constant vituperation against Churchill. The pig-headed British prime minister could not see sense and surrender to the inevitable—why did he not want peace?—but there was no obvious antipathy towards "England." The people were disappointed, of course, that Churchill refused to accept peace, without understanding that it was their own leader's insistence on imposing impossible terms on otherwise free peoples that was the real obstacle. Oddly, Smith noted, the Germans had a sneaking admiration for the British as they stoically coped with the Luftwaffe's air attacks on Britain, a subject that filled lurid headlines, day after day, in the German press.

Large crowds continued to attend music performances, and the churches were packed. But it didn't take long for air raids—or, rather, the fear of them—to become part of life in Berlin. On the night of August 25–26, 1940, ninety-five RAF bombers attacked Tempelhof Airport and the suburb of Siemensstadt. Shirer noted that the sirens sounded at 12:20 A.M., and the all-clear was sounded at 3:23 A.M., a mere three hours of disturbed sleep for a population told repeatedly that Berlin was safe from aerial attack. Despite the heavy concentration of antiaircraft fire, the searchlights did not find a single aircraft, and none were shot down. There were no casualties on the ground. Four nights later the attacks were renewed, with a total of ten killed and twenty-nine wounded in Berlin. Goebbels was apoplectic, his newspapers screaming loudly at the brutality of the enemy "terror fliers" who were setting out, supposedly on Churchill's direct orders, to indiscriminately massacre the innocent population of Berlin. There was nothing, Shirer noted, in the papers about their own air attacks on

British cities. Not surprisingly, the propaganda was effective. Bill Shirer had a conversation with his maid on the evening of August 31, 1940:

> I asked, "Will the British come over tonight?"
>
> "For certain," she sighed resignedly. All her confidence, all the confidence that five million Berliners had that the capital was safe from air attack, is gone.
>
> "Why do they do it?" she asked.
>
> "Because you bomb London," I said.
>
> "Yes, but we hit military objectives, while the British, they bomb our homes." She was a good advertisement for the effectiveness of Goebbels's propaganda.
>
> "Maybe you bomb their homes too," I said.
>
> "Our papers say not," she argued. She said the German people wanted peace. "Why didn't the British accept the Führer's offer?" she wanted to know. This woman comes from a worker's family. Her husband is a worker, probably an ex-Communist or Socialist. And yet she has fallen a complete victim to the official propaganda.

The bombing campaign developed slowly—Britain had few long-distance bombers, trained aircrews, or powerful enough bombs to inflict significant damage on Germany at this stage of the war—but it didn't take long for Berliners to start getting into the air-raid habit. Blackouts became mandatory, whether an air raid was expected or not, and heavy curtains had to cover every window from late afternoon onwards, as winter made the days shorter. Many air-raid sirens were in fact false alarms. Using the nominated air-raid shelter, or *Luftschutzkeller*, was obligatory, and the first time that Kenworthy was awoken by the siren he rushed downstairs to the basement. He found himself alone. "Obviously I had slept through the alert signal and thought the 'all is clear' alarm was the warning signal," he recalled. "So I trudged back to my room, thankful that no harm had come to me." His friend, the Reverend Stewart Herman, Lutheran pastor of the American Church in Nollendorfplatz since 1939 until it was closed at the end of 1941, suggested to him that the official *Luftschutzkeller* was more dangerous than remaining in one's room, as water or gas mains might burst under the bombing and kill everyone there congregated. Kenworthy decided to stay in his own bed when the sirens went off. One night, however, when Berlin experienced a noisy raid, he decided that he would henceforth obey the sirens when they began their doleful wails. Staying in his room was a fearful mistake:

> [A]t one point it seemed as if a missile had zoomed into my stomach. I lay there a while as if paralyzed, drenched in sweat. Then I got out of bed, took my bag, and scurried to the shelter, determined thereafter to heed the warning signal as soon as it sounded.

In early 1941, Wallace Deuel in Berlin experienced RAF bombing for the first time. It wasn't just the sound of bombs falling that made living in a city under attack harrowing, it was the entire sensory experience. It was one's nerves, as Kenworthy had discovered, that were the first victim. Each raid, starting with the eerily wailing sirens, induced a sense of fear. Where will the bombers drop their loads tonight? Even if there was only a handful of aircraft droning in the skies above a German city, they could keep the entire population awake, hidden in their shelters, nervously waiting to see, hear, and feel what happened next. It was the uncertainty of the process that was so unsettling. The first Royal Air Force raids on Berlin in August 1940 were a psychological jolt to the citizens, who had been assured by the Nazi propaganda machine that it was impossible for a single enemy plane to get to Berlin. The limited physical results of the bombing on the ground was a function of the tiny numbers of aircraft the RAF could put into the air, but what would happen if Britain was not subdued, and in time visited with ever-growing aerial armadas? In August 1941, Fred Salter, third secretary of the US embassy in Berlin, told Brigadier General Raymond Lee in London that the RAF attacks were disappointing. They were weak and ineffective, he reported.

In fact, Berlin was spared the horror of London's Blitz until late 1943. There were only four Allied (one French and three RAF) attacks on Berlin in 1940, and a mere eight in 1941, of which two were mounted by the USSR. There were no raids on Berlin during the whole of 1942, the RAF being fully occupied with bombing military targets across Germany and occupied Europe. Howard Smith was depressed by this lack of RAF attacks, as he saw that it emboldened the Germans, who became certain that it represented British military weakness, and made them ever more convinced that Germany would prevail. On one of the rare RAF attacks in 1941, in which bombs were dropped on the suburb of Babelsberg, Goebbels's Propaganda Ministry the following day delightedly showed the derisory results to those of the international press corps who remained in the city. Smith concluded that "Berlin was safe as any neutral city." But this didn't worry Bill Shirer or Deuel. The psychological impact of these admittedly limited attacks on the German population, and the fear and uncertainty they produced, were to both men all-important. On September 23, 1940, Shirer noted in his diary that after a week's absence, the British bombers came over that night and forced the entire population of Berlin to spend the night in their cold, damp cellars, wearing down their nerves. Given the Nazis' weak antiaircraft defenses, their papers could only rage impotently against the "British Air Criminals," "Terror Fliers," and "Pirates," with no attempt at self-reflection about their own behavior over Warsaw, Rotterdam, or London. But would bombing be sufficient to win the war? The attacks now were few, and bombs dropped tiny in the scale of things. Only time would tell.

Nevertheless, as 1940 neared its end, Bill Shirer acknowledged that German morale remained robust. Even though there was no popular enthusiasm for war and most Germans saw it as the regime's and not theirs, they still liked the fact that their armies had been victorious in battle. Hitler might be a nasty, working-class demagogue surrounded by a camarilla of gangsters, but he had undoubtedly united ethnic Germans under one flag (even though this had been done at the expense of Czechoslovakia, Poland, and Austria). He had made Germany feel strong again after the humiliation of Versailles, and he had reversed the shame of 1918. Many people were prepared to trade their dislike of the little man with the mustache and his extreme racial views for this newfound confidence and sense of historical mission. Hitler had made Germans proud again, Shirer concluded. George Keenan also noted that Hitler acted "in the best traditions of German nationalism, and his conception of his own mission [was] perhaps clearer than that of his predecessors because it [was] uncomplicated by any sense of responsibility to European culture as a whole." This was sufficient to ensure that most Germans were prepared to put up with the regime.

Like Smith, it didn't take Kenworthy long to realize that there was no widespread enthusiasm for the war. Most people he encountered appeared resigned to the fact that they were once again in conflict with their neighbors but hoped that the nastiness would all be over soon, when their lives could return to normality. Few could understand why war had returned, but most believed the rhetoric emanating from the Wilhelmstrasse: Europe was being unpleasant to Germany, and denying her legitimate birthright. Everyone hoped the fighting would be brief—as that in Poland and France had just demonstrated—and the boys would be home at the end of the summer, or at the latest by Christmas. He noted the widespread assumption that Hitler, as a veteran of the Great War, did not want this one to continue a minute more than was necessary, because of his fellow-feeling for the ordinary soldiers whose blood was being shed to protect the country from its numerous enemies. Kenworthy found that Hitler was well regarded by most. If they expressed any views directly, it was that Germany would be unequivocally triumphant, as the alternatives, such as the resurgence of 1920s bolshevism, would be disastrous. He concluded that even those who were opposed to Nazism as a political ideology nevertheless supported their country in this conflict. He rarely met anyone who openly expressed anti-Nazi views, which was probably because few were prepared to criticize the regime for fear of the consequences. Likewise, he came quickly to realize that it was not possible to speak openly about the war, or politics, or in any way criticize the country or its leaders. People used a special code when talking to disguise their real meaning. But they still enjoyed jokes at the expense of the regime, if told quietly and to friends. For instance, How could one tell whether someone in the *Luftschutzkeller* had slept that night? If they said "Guten Morgen," they had already slept; if they said "Guten Abend," they had not, and if they said "Heil Hitler," they were still asleep. Or, Did you hear that Hitler and Goering went on a trip on an airplane? Hitler soon fell asleep. When the Führer awoke, he surveyed the ground below and, seeing much destruction, exclaimed, "Magnificent. Wonderful"—to which Goering swiftly replied, "Wait a minute, Adolf—we are only flying over Kiel." Then again, Hitler, Goering, and Goebbels were flying together—so it was told—when their plane crashed. When the listener was asked, "Who was saved?" the answer was "The German people." Do you know the difference between Gandhi and Hitler? In India one starves for all; in Germany, all starve for one. Lothrop Stoddard heard one joke about rationing:

> Recipe for a good meal: Take your meat card. Wrap it in your egg card, and fry it in your butter or fat card until brown. Then take your potato card, cover with your flour card, and cook over your coal card until done. For dessert, stir up your milk and sugar cards; then dunk in your coffee card. After this, wash your hands with your soap card, drying them with your cloth card. That should make you feel fine!

But other groups did demonstrate fanatical adherence to Nazi nonsense, as Shirer attested in September 1940 when he witnessed Hitler manage an audience of women, nurses, and social workers with consummate skill. The war, of course, was blamed on Herr Churchill. Cheers and clapping. The air attacks on Germany would be responded to by the leveling of British cities, turning them to ash. Hysterical applause forced the Führer to stop. When silence returned, he said: "'We will stop the handiwork of these air pirates, so help us God."

> At this the young German women hopped to their feet and, their breasts heaving, screamed their approval. "The hour will come," Hitler went on, "when one of us will break, and it will not be National Socialist Germany." At this juncture the raving maidens kept their heads sufficiently to break their wild shouts of joy with a chorus of: "Never! Never!"

As Kenworthy observed in mid-1940, food was sufficient, if not plentiful or appetizing. Even a year later, in mid-1941, Smith could record, "Butter was not abundant, but it was sufficient. A goodly slab of meat, a medium-size *Schnitzel* or a couple of long, fat sausages were available before the war for almost every meal; and after the beginning of the war for a smaller but not insufficient number of meals. This, garnished with carrots, beans and potatoes, constituted a normal repast; thereto a crock of beer or a bottle of good Moselle wine. For a people engaged in a life-and-death war, in which absolutely everything was in the scales, the German people for two years of war ate amazingly well." It was the invasion of the Soviet Union in June 1941 that constituted the cliff edge over which the German availability of food fell. The quantity and quality of food available to the mass of ordinary Germans were dramatically reduced. Choice was a thing of the past. Queues grew. Berliners spent more and more time lining up for whatever they could buy, all of which was at inflated prices. By the time he left Germany in December 1941, Smith was reporting "for the first time that *the German people are undernourished.*"

> Most foodstuffs became worse and less in stages. But the main constituent of the German diet, the very stuff of German life, potatoes, disappeared with alarming suddenness one day in early autumn, the result of a poor harvest. For almost two weeks there were no potatoes in Berlin. The government also issued an appeal to the people (and an order to restaurants) not to peel potatoes before boiling them, for this wasted fifteen per cent of each potato and served to intensify the scarcity. Other vegetables came to count as luxuries. Tomatoes were rationed too for a while, then disappeared altogether to canning factories where they could be preserved and sent to the Eastern front. Two-vegetable meals became virtually extinct.

Real food became a thing of the past, replaced by synthetic, or ersatz, material. "Icing for the few remaining pastries tasted like a mixture of saccharine, sand and cheap perfume," recalled Smith. "White bread was issued after the third month of the campaign [in the East] only on the ration cards formerly for pastry. A red colored paste called *Lochs Galantine*, resembling salmon in color and soggy sawdust in taste, appeared in restaurants on meatless days. Several strange bottle sauces made of incredible combinations of acid-tasting chemicals made their appearance in shops to answer the public's growing demand for something to put a taste of some kind in their unattractive and scanty meals." In his diary on September 23, 1941, Bill Shirer noted that there hadn't been any oranges or bananas for a year. There were unlikely to be any this winter. Whereas the invasion of Denmark, Holland, and France the previous year had resulted in a short-lived glut of looted foodstuffs, the attack east had had the opposite effect: food left Germany to feed the Wehrmacht's millions, and nothing was coming back yet in return. With the cupboard in the West now bare, there was nothing to feed Germans at home, let alone the starving masses in the countries now under Nazi control, despite the starvation rations being imposed on those—in the East especially—who survived the deliberate thinning out of the native populations. "Well, if you think it's bad here," insinuated the [Ministry of Propaganda], "have a heart for those poor Britons, who are starving." Given the strength of German propaganda on the subject, when the third secretary of the Berlin embassy, Fred Salter, reached London from Berlin in August 1941, he did not believe Raymond Lee's protestations that there was still plenty of food to eat in Britain, with or without ration coupons. Britons were starving, Goebbels's ministry repeated endlessly, and the German people, given their own experience, had no reason to believe otherwise.

It wasn't just food in Germany that began to disappear. The tiny soap ration became even smaller, something to which the odor on the crowded Berlin subways attested. In summer, the smell was asphyxiating, Smith recalled. "Sometimes you just have to get out at some station halfway to your destination to take a breath of fresh air between trains." Cosmetics, shampoo, toothpaste disappeared, as did cigarettes and tobacco. Smith kept a record of the length of the queue outside his local tobacconist. It "increased from around twenty yards in length in the second month of the Russian war to ninety yards" when he was forced to leave six months later. Alcohol became the preserve of the Wehrmacht once the tidal wave of French booty in mid-1940 was exhausted. Beer became scarce, and what was available was watered down. By November, according to Smith, "there were only four places in all Berlin where one could get beer consistently, and their supplies were maintained for sheer propaganda effect, in the biggest hotels and the press clubs." Shops resorted to displays of colored water, simply for show, while under the counter the only alcohol available was home brewed concoctions sourced illegally from farmyard stills in the countryside. By the winter of 1941, he observed, Germany had become, reluctantly, "perhaps, the most temperate nation on earth."

For Germans, especially those in the big cities, life became harder each day. William Russell watched it. Coal was in short supply. In even shorter supply were the trucks to distribute it. They had all been requisitioned. Households had to trudge to the rail depots to collect it for themselves. "It got to be a common sight to see an old man of seventy-five or eighty years trudging along the streets with a heavy coal sack slung over his shoulder. Beside him usually walked a youngster pulling a toy wagon full of lumps of coal." They, the members of the American Embassy, could order domestic consumables from Denmark, like bacon, eggs, butter and ham, and buy things from the Embassy shop, shipped in from outside Germany, of items entirely unobtainable in the local shops, such as soap, torches, chocolate, sardines, coffee, dried fruits, milk and matches.

"An automobile? You cannot get permission to drive it.

Shoe laces. None.

Toilet paper. None

Braces. None.

All canned goods. Verboten.

Rubber bands and paper clips. Sold out.

Other things which one could not buy in German stores: shaving soap, electric wire, candles, any metal object, gramophone records (in order to buy a new record, the customer had to give up an old one), typewriters, electric razors, electric water heaters, clothing of all kinds (except on ration cards), furniture, thread (one spool a month), many kinds of paper and stationery, color film, vanilla, spices of all kinds, pepper, gelatine, leather goods such as suitcases and pocket-books, buttons, cigars (one to a person each day as long as they lasted)."

Clothing, likewise, became scarce. Coats simply disappeared in a massive series of collections. It was if the war in the East was a giant vacuum sucking the clothing off Germans at home to support the millions of men under arms on far-off battlefields. The piles of fur coats that had arrived during the previous year from Paris enjoyed a limited sojourn on their temporary German owners, as they, too, disappeared eastwards. So much for the spoils of war. "But by the time the Germans entered Kiev, clothing rationing had become purely theoretical," recalled Smith. "Clothing simply ceased to exist. . . ."

Scarcity drove up prices to astronomical levels for the food and consumables that were available on the black market, a trade which the Nazi authorities attempted to stamp out with increasing brutality. "Suburban farmers around Berlin are being offered from three to ten times peace prices for butter, eggs, meat, or, indeed, anything edible, by city dwellers," Howard Smith noted. "At Christmas time farmers were getting hundred marks each for Christmas geese. Bad, home-fermented liquor brought many times peace-time prices of high grade schnapps." Those caught dealing this way, however, faced extraordinary penalties. In September 1941, for instance, the newspapers reported that "a farmer in Rostock on the Baltic coast was beheaded for slaughtering a single hog without permission." The harsh reality of war was still far from the experience of most Germans, but the multitudinous effects of war-induced deprivation were at last beginning to be felt by the bulk of the population. The future looked bleak: only ultimate victory in wars to both east and west, which invariably implied economic exhaustion, or defeat at the hands of her enemies, which implied something far worse, could now return Germany to peace. "What have we got to live for? What is there to look forward to?" asked one of Smith's acquaintances. She didn't expect an answer, although the answer was clear to Smith. Many Germans were now frightened of the terror they had unleashed on Europe, aware that the destiny of the country was not now entirely in their hands. Victories—and ultimate victory—could not be guaranteed. The early defeats in the West and the East were because the enemy weren't prepared for war in the first place. Early successes in the East and the West had been achieved not because of Wehrmacht brilliance but because Germany's neighbors had naively believed that the Great War had been the war to end all wars, and had failed to protect themselves. In the battles of 1940 Germany outgunned and outthought their opponents because they had been thinking of nothing else since 1933. But would it last? Even in 1941, to this Berlin *hausfrau*, the evidence did not suggest so. In Smith's view, only a tiny fraction of Germans held any Nazi ideas. But concern for the future now began to bind them together in a way that fear of their leaders never could. Germans, he considered, were "attached to the Nazis like the man who unexpectedly found himself holding on to a lion's tail, and kept right on holding on, not because he enjoyed the lion's proximity, but because he was scared speechless at what might happen if he let go. . . . The main reason the Germans cling to the lion's tail is that they are terrorized by the nightmare of what will happen to them if they fail to win the war, of what their long-suffering enemies will do to them; of what the tortured people of their enslaved nations, Czechoslovakia, Poland, France, will do when there is no longer a Gestapo to hold them down. The German people are not convinced Nazis, not five per cent of them; they are a people frightened stiff at what fate will befall them if they do not win the mess the Nazis have got them into." Shirer agreed. "You don't have to be profound to conclude that the rule of brute force now exercised by the Germans over the occupied territories can never last very long. For despite complete military and police power, which the Germans admittedly have, you cannot forever rule over foreign European peoples who hate and detest you."

Smith described Berlin in late 1941 in the months following the onset of Operation Barbarossa, the Wehrmacht's code-name for the invasion of the Soviet Union, as a shadow of its previous self. The cafés, restaurants, and bars along the Unter den Linden had no alcohol, and menus were limited to one or two choices of foul, artificial food. Buildings damaged by bombing were not being repaired, there being no workmen left in the city to carry out the work. Fuel was short, which meant that buses no longer ran with any frequency. Shops soon ran out of goods and closed. The window of the empty American Express Company building, which before the war had been a thriving tourist hub, featured a solitary poster in the window encouraging people to "Visit Medieval Germany." The Nazis did not understand the irony of this message and left it there unmolested. Coca-Cola GmbH could no longer import its syrup from the United States because of international sanctions, so it invented a drink to keep its plant operating. Made from cider pressings and whey, it was called Fanta. The famous Pschorr Haus on the normally busy Potsdamer Platz, a typical, large *buergerliche* ("good, plain cooking") restaurant in Berlin, "is now dingy and dirty," Smith remarked, "and so much bad fish has been served on its white wooden tables that the whole place smells like bad fish."

> People from the Potsdamer railway station next door sit at its tables and sip chemical lemonade and barley coffee between trains, as the Pschorr breweries, which own the big restaurant, are no longer making very much beer. I have a menu from the Pschorr Haus somebody gave me dated November, 1916, and on it are nineteen different meat dishes to choose from. Today, also after two years of war, there are only two meat dishes on the menu, one of which is struck through with a pencil mark along the strategy of the Kaiserhof Hotel. The other is generally two little sausages of uncertain contents, each about the size of a cigar butt. Before the meat they give you a chalky, red, warm liquid called tomato soup. . . . With the meat you get four or five yellow potatoes with black blotches on them.

Children, Smith noted, were easily the most fanatical of Hitler's supporters, and the German leader made much of them. They loved the tinsel and baubles of Nazidom, the marching, drums, and trumpets. They ached to get into the fight. It was always children, boys and girls, who made the rounds for the Nazi Winter Relief collections. "I have never seen so completely military a German as the little seven-year-old boy who knocked on my door one day and, when I had opened it, snapped to rigid attention, shot his arm high and shouted at me a falsetto 'Heil Hitler!' after which he asked me in the clipped sentences of a military command would I donate twenty pfennigs to 'support the Fuehrer and the Fatherland in this, our life-and-death struggle.'"

—⁓—

For Germany, late 1940 and early 1941 represented the peace before the storm. For Germany, the beginning of the end of the Second World War began on Sunday, June 22, 1941. This was the ill-fated day that hubris finally overcame the German dictator and the long, slow journey to ultimate destruction began. It would take nearly four more years, and millions more deaths, but the process had begun. Howard Smith was first alerted to the event when his bedside telephone rang at 3:00 A.M. on Sunday morning and jolted him from sleep. The voice at the other end of the phone told him that there would be a special press conference at the Foreign Ministry at 5:00 A.M. if he wished to attend. He quickly got dressed and stumbled out into the moonlit darkness of the midsummer's night. "Being called out of bed at three in the morning, I knew from several past occasions," he later observed, "meant but one thing: Germany was going to save the world from somebody again . . . it was the familiar routine of committing the crime, then justifying it to the world." He was soon to discover the cause of his early morning call: it was the start of Operation Barbarossa, Germany's invasion of the Soviet Union. When he returned home, he switched on the radio:

> Radio reports straight from the eastern front were coming through; soldier-reporters were breathlessly talking about the flashes of shell explosions over there in the Russian lines. The first Russian barracks had been taken. Surprised Russian prisoners were described. That was Nazi, perfectly Nazi. Everything so beautifully arranged that radio reporters in soldiers' uniform had

hooked up their apparatus on the front and, long before the High Command issued any communique, were describing what was happening blow by blow. The Russians were already collapsing. It wasn't war. It was a national sport and the reporters were right on the sidelines giving a play-by-play description.

Gradually, the enormity of what the German state had and was doing as part of its massive attack eastwards became apparent to the German public. Smith noticed for the first time a drop in public morale, and a mood swing away from the war. The grumbling now became more open, as domestic consumables became scarcer, the burden of work increased, and hospital trains bringing the wounded back to hospitals in Berlin from the east grew more numerous and longer. People were careful to hide their complaints from the police, but discontent was self-evident. Every rumor that suggested the war was nearly over represented a false dawn for the increasingly war-weary German public. But they could no longer control the trajectory of their country's fate, or the speed at which they were hurtling to destruction. When they emerged, from who knows where, rumors acted like manna to a starving people. The idea that the horrible slaughter of Germany's best sons was nearing an end and that the boys would be taken out of their panzers by Christmas was, as Smith described, "to parched desert-dwellers, as if the rains had come. Even as God had promised, and His apostles confirmed. And grateful worshippers were wallowing joyously in the coolness of it."

It is hard to realize what this meant to the German people, unless you have lived through those two years of war with them, and watched them suffer. As the core of a strong, steel-willed leadership, they have been remarkably timid and sensitive to trends. They have detested this war from the moment it broke out, and they, the People, have been willing to end it at any juncture. Before it came, they feared it far more than the peoples their leaders and their army threatened with annihilation. On the few occasions on which the end appeared to be in sight, they have been gleeful as children.

In response to this decline in morale, Smith noticed a distinctive up-gearing of the Nazi propaganda machine. One very distinctive aspect of the new, strident rhetoric emanating from Goebbels's Propaganda Ministry was an intensified level of hate for the Jews. Their persecution—the long, slow drip-drip of hatred, alienation, and petty hostility at the hands of the state, beginning in 1933 and reaching a new level at Kristallnacht in 1938—redoubled when war began in September 1939, and was again accelerated in the months after Operation Barbarossa. Why was this? Was it because the offensive in the east was getting bogged down, and animosity against the old enemy within needed to be whipped up to distract attention from the regime's failures? Suddenly, an announcement was made in September 1941 that every Jew in Germany and Bohemia was required by law to wear a yellow six-pointed Star of David, marked *Jude* for Jew. Smith came face-to-face with the terror of this persecution, although to his shame he acknowledged that he failed to understand it fully at the time. Late one night in October 1941, a Jewish friend, Fritz Heppler (not his real name: even in 1942 Smith was trying to protect the identity of a Jewish man in Germany), knocked in terror on his door. His house had just been raided by the police. He hadn't been arrested, but he was terrified. Arrest was inevitable, and soon. He was desperate to leave Germany. Could Smith help? Smith didn't give it much thought and didn't understand his friend's terror. He made some weak promise to do what he could, shut the door, and quickly forgot the incident. He never saw Heppler again.

> For people living outside Germany . . . it is hard to conceive, to the full sympathetic extent, of the fear with which utterly helpless Jews—completely at the mercy of heartless brutes who do not even consider them as entitled to as much consideration as stray curs on the streets—watched every little indication of events inside Germany that might bear on their fate. It is hard to feel with them the paralyzing fear that gripped their hearts even at something so trivial as an unconscious stare at them from some uniformed Nazi on the streets. They lived in the terror of expectancy, which is always more horrible than actual persecution itself.

One night he saw that the door on the apartment next to his, which was owned by the Bernsteins, a quiet, elderly family, had been closed up by the Gestapo. There was a piece of official-looking paper affixed to the door, with a stamp on it depicting "a spread eagle, gripping a swastika in its claws and around it in a circle, the words: 'closed by the *Geheime Staatspolizei.'*" The Bernsteins had gone, presumably, he thought, on an involuntary colonizing mission to the east. What could they do, at their age, to resettle the east? Little did he know, little could he imagine, that the Bernsteins would fertilize the east, rather than populate it. The very consideration of such a ridiculous notion did not pass his mind. It was the sheer enormity of the hidden crime that prevented it being exposed. He hadn't noticed their quiet departure.

The Gestapo made sure of that. They arrived quietly, in the dead of night, to hide themselves—and what they did—under the veil of darkness. Their victims were given a few minutes to pack a small bag, sign over the remainder of their lives and belongings to the state, be pushed into a truck en route to a train station, and then to who knew where? The affairs, homes, friendships of a lifetime ended with an authoritative knock on the door. The Bernsteins' sudden departure, as well as the strange affair in the middle of the night with Fritz Heppler, forced Smith to ponder the fate of this benighted nation-within-a-nation. For years, Jews in Germany had led a miserable existence, one they had taken with considerable grace and fortitude. There had been no Jewish uprising to condemn their fate, and no popular movements by Germans to defend the liberties of their fellow countrymen. It was as if a whole section of German society was being publicly drowned in a hot bath of hate, with the rest of Germany standing quietly watching, at a distance, some even complicit in this public destruction of a race—especially the screaming, hate-filled press. No one seemed to be prepared to stand up in the defense of those being publicly erased from German life and society. Perhaps those people, the ones who would have stood up for the Bernsteins had they been there, had already gone to the concentration camps? It wasn't just the Jews who, being led like lambs to the slaughter, were dumb: it was the whole of German society which was insisting on being dumb to the fate of their countrymen. According to Smith,

Nazi policy, at least until he left Germany in late 1941, constituted a long, slow, gradual drowning of the Jews:

> The Nazis have pilfered [the Jews'] possessions and withdrawn every right from them, but have not, since that time, actively and physically molested them. When the war began they were made outright helots. They were drafted into factories and made to do all forms of manual labor from twelve to fifteen hours a day regardless of age or sex. Seventeen-year-old Jewish girls and sixty-year-old men alike were forced to labor over dirty jobs for ninety hours a week at a wage which, when taxes and "contributions" had been subtracted, amounted to twenty marks a week. A Jewish curfew began at nine o'clock, and Jews caught on the streets after that time were subjected to heavy money fines and prison sentences. They were allowed small rations of a few staple foodstuffs, but forbidden luxuries such as fruit, or tomatoes or cheese or tobacco or alcohol. They were allowed to do their shopping only between the hours of four and five o'clock in the afternoon, when shops were so crowded that a Jew could seldom visit more than two stores a day; their ration cards were spotted with little purple "J"s for Jew to prevent them buying outside this time, and even within the single shopping-hour shopkeepers were expected to serve Aryan customers first, no matter how long the Jews had been waiting in queues outside the door.
>
> They were not allowed to buy clothing during the war, but, if they could prove they were unable to continue working without it, they were granted a permit every six months to buy twenty pfennigs worth (about three pennyworth) of cheap yarn for mending purposes. . . . Every amenity was strictly forbidden! No cinemas, no theatres, no taverns, no wireless sets, no telephones. Actually, they did not require means of recreation, for they were given no time for it. The few hours of freedom they enjoyed between the end and beginning of their workdays, they used in trying to restore fitful sleep in the tissues that were overworked and undernourished beyond restoration. On Sundays, they were not allowed

to use the trams car buses or the underground to go outside Berlin for fresh air and a walk (eventually, they were forbidden to leave their districts of the city for any purpose at any time), and were not permitted to walk in parks inside the city.

The attempts by the Quaker International Center to resettle Jews abroad was made immeasurably difficult by the fact that the country was now at war and it was increasingly difficult to get travel permits, as well as the general bureaucratic harassment meted out to the unfortunate Jews who wanted so desperately to flee. The world, too, was reluctant to open its doors to German Jews, little understanding the terror that awaited them in Europe (even though Germany had not yet instituted its program of mass extermination) and fearful of threatening their labor markets and, far worse, potentially importing fifth columnists. The bureaucracy involved in attempting to leave Germany, assuming one had secured a country to go to, was immense. Long hours of queuing for the obligatory *ausweis* (pass) was the least of people's problems. "Emigrants also had to obtain a certificate of residence and one of good conduct," Kenworthy noted. "In addition, each person leaving the country had to obtain several tax papers and affidavits about his or her personal belongings and a certificate that all taxes had been paid." A specialist bureau had then to be approached, which proved to be a formal means by which the German state robbed the emigrating citizens of whatever money they had left, as it determined what they could and could not take with them. Valuable property and possessions were compulsorily "sold" at knocked-down prices to the government. This assumed, of course, that the receiving embassy or consulate had themselves processed the necessary visas and travel documents for the lucky few who had been granted permission to emigrate. The Quakers set themselves the task of doing what they could to facilitate this process for those who asked for help. "So there were the seemingly endless trips to the banks, steamship companies, airlines, and embassies and consulates," Kenworthy recorded. "Most officials were helpful, but the transactions were almost always complicated and slow." The number of those so aided, however, given the vast tide of humanity who needed help, was tiny. Kenworthy's predecessor in Berlin, Howard Elkinton, managed to help over one thousand professional Jewish women to emigrate to Australia. The Quakers assisted perhaps one thousand to escape before the operation was closed completely in 1942, making only about 150 rescues in the year Kenworthy was in Germany.

Most of those who did escape managed to find their way to places like Ecuador, Cuba, the United States, Mexico, Japan, Brazil, Shanghai, and the Virgin Islands. Before the war, France had maintained a relatively benevolent immigration regime for the persecuted of Europe: after the German invasion, those who had previously fled from Germany, Austria, and Czechoslovakia had once more to flee, or hide, as the terms of the French armistice demanded that they be "surrendered on demand" to the German authorities. Kenworthy's friend, 25-year-old Tracy Strong of the European Student Relief Fund, helped set up escape routes for young Jews trying to get to Switzerland. It wasn't easy. He rented an old hotel—La Maison des Roches—in the fervently Protestant Haute-Loire town of Le Chambon-sur-Lignon, which became famous for its steadfast protection of fleeing Jews during the Vichy and Nazi persecution in France. Strong used the hotel for students, mainly Jewish, who needed help. But nearby Switzerland was reluctant to offer sanctuary to any of these young people. "There were five or six students I knew particularly well who tried to get into Switzerland once with help from young Frenchmen who knew the mountain passes," Strong recounted. "The first time, they were turned back by the Swiss, and the second time we got them visas. It wasn't easy; the Swiss were very reluctant to give out visas. But we were located in Geneva—our headquarters were—and we had people there who knew people in the government and could intervene. Sometimes it worked, sometimes not." After 1942 the Nazi regime sought to bring back the European Jewish and refugee diaspora to Germany to exterminate them in the gas chambers of Auschwitz and elsewhere as part of the "Final Solution" (all other solutions having failed to eradicate the fact of European Jewry), although in 1940 and 1941 they were content to allow those who could afford to buy their way out of Germany to do so.

A foretaste of the horror facing Jews came in their mass deportations by train from Vienna to occupied Poland in February 1941. Between February 15 and March 12, five trains took 5,056 Jews to ghettos in Poland on the first stage of their extermination. Kenworthy received a phone call from Frau Neumeyer, the director of the Vienna bureau. "They are being put onto trains, a thousand a train. Two trains have left. We are doing what we can. Can you come?" He grabbed his bag and made the next train to Vienna. The days that followed were, he described, "the worst of my life." Hundreds of frantic people sought sanctuary at the Quaker offices, desperate for a way to escape. Little could be done for them, however, except alleviating the misery of the journey by providing blankets and food. The men and women at the bureau were powerless to stop the trains as they rolled eastward. The most desperate experience was that of deciding who could not be helped. It was like playing God. One day a blind man pressed into Kenworthy's office:

> With bitterness he told me that I was not saving his life because he was blind. What does one say to a man at such a time? All I could say was that I was doing the best I could in a tragic situation completely beyond my control. From time to time, however, the memory of his face and his forefinger jabbed into my face, still haunt me.

The strongest memories Kenworthy took from his yearlong sojourn in Hitler's Heart of Darkness were of those many people for whom Quaker diligence, faithfulness, hard work, and prayer came to nothing in the face of Nazi indifference to their fate. These people lay on Kenworthy's conscience for the rest of his life. "One was an old lady, her face hardened by bitter experiences, her eyes almost closed, her jaw determined," he recalled. "In her hand she flourished a cane as she vented her wrath on all those she could name, ending with a curse on me for not helping her in her plight."

CHAPTER FOURTEEN

London

During the attacks by the Luftwaffe on London in 1940 and 1941, American observers were keen to understand whether Britain and its put-upon citizens had much stomach for the fight. It didn't make any sense to throw oneself into a war for a cause doomed to failure. Of real concern, at the point at which France fell, was whether Britain would do a separate deal with Hitler and hand over her fleet and aircraft as part of an accommodation with Nazism. This was, fleetingly, a fear expressed to Roosevelt by Bullitt. Clearly, America would not want to commit herself to providing armaments to a country that might soon be batting for the other side. In addition, American capital had considerable investments in Germany, which would be put at risk by war. It made sense to see which way the wind blew, before committing the country to one or the other option. In the weeks following the disaster in France, Churchill made clear, through speeches to Parliament, public radio, and private letters to the US president, his unambiguousness as to Britain's complete commitment to fighting the Nazi menace.

Britons observed two sorts of responses from Americans when Great Britain and Northern Ireland found itself standing alone following the humiliation of Dunkirk and the subsequent fall of France. "Let the British move up; God bless your arms" was the first, welcome, though somewhat unneutral, message that Lord Hastings Ismay, secretary of the Committee of Imperial Defence, received from his friend Raymond Lee in Washington on September 3, 1939. Lee had just returned to the United States following several years as the US military attaché to the United Kingdom. He returned to London to resume this post in June 1940. From the beginning, Lee believed that although it would be a close run, Britain would beat back the invader and survive. It would only do so, however, with the help of Uncle Sam. And it would take time.

There weren't many, in mid-1940, however, who agreed with him. Joseph Kennedy, the US ambassador, who was representative of the second response, lost no time in telling as many people as would listen that he predicted a Nazi triumph in Europe. From the time he had arrived in London in March 1938, Kennedy had aligned himself closely with the appeasement body in British politics, a powerful cross-party grouping who considered Britain's best policy towards the dictators to be to ameliorate their worst excesses by diplomatic and political action. On September 9, 1939, Kennedy warned King George VI that England would bankrupt herself in this new war and should get out while she could. Filled to the brim with terrifying (and subsequently disproved) arguments from Charles Lindbergh about the size and destructive power of the Luftwaffe, Kennedy could not see how an unprepared Britain could possibly survive a bombing onslaught by Nazi Germany. Like many others, he believed that it was better, given the militarily unprepared state Britain found herself in, to surrender to German aggression than to fight back, when fighting would merely cause massive bloodshed and ultimately fail to succeed to stop the invincible Wehrmacht. Like Kennedy, Nazi Germany also expected Britain to fall and determined that it need not waste undue effort in hastening the inevitable. French general Weygand, looking forlornly in June 1940 at the ignominious collapse of his own country, predicted—perhaps even desired—the same fate for Britain. In three weeks, he declared, her neck would be wrung "like a chicken."

It was hard not to agree with this assessment. In June 1940 Britain stood on the precipice of defeat. The bulk of her deployable prewar professional army had been destroyed in France, and its equipment left there and on the beaches at Dunkirk: 12,200 artillery pieces; 1,350 anti-aircraft and antitank guns; 6,400 antitank rifles; 11,000 machine guns; 75,000 vehicles; and virtually all its tanks. From as early as the fall of France, most intelligent opinion gave Britain little hope of survival. Captain Basil Liddell Hart, a noisy and initially influential English prewar military theorist, despairing of the imminent demise of British civilization, started circulating papers advocating surrender. This was grist to Kennedy's mill, who regularly reported Britain's impending ruin to Washington. Fearful of mass death from the air, he packed his wife, Rose, and nine children off to Boston in mid-September, by means of two different ships and the Pan Am Clipper service. He angrily reported to Rose on March 20, 1940, that the gossip in London was that he was a coward and had fled to his country home, Wall Hall in Watford, to escape the bombing. "You would never believe the way public opinion in this country has turned anti-American and inciden-tally anti-U.S. Ambassador Kennedy," he wrote. "The things they say about me from the fact I've sent my family home because they were afraid, to the fact that I live in the country because I am afraid of being bombed etc. etc. All rotten stuff but all the favorite dinner parties at Mayfair go right to work."

To be fair, Kennedy was only taking his own advice to send his family out of harm's way. Many other Americans sought the earliest vessel home. Raymond Lee noted the Americans in Britain who, from the advent of the war, had "been howling [at their government] for a passage home. . . ." Even those who had been in Britain for many years did what they could to send their families to a place of safety. "Chips" Channon and his wife, Honor, took their five-year-old son, Paul, to Euston railway station early on June 24, two days after France fell, en route for the sanctuary of the New World. Outside the sta-tion, Channon observed a long "queue of Rolls-Royces and liveried servants and mountains of trunks. It seemed that everyone we knew was there on the very crowded platform." He pondered in his diary on June 2 whether this was the end of life as they knew it. "I wonder as I gaze out upon the grey and green Horse Guards Parade with the blue sky, the huge silver balloons like bowing elephants, the barbed-wire entanglements and soldiers about, is this really the end of England? Are we witnessing, as for so long I have feared, the decline, the decay and perhaps extinction, of this great island people?" On the day Paris fell, Channon considered that Britain too would fall soon. If the United States didn't make an immediate decision to declare war on Germany, all would be lost:

> Paris was occupied by the Germans early this morning, although some advanced troops entered the capital late last night. Thus Hitler's boast that he would have conquered the city before 14 June has come true. Little news has come through, other than that the French have further retreated. The question is, will France go on fighting? M. Reynaud has asked to be released from his promise not to negotiate a separate peace, and has Marshal Petain behind him. Winston [Churchill] and [Lord] Halifax flew yesterday to see Reynaud at Tours to try and dissuade him from giving up, and he said that he would make one more appeal to President Roosevelt for American help; if it were not forthcoming it was probably that the game was up, as the Army could not hold. Halifax and Winston are back, and the situation is very grave indeed; meanwhile all hangs on Washington. What will Roosevelt decide tonight? If he refuses to come in, it would seem that the war must come to an end, and this great Empire will have been defeated and humiliated. Today and tomorrow are probably the most vital days in our history. . . .

Channon wasn't alone in making the connection between the fall of Paris and the expected demise of London. Britain was now threatened by invasion from France and the Low Countries, and faced desertion by her allies. True, the British Commonwealth had responded quickly to the threat faced by Britain, but France, the old ally, now represented by Vichy, not only turned its back on Britain but also actively sought to support the victor. Jock Colville, Churchill's private secretary, wrote despondently in his diary at the end of 1940 about the consequences of possible defeat: "Western Europe racked by warfare and economic hardship; the legacy of centuries, in art and culture, swept away; the health of the nation dangerously impaired by malnutrition, nervous strain and epidemics; Russia and possibly the U.S. profiting from our exhaustion; and at the end of it all compromise or Pyrrhic victory."

Roosevelt, despite having his radius of action limited by the Neutrality Acts, nevertheless made his affections and intentions clear. He would do what he could to assist Britain to defend herself against the current threat. When British, French, and Belgian troops were being evacuated from Dunkirk, he told Americans that the country would "pursue two obvious and simultaneous courses: we will extend to the opponents of force the material resources of this nation; and at the same time we will harness and speed up the use of those resources in order that we in America may have equipment and training equal to the task of any emergency. . . ." Roosevelt had no political mandate to bring a reluctant United States into the war, and he didn't have the legal authority to do so either. Anything he did in terms of carrying popular and political opinion with him needed to be done carefully and gradually. In secret, Roosevelt was already pulling hard in support of beleaguered Britain, in the hope that his oft-quoted phrase "All things short of war" would actually win the fight. He had begun a secret correspondence with Churchill when the latter had been reappointed first lord of the admiralty, on September 11, 1939, and thus a member of Chamberlain's cabinet. Roosevelt chose to write to the one man in the British government who most strongly opposed the policy of appeasement. Roosevelt had always favored an American policy of international cooperation and collective security, although he was, especially in an election year (1940), sensitive to the impulses of an American electorate that, for the time being at least, preferred a more distant stance. The sudden and unexpected collapse of France shocked Americans into realizing that there was no guarantee that the Allies would prevail, and that there was a very real prospect of the Germans conquering and subjugating all of Europe. If this happened, it was logical to assume that America would be next in the firing line. This highly irregular correspondence remained secret for a further thirty-five years. Roosevelt, who used the label POTUS (President of the United States), sent his messages to Churchill as "Naval Person." When Churchill became prime minister, this became "Former Naval Person." The dialogue was an extension of the private discussions Roosevelt had enjoyed with King George VI that June in Washington, where the US president had assured the British king in no uncertain terms that he, personally, would remain Britain's firmest of friends in the event of war.

From the point at which he became prime minister, Churchill was eager to make Roosevelt's job in America easier so as eventually to have the United States as a cobelligerent. To do so, Churchill mounted an offensive designed to enable the United States voluntarily to side with her in the fight against the Axis powers now rampant in Europe. Even before he became prime minister, Churchill had been convinced of the need for a trans-Atlantic alliance of the democracies to stand up to totalitarian aggression in Europe. He realized nevertheless that it would not be easy to convince the American public, in the face of acute domestic pressure to isolate herself under the banner of America First, that this war was one for the survival of the free world and required action by the United States. His solution was to open himself, and all the appendages of the British state, to American scrutiny, and to secure the understanding and goodwill of President Roosevelt. The year 1941 was the battle for the heart and mind of America. Would she, under Roosevelt's leadership, unilaterally declare war on fascism, and thus side again with Britain against Germany, or would she stand back and proffer balm to the innocent victim, without doing anything to restrain the attacker?

American opposition to any notion of military intervention was strong. In London, Kennedy led the Pessimist Brigade. Representing Irish-American and isolationist groups, his attitude to appeasement before the war mirrored the prevailing view of many in the British political classes, some of whom had pro-Nazi, authoritarian, antidemocratic views. They were disenchanted with the inability of capitalism to provide full employment, and had a visceral fear of bolshevism, which they thought would overturn the entire world order and replace rule by the elected minority with rule by the unelected proletariat. Many flocked in the prewar years to Nazi-type views of social order and cultural discipline, including "Chips" Channon and those (at least according to socialist polemicists) in the so-called Cliveden Set around American-born Member of Parliament Lady Nancy Astor, such as Geoffrey Dawson, editor of the *Times* (London); Philip Kerr (Lord Lothian), British ambassador to the United States; and Edward Wood (Lord Halifax). They did not yet comprehend the malevolent underpinnings of Nazi racial and economic theories, in which the world would become the slaves of an Aryan master race. It was only the arrival of war that made the true nature of Nazi plans unequivocal. Even once the war was underway, Kennedy scorned Churchill's open patriotism and public defense of democracy, accusing him to his face of fighting the war simply to retain the empire. He scoffed at Churchill's repeated assertions—made to Kennedy privately, as well as those Churchill made publicly—that Britain would fight on regardless of casualties or material punishment, and urged all with whom he conversed to make peace with Germany.

When in Washington in 1940, Lee had been shocked at the extent of the pessimism he encountered across America about the survival chances of the European democracies, and the defeatist talk he heard everywhere. Where, he asked himself, was the old American adage "God hates a quitter"? Were freedom and democracy not worth fighting for? In London, Kennedy told Lee on June 17, 1940, that he believed not just that the British were going to be beaten but that the United States must not intervene to prevent it. This was not America's war. German victory was inevitable, he argued. Britain's weakness in the air was combined with an increasingly worrying situation on the high seas, where German U-boats were causing mounting losses of the scarce shipping that was keeping Britain supplied and fed. Kennedy had personal experience of the U-boats. On September 10, 1940, he wrote to Rose, safely at home in Boston, "I bought quite a lot of French wine from French Ambassador Corbin and sent it to you in America last week, and got the very good news on my birthday that the Germans had sunk the ship. So that's that."

Kennedy represented many for whom any form of intervention in another country's war was anathema. Part of Kennedy's ultimate failing was a blindness to the evil that lay at the heart of German totalitarianism. His belief in laissez-faire internationalism meant that for him, war in Europe was none of America's business, regardless of who was fighting it. America certainly needed to arm herself to protect her own interests, but this did not extend to providing military protection to others who might be threatened by the dictators on far distant shores. Soon after he took up his appointment in March 1938, Kennedy made a point of asserting to his British hosts at the Pilgrims' Society dinner that they should not look to the United States for support in the advent of a European war. If Europe collapsed once more in violence, it would have to look to itself to solve its problems. Britain could not again rely on the traditional bonds of friendship between the English-speaking peoples to suborn American assistance. Europe's fight wasn't America's. If Britons knew that America would not come riding over the hill as her knight in shining armor (or perhaps, more aptly, as the sheriff), they might be more inclined to see sense and secure a modus vivendi with Germany. There was an underlying fear at the heart of American diplomacy that somehow the perfidious British would deploy sophisticated seduction techniques to draw the United States into Britain's self-serving web, from which the States would not be able to extricate itself, at great cost to American national interests. There were many who continued to argue that this is what happened in 1917.

This expression of American neutrality was combined with Kennedy's assumption that the democracies had no choice but to co-inhabit the world with countries that possessed differing political systems and should do nothing militarily—which always resulted in great cost in blood and treasure—to upset that reality. His views could not be described simply as an avowal of isolationism; they were rather a rejection of the arguments for military interventionism, whether these were based on moral, internationalist, humanitarian, or legal grounds.

The thought of American blood being shed once more in a conflict far from American shores was anathema to him, but he was never averse to the idea of selling Britain weapons to enable her to prosecute her own defense, in an impulse that spoke somewhat to his instinctive capitalism. He did not ameliorate his views—as did most others—when the facts of German brutality became apparent to the world when Hitler unleashed the dogs of war on Poland on September 1, 1940. Raymond Lee struggled to understand Kennedy's perspective on Britain's lonely struggle against Nazism. He wrote in his diary: "He has been wrong on many points about the war and I don't believe Churchill has had much use for him, preferring to deal directly with Roosevelt, or go through [Lord] Lothian. Kennedy likes the limelight too much to be satisfied with this. Furthermore, he disagrees completely with what he says are Roosevelt's policies which are leading us straight into war." Roosevelt increasingly circumvented his ambassador. The dispatch to Europe in March 1940 of Sumner Welles to explore the possibilities of peace was one such occasion, and that of a string of other visitors to Great Britain, such as Bill Donovan and the writer Edgar Mowrer. The latter had been thrown out of Germany in 1933 following publication of *Germany Puts the Clock Back*, and was now working for Frank Knox's *Chicago Daily News*, whose editorial line was strongly for intervention.

In Kennedy's view, the one man who represented ill-founded, jingoistic, and moralistic adventurism was Churchill. In fact, as he admitted to the privacy of his diary, Kennedy loathed the man. After one meeting with the prime minister, Kennedy wrote, "He kept smiling when he talked of 'neutrality' and 'keeping the war away from U.S.A.' I can't help feeling he's not on the level. He is just an actor and a politician." He felt that Churchill would do anything, such as blowing up the American embassy and blaming it on the Germans, if it would get the United States into the war. "Maybe I do him an injustice, but I just don't trust him." Churchill was open with Kennedy about his hope that one day soon the American people would authorize their president to go to war against Nazi Germany. On June 14, 1940, Churchill told Kennedy that he was confident that he expected the United States to be "in right after election [i.e., that coming November], once the people in the U.S. see the towns and cities of England after what so many U.S. cities and towns have been named, bombed and destroyed, they will rise up and want war." These comments seemed to reinforce Kennedy's determination to prevent, at all costs, the expenditure of scarce American resources (and lives) on what he considered the center of a defunct and rapidly declining empire. All empires came to an end, he believed, and he was merely lucky enough to be an observer at the point at which Britain's was ending. Kennedy reported that the barometer of British morale was being lifted on every positive political message from America, reported in "clippings from the NY Times, Herald Tribune and political speeches." This was giving Britain false hope. Uncle Sam would not be riding across the prairie to the rescue if he could help it.

It was Kennedy's continuing commitment to these views that caused his increasing divergence from Roosevelt, and the growing closeness between Washington and London as the German air attack on Britain intensified during the fall of 1940. Kennedy could not see that nonintervention at all costs, the defining principle in his conception of the United States' relationship with the world, was no longer Washington's view. Nor could he understand the growing closeness between the two countries as America slowly began to understand that Britain's war was also her war. So far as he was concerned, Britain was merely fighting for herself, her empire, and her survival. The war had nothing to do with democratic, liberal, or moral necessities. Roosevelt encouraged him to resign in November. The straw that broke the camel's back seemed to be an interview published in the *Boston Globe* in which Kennedy argued that the only reason for America to support Britain was "to give us time. . . . As long as she is in there, we have time to prepare. It isn't that [Britain is] fighting for democracy. That's the bunk. She's fighting for self-preservation, just as we will if it comes to us."

—✕—

As the war entered its second year, Lee was concerned to observe the deteriorating situation for the British Empire. The idea that Britain might find itself able to win this war in a short time by itself was a fool's notion. Britain was too weak, its forces dispersed. "The forces which Germany can exert are too enormous to be halted at once. They are like a flow of lava, irresistible and overwhelming," he wrote. But he was still confident that in time—years perhaps—German strength would ebb, and British strength would grow. The commonwealth held vast stocks of willing manpower, material, and wealth: it merely needed to be mobilized. He was confident that the British would manage to overcome any immediate attempt to invade their islands. Nevertheless, he was convinced that they could not win the war "without the help of God or Uncle Sam":

> Perhaps it will take both. God has undoubtedly been on the side of the big battalions so far, but may change sides. The equation at present is too unbalanced: 80,000,000 Germans in one lump + the labor of n slaves 4–8 years of intense rearming and organization + frenzied fanaticism > 70,000,000 British in 4 continents + zero slaves + only 3 years of real rearmament and no industrial mobilization + dogged determination.

Even he didn't know what US policy towards fighting Nazism was, or would be, but he was disappointed that the American government tended to respond to events, rather than try to preempt them. "From here our steps [in support] of Britain appear to follow along well behind the development of events," he noted. "The lag is great and may prove too much. It seems already to have had its effects in the slow and discouraged crumbling of France." America needed to be fully, wholeheartedly involved, in his view. "Total war requires throwing everything available at once, military, naval, air, economic, moral—including the kitchen stove, and following this up with everything else as soon as it can be got to working." In July 1941, he wrote his wife a letter, asking a question that could have been asked at the time by every American in London (and many Britons, too): "What is the U.S.A. going to do? It is all very well for us to take a reasonable time to make up our mind but we can't afford to hesitate and dilly-dally forever. . . . I fear that we will still be persuading ourselves that there is some magic way of winning—or that wars are won merely by spending vast sums of money. That is not what is winning for the Germans, who are under no illusions as to what wins wars." It seemed to some that the president was keen to fight the war to the last drop of British blood, certainly the last pound.

Roosevelt's rhetoric was, it was true, unassailable. The day after the German attack on France and the Low Countries on May 10, 1940, Roosevelt warned Americans that geography was no guarantee that America would be protected from the ravages of war. The president's language stirred up paroxysms of rhetorical fury from Germany, which—ironically—accused America of warmongery. Roosevelt's actions, however, were more ambiguous. Roosevelt had to tread a fine line between advocacy for Britain and the retention of the popular vote at home. A positive view of the president's position was that it would have done the British no favors if he had taken a more aggressive stance on supporting them, only to thereby lose the public vote and be replaced by someone more stridently isolationist. In the middle of that month, polls published in the *New York Times* found that whereas 82 percent of Americans had believed in the previous September that the Allies would win, only 55 percent did so. The question now was whether America would be forced to become involved. In June, a further Gallup poll suggested that 65 percent of Americans believed that if both France and Britain fell, Germany would seek to attack the United States, while 75 percent did not believe that America was giving the European democracies enough help. But although most Americans in mid-1940 were fearful of Hitler and instinctively supported Britain, American isolationist and "wait-and-see" imperatives remained strong, with less than 7 percent of voters believing that America should declare war on Germany in defense of democracy. It was this poll result more than anything that explains Roosevelt's hesitancy that year to declare war.

But a full year on, Lee found himself unable to change his view about Roosevelt's unwillingness to declare war, even with the elation in the US embassy in London on hearing the news that Hitler had launched a massive attack into the Soviet Union. Britons remained stoical in the face of adversity, although Lee reported that, "there is a profound realization that Britain alone cannot win, and a desperate anxiety lest America take too long in coming to a decision." On July 2, 1941, he recorded in his diary that FDR would be broadcasting to the nation again that night. It wouldn't go down well in Britain, he concluded, if the speech, yet again, was one "of glittering generalities." The result would be that "people here are going to begin to feel real discouragement and forlornness." They wanted action, not just fine words, from the president who said he upheld the right of free peoples to live as they wanted.

Lee's concern that Roosevelt would *never* go to Congress to advocate for a declaration of war against Germany for fear of the political consequences was confirmed by a meeting with Eugene Meyer, proprietor of the *Washington Post*, in London in mid-August 1941. Meyer's view was that "FDR is turning timid in his leadership of the country and feels very much bound by his sweeping campaign promises to keep the country out of war."

—⁂—

The gloom entertained by some in mid-1940 was not, however, all-pervasive. It remained inconceivable to most Britons that the country should merely await its fate and surrender meekly to the Nazis. One of the reasons for Churchill's popularity in 1940 and 1941 was that he embodied the will of the common people to fight back. They did not share the fears of those natural pessimists for whom any struggle against vast odds constituted pointless effort. The overwhelming feeling of the clear majority in Britain was that they had to resist tyranny at all costs. In London, the fight against pessimism was led very publicly by the prime minister himself. Whatever his private fears, the public face of Britain in the years following 1939 was of bulldog-like resistance, a refusal to accept failure or surrender. "Here is the answer which I will give to President Roosevelt," he told the nation in a BBC radio broadcast on February 9, 1941. "We shall not fail or falter; we shall not weaken or tire. Neither the sudden shock of battle nor the long-drawn trials of vigilance and exertion will wear us down. Give us the tools and we will finish the job." When the incoming American ambassador, John Winant, arrived in March 1941, he agreed. He recalled in his 1947 memoir that he "did not find a war-weary people, but a taut, disciplined, alert nation restless to be at the enemy."

Raymond Lee noted in August 1941 that in his view, Britain had come together remarkably well following the political divisions of the 1930s. The most significant part of this unity was how all classes were fighting together for their country, and how "the rich are quite as prepared to give up everything they have and to lose their lives as anybody else." He sat after supper one night listening to one of Churchill's broadcasts. "For thirty minutes," he recalled, the prime minister "hurled defiance at the world, and with his incomparable oratory bolstered the morale and fostered the fighting spirit of his race. Whatever his faults may be as an administrator, he is a great leader, and so long as he is in the office of Prime Minister the British will fight, and if after the war he remains as Prime Minister, I have no fear of a violent revolution here. The British will follow Winston even though he is the greatest aristocrat of them all." Eric Sevareid agreed. This was a war in which all Britons were participating, rich and poor. "One witnessed terror at times in West End and East, and I do not think class was a working differential in the matter of courage. The poor took the hardships better, true, but the nerves of the upper class were equally sound. Whatever the faults of the British ruling class, they are not a very 'soft' people; the tradition of physical courage, however poor a substitute for intellect, is with them still, and it has its uses in preserving empire as well as in building it."

The problem for Britain in 1941 was that Roosevelt spent the entire year on the fence. In the end, it was the Japanese attack on Pearl Harbor on December 7, and Hitler's subsequent declaration of war on the United States, that made the decision for him. It appeared that he was determined to not go down in history as the man who had initiated American involvement in yet another ruinous war in the teeth of opposition from the American people. As the year progressed, he did more and more to assist Britain, but he refused to commit himself to advocating war itself. And yet he flooded Britain with visits from men, experienced political operators, administrators, servicemen, and writers, who to a man *wanted* America to become a cobelligerent, and who attempted to persuade Britons that America was on their side. To be fair, they also attempted to persuade the president that if he was serious about defending the principle of liberty under the law, he needed to declare war on Nazi Germany without delay. If he didn't, they argued, he couldn't guarantee the survival of Britain, and that would place the United States on the front line of what was clearly now a global war between democracy and totalitarianism. He was never to do so, however. It almost seemed as if the multitude of men whom he sent to London acted as a buffer between anxious Britons and his own determination not to commit to war. Did he send these men across the Atlantic because he knew that they would be supportive of Britain, and therefore earnestly desirous to assist in her survival against the greatest threat in her long island history? It is certainly possible that he thought that they would be the Americans on whom Churchill and the British could rely for their moral sustenance, deflecting increasingly desperate British calls to arms to Roosevelt by means of their own increasingly passionate commitment to Britain's survival.

As part of Britain's commitment to hold nothing back from the United States, and in exchange for aid, in August 1940 Churchill authorized handing over a raft of scientific plans, papers, drawings, and blueprints for a wide range of Britain's most secret technical and scientific innovations. These included the cavity magnetron (a device that allowed for the miniaturization of radar), early jet engine designs, and, most importantly of all, nuclear fission. The Nazis were working to create a fission bomb from uranium, work that Britain was also fast developing. The owners of such a dramatically destructive weapon would be able to force the world to its knees. If Britain were to fall to the Germans, and British research captured or destroyed, that chance was suddenly more likely. Churchill hoped that Roosevelt would recognize that with this weapon, a Nazi victory would almost certainly also lead to the defeat of the United States if Germany managed to overcome the British Isles. In this argument Britain was, in every sense, the front line of America's defense, and that of the free world. It was critical that

Britain not be starved of the wherewithal to continue to fight. But would Roosevelt grasp the nettle?

In Churchill's view, handing over such secrets to her biggest trade competitor was an economic, but not a political, gamble. It would, Churchill believed, vouchsafe Britain's determination to work with the United States against the enemy, and ensure that Britain could never be accused of holding anything back if this argument was ever used to prevent American participation in the war. It was a valid criticism of Britain by many Americans that she had done very little, until 1938, to prepare for war. Why should she be so desperate for help now, after the balloon had gone up, when her own lack of preparation, and her constant appeasement of Nazi Germany during that decade, had led in part to the current catastrophe? Churchill accepted these criticisms, but by handing over the full suite of Britain's secrets, he could now argue that the country was fighting with every ounce of its power, blood, and treasure. Everything Britain had was being thrown lock, stock, and barrel at this struggle for its existence. It would also enable the United States to develop this British-initiated scientific and technological work far from the danger of falling bombs. The hope in London was that in time, the benefits of America's political investment in Great Britain would be considered a sound one, and the basis for an enduring partnership in the defense of liberty.

Britain's secrets were channeled through a man with the code name "Intrepid." Sir William Stephenson first arrived in the United States in June 1940. A senior member of the Secret Intelligence Service, he was to act as the conduit for British intelligence to the United States, to coordinate the purchase of war materials allowed under the Neutrality Acts, and to serve as a secret go-between for Churchill and Roosevelt. He was also responsible for ensuring that the "support-for-Britain" message within the United States was clearly and forcefully articulated. This was no time for half-measures, and if active propaganda in the United States in favor of American intervention was the worst that could be done, so be it. Stephenson flew regularly to the United States in a converted bomber via Iceland and Greenland, and could make the journey between London and New York in twenty-four hours.

In return, and circumventing his ambassador (to Kennedy's fury), Roosevelt—with Churchill's active encouragement—dispatched to Britain a handful of advisers, independent of the embassy, to evaluate the situation and report to him directly on their findings. Britain offered full transparency to these official visitors (although not Ambassador Kennedy, in the months prior to his departure in November 1940). One of the first was Colonel "Wild Bill" Donovan, veteran of 1914–1918 and well-connected lawyer with political aspirations (and friend of Roosevelt's) whom Stephenson knew from the Great War. Donovan arrived in London from Lisbon on a Pan American Clipper flying boat on July 14, and spent two weeks immersed in Britain's war plans. He was given access to everyone of consequence, from King George VI down. He met Lee to compare notes at the end of his visit. Donovan's conclusion was the same as Lee's; he gave odds of 60:40 that the British would beat the Germans, but it would be a hard fight, and the support of the United States would be essential to ultimate victory. Most of the professional US servicemen on duty in Britain at the time believed that the country was doomed. The Wehrmacht was simply invincible. In his memoirs, John Winant recalled a conversation with General "Tooey" Spaatz, who had met with Donovan during his first visit to London in August 1940. "He explained that Colonel Donovan . . . called a meeting of the army air force observers, namely himself, Lt.-Colonel 'Monk' Hunter, Major McDonald and Captain Kelsey, and also a number of resident naval and army observers. The story goes that the naval and army observers, when asked what they thought of the British chance of survival, replied they had not got a hope. Lt.-Colonel Spaatz, on the other hand, said that he and the army air force observers were convinced that the British would pull through because the Germans could not beat the R.A.F. and they would not invade until they had."

On his return home on August 4, 1940, Donovan's report was succinct: "The British would fight on; they would not surrender their fleet; their morale was high, but their equipment was deficient." They urgently needed American industrial ingenuity and capacity if they were to survive. Other visitors agreed. On September 23, the *Times* (London) carried an interview with General Strong following a visit to London, in

August 1940, with General Delos Emmons on behalf of the US Army chief of staff, General George C. Marshall. Strong had said, "Britain is determined to win if it is humanly possible. If she cannot win, she is going down with every man fighting and the flag flying." He believed that Britain would succeed without America's military intervention but with access to her industrial capacity.

Gradual steps were being made to relieve some of Britain's burden, although the pace of American support was considered slow by most Britons at the time. Roosevelt, in May 1940, successfully persuaded Congress to allow the purchase by Britain of American fighter planes, despite the "cash-and-carry" prohibition on the export of warlike material. Ingeniously, the excuse used for this transaction was that the aircraft could receive operational testing in a real-life environment, and that British money would assist in the jump-starting of the American aviation industry. Then, to Churchill's urgent pressing, the day after Dunkirk the president ordered that vast quantities of arms owned by the US government be sold to Britain. Forty-three million dollars' worth of Great War vintage rifles, machine guns, and ammunition (all .3 caliber, and not compatible with the British .303), as well as 895 French-designed, British-built 75 mm artillery pieces, together with a million rounds of ammunition, were taken from deep storage in arsenals across the United States and shipped to Britain. The justification on this occasion was that this material was obsolete and of no use to the US Army. The gesture was appreciated, but no round of this ammunition was ever fired in anger. Then, in September 1940, following months of urgent requests from London and following the return to Washington of Bill Donovan, the United States "sold" Britain fifty old—and frankly decrepit—destroyers in exchange for ninety-nine-year leases on naval bases in the West Indies, Bermuda, and Newfoundland. It was a hard bargain, and caused intense grievance in London. American hard bargaining appeared to be a process of asset-stripping when the market was depressed—Colville's "profiting from exhaustion." Nevertheless, Roosevelt's reelection to a third term as president on November 5, 1940, provided him with the mandate to help Britain through "all means short of war," principally by allowing

America to become, as he described it, the "arsenal of democracy." Roosevelt's electoral success had long been desired by London. When the news came through, Channon noted in his diary, "President Roosevelt has had an even greater triumph than anyone anticipated. A real landslide, and I have yet to see anyone who is not delighted."

Unexpectedly, the presidential election served to unite the Republican and Democratic leadership in their support of active measures to assist Britain. After losing the election on the Republican ticket, Wendell Willkie, against the instincts of many in his party, decided to nail his colors firmly to the interventionist "aid to Britain" mast, one that up to that time had been a Democratic preserve. At a stroke, this united the senior Republican and Democratic leadership in a commitment to doing all things short of war to support beleaguered Britain, making the prospect of winning the debates in Congress that much simpler. Following a three-week visit to Britain in late January 1941, during which he was courted assiduously by Churchill, Willkie was back in Washington by mid-February to testify before Congress in favor of the Lend-Lease Act, the successor to the "cash-and-carry" clause of the previous year, which allowed exports to warring nations so long as the exports were not war materials. The problem for Britain was that it was fast running out of cash. On December 8, 1940, Churchill wrote to Roosevelt saying that the time would soon come when Britain would have no more money to pay for essential war supplies. What followed was the Lend-Lease Bill, which passed through Congress in March 1941, replacing the cash-and-carry policy hitherto in place, and extending to the now poverty-stricken country an almost endless line of credit. In Parliament, Churchill described it as the "most unsordid act in the whole of recorded history," although it was to prove very hard to persuade American manufacturers to meet many of the orders placed by Britain, as US domestic demand was also running high, and factory owners were loath to switch to building war material at unknown cost and uncertain margins. In the course of 1941, industrialist Averill Harriman was sent to London to oversee the practical working out of this act. Berlin saw the implications of this act very clearly, and from that moment on the lives of all free Americans in Germany became

severely constrained. Howard Smith recalled that even before Operation Barbarossa, "Roosevelt had already displaced Churchill as the
Nazis 'World-Enemy Number One'":

> While Chamberlain appeased, and the German-Russian friendship
> agreement was a mere prospect, Roosevelt had sworn opposition
> to Hitlerism, and begun, in his own way, to act upon it. If there
> was one man in the world who directed foreign policy with the
> same consciousness and purposefulness as Hitler, but against
> Hitler, it was the American President; and he did not swerve from
> his course until events he rightly predicted changed it from an
> outlook shared only by a few intelligent liberals in America, to
> a national one.

Willkie's whirlwind visit to Britain continued Roosevelt's strategy
to send an array of advisers to London to concrete the activities necessary, at both political and administrative levels, for both countries to
work together, in secret if necessary. Willkie's visit was followed by
that of Harry Hopkins, who arrived in January 1941 for three weeks
in the role of "roving ambassador." Passionately anti-Nazi, he wanted
to understand what more America—in its current noninterventionist
state—could do to aid Britain. His visit was a spectacular success. On a
return to London from a trip with Churchill to Scapa Flow, the Royal
Navy's port in the Shetland Islands, Churchill hosted a dinner in Hop-
kin's honor in Glasgow. At the table, the prime minister asked him to
speak. Standing up and looking around him, Hopkins said, "I suppose
you wish to know what I am going to say to President Roosevelt on
my return. Well, I'm going to quote you one verse from that Book of
Books in the truth of which [I was] brought up: 'Whither thou goest,
I will go, and where thou lodgest, I will lodge; thy people shall be my
people, and thy God my God.'" Then he added very quietly, "Even to the
end." It was as close a commitment to Britain as he could make without
committing America to war, and, recalled Hastings Ismay, it "moved us
very deeply." Ismay observed of Hopkins that "When the time came for
him to leave our shores, he had got right inside Churchill's mind and

gained his complete confidence; he had won the hearts of us all, from the highest to the lowest; he had seen everything. We felt sure that he would report to his chief that we were worth backing to the limit. Henceforward he was not only Roosevelt's principal adviser, but also a 'precious link' between his chief and Churchill."

If we were to discount the remarkable impact made on American attitudes toward Britain by Ed Murrow and his "boys," by far and away the most significant American in London from March 1941 onwards was Roosevelt's choice as new ambassador, John (Gil) Winant. An old friend of the president and an experienced political operator, organizer, and administrator, Winant had operated at the periphery of the president's circle rather than a member of it. His instructions from Roosevelt were "to keep Winston Churchill and the British Government patient while the American people assessed the issues which faced them." He was to reassure Britain that the United States "believed in their cause, that Nazism and Fascism were incompatible with the American way of life . . . [that] American industry was keying to war production, Lend Lease was pending before Congress, and the transfer of fifty destroyers had already been accomplished. We had made our decision to do everything short of war." It did not take long for Winant to begin to urge Roosevelt to go one step beyond this, however, and join Britain in the war against Germany. A naturally quiet, reticent man, with the traditional stoop of the very tall, Winant was probably the most important person in Anglo-American relations since they had broken down so irrevocably in 1776. If there has ever been such a thing as a special relationship between the countries since the war, it is because of Winant. In 1941 every Briton recognized that the United States, as the potential arsenal of the free world, had a key role in ensuring the survival of democracy and liberty, by supporting Britain's lone fight against fascism. Under Kennedy, Britons had been forced to the conclusion that America was not interested in her survival. Under Winant, the very opposite message was quietly, but consistently and forcefully, conveyed. Winant joined a small but important phalanx of American men and women in Britain who worked assiduously not just to enable Britons to understand America but to encourage Americans to move away from active neutrality into active engagement in support of Britain against Germany. He already knew Europe well, had been in Prague when Germany occupied it in March 1939, and only escaped from Paris days before they arrived on June 14, 1940.

He made an immediate impact on British public opinion. Here was someone fundamentally different from his despised predecessor, someone who was not afraid to state publicly that he represented a president who stood firmly behind Britain in her hour of need. In his first public utterance on British soil, he said simply (for he was no public orator) that there was no place he "would rather be at that time than England." It helped that he arrived at a point in time when Congress overwhelmingly endorsed the Lend-Lease Bill.

Behind the scenes, and despite the Neutrality Acts, a raft of secret relationships was fast developing, enabling detailed cooperation across the widest of areas, from the make of tank treads to radar, ballistics technologies, and advances in combat medicine. America was yet to declare war, but to all intents and purposes she was already fighting it on Britain's behalf. Most Britons, with a sketchy understanding of recent American history and politics, couldn't understand why the United States didn't just declare war, and they listened despairingly to what they considered "fine words" from Roosevelt that were not followed by seemingly concrete actions. But behind the scenes, the full weight of American industrial, scientific, and political might was now unequivocally (if secretly) supporting Britain. Secret staff talks were completed in January 1941, leading to the "Germany First" policy, which committed both countries to defeat Germany first if they ended up having to fight Germany and Japan at the same time. Naval and army missions were established in London to help coordinate the design and construction of equipment ordered by Britain; cement operational relationships between the two navies; and coordinate the movements of each other's vessels in relation to the U-boat threat. The Atlantic Charter was publicly announced in August, articulating America's unequivocal commitment to the defense of democratic liberty. The size of the work being undertaken by the American government in Britain can be understood through Winant's efforts; once he restructured the

embassy to better meet the needs of the new transatlantic relationship, it had four thousand employees supporting twenty-two separate
British government ministries. As a result, he wrote in 1947, "There
was no phase of fighting equipment, tactics or strategy that the British
developed from their war experience that was not known to us before
Japan struck at Pearl Harbor."

Winant's perspective was objective, yet intense. Living through
what he described as Britain's "grim struggle for existence" gave him a
unique perspective on the mentality of this island people: their sense of
history and of destiny; their stoicism; their pig-headedness and refusal
to bow to what might seem the relentless tides of history; their pride
in their achievements and their liberties; their role in stemming the
aggrandizing ambitions of the kaiser in the Great War; the loyalty
of the scattered dominions and colonies "upon which the sun never
set"; the discomfort they were forced to live through (by both Blitz
and U-boat-induced deprivation); and their daily sacrifice, of people
at home and in the field. The Germans had failed, against all expectation, to invade in 1940, but until Operation Barbarossa in June 1941
proved unequivocally to Britons that Hitler was a strategic nincom-
poop, they waited with bated breath for the news that the Wehrmacht
suddenly was in Kent, or Dorset, or the Norfolk Broads. Until then,
he observed, all they could do was launch puny air raids against Germany, husbanding their weak air forces while progressively building
up their fighting strength across the board, replacing what was left
on the beaches of Dunkirk, and successfully protecting their flanks
in the Near East—in Iraq, Syria, and Iran. From his vantage point in
London, John Winant had a powerful grasp of British strategy, and he
played a significant role in allowing that viewpoint to be understood
in Washington. The odds against Britain were formidable:

> In this year of 1941 the Germans had a total of two hundred and
> fifty divisions in the field. They were powerful enough to fight
> the Russians in the East, and they maintained forces in Western
> Europe which the British could not tackle single-handed. This
> limited British strategy to the destruction of the foundations

upon which the German war machine was built—by blockade to strangle its economy; by bombing to destroy its factories and transport, and unsettle its morale; by subversive activities and propaganda to encourage and sustain resistance in occupied countries and to win the support of neutrals; but, meanwhile, to build up slowly but surely the forces and accumulate the stores of material needed for an eventual return to the Continent.

Britain, he concluded, needed time, and this was something that could be gained through the support of the United States. Two weeks after his arrival in London, Winant attended the annual Pilgrims' Dinner as the guest of honor. Churchill invited him to speak. He did so without any of the prime minister's oratory, but with unquestionable sincerity. America, he insisted, was on Britain's side, the side of freedom. He paid tribute to Britain which had "the honor and destiny to man the bridgehead of humanity's hopes" against "ruthless and powerful dictators who would destroy the lessons of two thousand years of history." America, energized and vigilant, stood behind her, and would "provide the tools—the ships, the planes, the guns, the ammunition and the food—for all those here and everywhere who defend with their lives freedom's frontiers."

Although dark years lay ahead, Britain had found her champion, and liberty her voice. America was now fully and utterly committed to a war against the dark forces that had threatened to stamp out the lamp of liberty across the Old World of Europe and, in Edgar Mowrer's words, "put the clock back." Liberty under the law would once again prevail—at least in those parts of Europe unshackled from the fascist yoke—when the war ended in 1945. For other parts, remaining under the Communist jackboot, it would take until 1989, and 1990. It was a war that had to be fought at great cost in life and treasure, one that arguably hadn't needed to be paid if Europe had been alive to the dangers of totalitarianism when it had the chance. Americans at home now realized—as most Americans abroad had already done—that if democratic liberties were worth preserving, they were worth fighting for.

EPILOGUE

Drue Tartière spent Sunday, December 7, 1941, at her rented home and refuge in Barbizon. She had as weekend guests her friends Dr. Robert Lamour and his wife, Annie. Jean Fraysse had gone to pay a visit to his friend, Max Jacob, the writer and painter, at St. Benoit-sur-Loire. After a day spent quietly walking on the plain and relaxing from the week's chores, they turned on the radio to listen to the regular nightly broadcast from London. As the news came over the air that Pearl Harbor had been attacked by the Japanese, they felt the hope and encouragement in the BBC announcer's voice at this new development, which so suddenly brought the United States into this global war. Tartière recalled in *A House Near Paris*:

> "This is the end for the Nazis," Robert Lamour said exuberantly.
>
> I wondered what the people I had known in the United States were thinking and how they were reacting to this, their greatest crisis. America seemed far away, and it was impossible within these prison walls of conquered France to get any conception of the feelings and developments there with respect to the events which had brought crises and war to the whole world.

America's ever-deepening involvement in the war, as a nonbelligerent ally of Great Britain and, by default, a nonbelligerent enemy of Nazi Germany, raced to its inevitable denouement in December 1941. The crisis was initiated by the Japanese attack on Pearl Harbor. What would Germany do? In Berlin, George Keenan could sense only that events were out of everyone's control. He wasn't just referring to the hapless souls manning the shell of the US embassy; he was referring to the entire world as it clashed and crashed towards a Nazi-initiated Armageddon. No one seemed to know how to stop it. Things just went from bad to worse. Did anyone know what was going to happen in Europe? Did the Germans? Was hubris the inevitable consequence of the easy victories of the previous year? Possibly, Keenan thought, as he watched the German units on his map wall crawling towards Moscow, mirroring with striking similarity the advance of Napoleon's army in 1812. For the four days that followed Pearl Harbor, Keenan's group waited quietly for the inevitable. Their country was at war with Germany's ally, and a declaration of war was therefore expected. Surely the Germans would support their Japanese allies? They burned their codes. The embassy telephones were mysteriously cut off. The inevitable came on Friday, December 12, 1941. The telephone mysteriously sprung back to life, summoning Leland Morris, the chargé d'affaires, to Ribbentrop's office in the Foreign Ministry on the Wilhelmstrasse. According to Keenan, the event was a farce—Ribbentrop, striking ferocious attitudes, read out loud the declaration of war and then screamed at him, in German, "Your president has wanted this war; now he has it." That was it. America was at war with Germany, eight years and eleven months after Hitler and his gangsters had stolen power in the heart of Europe.

Since early 1933, the history of Western Europe had been dominated by the ruthless, relentless militarization of an entire nation under the banner of pan-Germanism, and its subsequent racial aggrandizement by a new, united, and purposeful Germany. Nazism had worked hard to ensure that this cult bound the Aryan race together while disposing of those who were opposed to, or posed a threat to, this new political movement, which was determined to divide Europe into slave and free. It was remarkably successful for a time, but in its once-rapid growth could be discerned the seeds of ultimate disaster. The movement was based on German exception-alism, and it was fed and watered by hate. Neither, ultimately, could stand against its enemies. The tragedy was that by the time it died, so too had many, many millions of its victims.

PROGRAM OF THE NATIONAL SOCIALIST GERMAN WORKERS' PARTY, MUNICH, FEBRUARY 24, 1920

THE PROGRAM

1. We demand the union of all Germans to form a Greater Germany on the basis of the right of the self-determination enjoyed by nations.

2. We demand equality of rights for the German People in its dealings with other nations, and abolition of the Peace Treaties of Versailles and St. Germain.

3. We demand land and territory (colonies) for the nourishment of our people and for settling our superfluous population.

4. None but members of the nation may be citizens of the State. None but those of German blood, whatever their creed, may be members of the nation. No Jew, therefore, may be a member of the nation.

5. Anyone who is not a citizen of the State may live in Germany only as a guest and must be regarded as being subject to foreign laws.

6.   The right of voting on the State's government and legislation is to be enjoyed by the citizen of the State alone. We demand therefore that all official appointments, of whatever kind, whether in the Reich, in the country, or in the smaller localities, shall be granted to citizens of the State alone.

    We oppose the corrupting custom of Parliament of filling posts merely with a view to party considerations, and without reference to character or capability.

7.   We demand that the State shall make it its first duty to promote the industry and livelihood of citizens of the State. If it is not possible to nourish the entire population of the State, foreign nationals (non-citizens of the State) must be excluded from the Reich.

8.   All non-German immigration must be prevented. We demand that all non-Germans, who entered Germany subsequent to August 2nd, 1914, shall be required forthwith to depart from the Reich.

9.   All citizens of the State shall be equal as regards rights and duties.

10. It must be the first duty of each citizen of the State to work with his mind or with his body. The activities of the individual may not clash with the interests of the whole, but must proceed within the frame of the community and be for the general good.

We demand therefore:

11. Abolition of incomes unearned by work.

ABOLITION OF THE THRALDOM OF INTEREST

12. In view of the enormous sacrifice of life and property demanded of a nation by every war, personal enrichment due to a war must be regarded as a crime against the nation. We demand therefore ruthless confiscation of all war gains.

13. We demand nationalisation of all businesses which have been up to the present formed into companies (Trusts).

14. We demand that the profits from wholesale trade shall be shared out.

15. We demand extensive development of provision for old age.

16. We demand creation and maintenance of a healthy middle class, immediate communalization of wholesale business premises, and their lease at a cheap rate to small traders, and that extreme consideration shall be shown to all small purveyors to the State, district authorities and smaller localities.

17. We demand land-reform suitable to our national requirements, passing of a law for confiscation without compensation of land for communal purposes; abolition of interest on land loans, and prevention of all speculation in land.

18. We demand ruthless prosecution of those whose activities are injurious to the common interest. Sordid criminals against the nation, usurers, profiteers, etc. must be punished with death, whatever their creed or race.

19. We demand that the Roman Law, which serves the materialistic world order, shall be replaced by a legal system for all Germany.

20. With the aim of opening to every capable and industrious German the possibility of higher education and of thus obtaining advancement, the State must consider a thorough re-construction of our national system of education. The curriculum of all educational establishments must be brought into line with the requirements of practical life. Comprehension of the State idea (State sociology) must be the school objective, beginning with the first dawn of intelligence in the pupil. We demand development of the gifted children of poor parents, whatever their class or occupation, at the expense of the State.

21. The State must see to raising the standard of health in the nation by protecting mothers and infants, prohibiting child labor, increasing bodily efficiency by obligatory gymnastics and sports laid down by law, and by extensive support of clubs engaged in the bodily development of the young.

22. We demand abolition of a paid army and formation of a national army.

23. We demand legal warfare against conscious political lying and its dissemination in the Press. In order to facilitate creation of a German national Press we demand:

> (a) that all editors of newspapers and their assistants, employing the German language, must be members of the nation;
> (b) that special permission from the State shall be necessary before non-German newspapers may appear. These are not necessarily printed in the German language;
> (c) that non-Germans shall be prohibited by law from participating financially in or influencing German newspapers, and that the penalty for contravention of the law shall be suppression of any such newspaper, and immediate deportation of the non-German concerned in it.

It must be forbidden to publish papers which do not conduce to the national welfare. We demand legal prosecution of all tendencies in art and literature of a kind likely to disintegrate our life as a nation, and the suppression of institutions which militate against the requirements above-mentioned.

24. We demand liberty for all religious denominations in the State, so far as they are not a danger to it and do not militate against the moral feelings of the German race.

The Party, as such, stands for positive Christianity, but does not bind itself in the matter of creed to any particular confession. It combats the Jewish-materialist spirit within us and without us, and is convinced that our nation can only achieve permanent health from within on the principle:

THE COMMON INTEREST BEFORE SELF

25. That all the foregoing may be realized we demand the creation of a strong central power of the State. Unquestioned authority of the politically centralized Parliament over the entire Reich

and its organization; and formation of Chambers for classes and occupations for the purpose of carrying out the general laws promulgated by the Reich in the various States of the confederation.

The leaders of the Party swear to go straight forward—if necessary to sacrifice their lives—in securing fulfillment of the foregoing Points.

Source: Kurt G. W. Ludecke, *I Knew Hitler* (New York: Charles Scribners Sons, 1937)

A Guide to Further Reading

Rather than provide the traditional extensive list of my own research into these incredible years (Max Hastings's "peacock display"), I thought it would be helpful to refer readers to material that they could examine for themselves, both in published and unpublished sources, and which I would recommend for reexamination. Books are mentioned at the point at which they are first referenced in the narrative. The list below is not meant to be comprehensive; it is based on accessibility, either in public libraries, research centers, and the internet. Please note that unless otherwise noted, all references in the text are made to books in this list.

CHAPTER ONE: "NAZI GERMANY MEANS WAR"

Matthew Halton's *Ten Years to Alamein* was published in 1944, and his son has written an excellent biography, *Dispatches from the Front: The Life of Matthew Halton, Canada's Voice at War* (McClelland & Stewart, 2014). Leland Stowe's *Nazi Germany Means War* (1933); Dorothy Thompson's *I Saw Hitler* (1932); Wallace Deuel's *Hitler and Nazi Germany* (1941) and *People Under Hitler* (1942); Howard Smith's *Last Train from Berlin* (1943); Lothrop Stoddard's *Into the Darkness: Nazi Germany Today* (1940); and John Raleigh's *Behind the Nazi Front* (1941) are all highly recommended as firsthand accounts by American journalists in Hitler's Germany. The Rev. Stewart Herman's story is in *It's Your Souls We Want* (1943). Janet Flanner's story is in Irving Drutman (ed.) *Janet Flanner's World: Uncollected Writings, 1932–1975* (1981). The book that had Edgar Mowrer thrown out of Germany was his 1938 *Germany Puts the Clock Back*. One of the most important commentators on Nazi Germany was William ("Bill") Shirer. Both his *Berlin Diary: The Journal of a Foreign Correspondent, 1934–1941* (1941) and *The Rise and Fall of the Third Reich* (New York: Secker & Warburg Ltd, 1959) are indispensable. His colleague Louis Lochner wrote *What About Germany?* in 1942. Of the early years (1933–34) Erik Larson's account of the voyage of discovery for US ambassador William Dodd and his family—*In the Garden of Beasts: Love and Terror in Hitler's Berlin* (Transworld, 2011)—is superb. A fascinating story about the American-German "Putzi" Hanfstaengl is Peter Conradi's *Hitler's Piano Player: The Rise and Fall of Ernst Hanfstaengl* (2005). A comprehensive account of American witnesses to Hitler's rise to power is in Andrew Nagorski's *Hitlerland: American Eyewitnesses to the Nazi Rise to Power* (2012), and Henry Gole has told the story of a US military attaché in his 2013 book, *Exposing the Third Reich: Colonel Truman Smith in Hitler's Germany*.

CHAPTER TWO: PARIS IN SPRINGTIME

Julian Jackson's books on this period are an indispensable first point of reference. They include *The Popular Front in France: Defending Democracy 1936–38* (1990); *The Fall of France: The Nazi Invasion of 1940* (2003); and *France: The Dark Years, 1940–1944* (2001). Sylvia Beach wrote of her experiences in *Shakespeare and Company* (1959). Josephine Baker has had several biographers, the most important being her Deuxième Bureau handler, Jacques Abtey. Abtey's discovery of Baker and her work for the French Secret Service and General de Gaulle's Forces françaises libres is contained in Abtey's *La guerre secrète de Joséphine Baker* (1948) and *2d Bureau contre Abwehr* (1966). Unfortunately, these are only available in French. Dr. Sumner Jackson's story is brilliantly covered by, among others, Alex Kershaw in *Avenue of Spies: A True Story of Terror, Espionage, and One American Family's Heroic Resistance in Nazi-Occupied Paris* (Random House, 2015). Dr. Charles Bove wrote his autobiography *A Surgeon in Paris* in 1956. The life of Pauline Crawford has been captured by Charles Robertson in *An American Poet in Paris: Pauline Avery Crawford and the "Herald Tribune"* (2001). William ("Bill") Bullitt's papers were organized and edited by his brother, Orville, in *For the President Personal and Secret: Correspondence Between Franklin D. Roosevelt and William C. Bullitt*, and his biography, *So Close to Greatness: The Biography of William C. Bullitt*, was written by Will Brownell and Richard Billings. Clare Boothe Luce's account of her time in Europe in 1940 is in *Europe in the Spring* in 1940, and Virginia Cowles's account of these times is in *Looking for Trouble* (1941).

Charlie Scheips has beautifully captured the last days in Paris of Elsie Mendl in *Elsie De Wolfe's Paris: Frivolity Before the Storm* (2014).

CHAPTER THREE: THE GATHERING STORM

Al Wedemeyer's autobiography, *Wedemeyer Reports,* was published in 1958. Ed Beattie wrote *Freely to Pass* in 1942 and *Passport to War* the following year. Jimmy Sheean caught the extraordinary feel of the times in his books, including *Not Peace but a Sword* (1939), an account of events in Prague, Madrid, London, Paris, and Berlin during the twelve fateful months following March 1938; and *Between the Thunder and the Sun* (1943), an account of being in England during the Battle of Britain. Raymond Gram Swing's account of his time as a broadcaster in Europe is in *Preview of History* (1943), and his autobiography was published as *Good Evening!* in 1965. George Keenan's *Memoirs: 1925–1950* was published in 1967. Martha Gellhorn can be accessed through *The Face of War: Writings from the Frontline, 1937–1985* (2016); *The Face of War* (1998); and an excellent biography by Caroline Moorehead, *Martha Gellhorn: A Life* (2003).

CHAPTER FOUR: "A LONG, AGONIZING ILLNESS"

Ronald Blythe's *The Age of Illusion: Glimpses of Britain Between the Wars, 1919–1940* (1984) is an indispensable guide for foreigners in time and space attempting to understand Britain between the wars. Amanda Smith has edited Joseph Kennedy's diaries in *Hostage to Fortune: The Letters of Joseph P. Kennedy* (2001). William Russell's superb *Berlin Embassy* was published when he reached Britain in 1941.

CHAPTER FIVE: THE NINETY PERCENT

Virginia Lake's story has been told through her diaries by Judy Barrett Litoff in *An American Heroine in the French Resistance: The Diary and Memoir of Virginia D'Albert-Lake* (2008). Ralph Ingersoll published his *Report on England* in 1942 following his visit in 1941.

CHAPTER SIX: *LE DRÔLE DE GUERRE*

Abbott Liebling's experiences are covered in *The Road Back to Paris* (1944), while Raymond A. Sokolov wrote his biography, *Wayward Reporter: The Life of A. J. Liebling* (1980). The story of Sumner Welles's ill-fated peace mission in 1940 was published in 1944 as *The Time for Decision.* Eric Sevareid's account of his time in France and Britain in 1939–40 is contained in *Not So Wild a Dream* (1946).

CHAPTER SEVEN: THE OFFENSIVE IN THE WEST

The best book on the German invasion of France in 1940 remains that by Alistair Horne, *To Lose a Battle: France, 1940* (1969). The extraordinary story of Johnny Dodge is brilliantly told by Tim Carroll in *The Dodger: The Extraordinary Story of Churchill's Cousin and the Great Escape* (Edinburgh: Mainstream Publishing, 2012). The story of Drue Tartière is told in her *A House Near Paris* (1946). The Tartière Family Papers (1920–1950) are in the United States Holocaust Memorial Museum Archives. Quentin Reynolds published some twenty-five books, including *The Wounded Don't Cry* (1941) and *London Diary* (1962). Robert Murphy's autobiography is entitled *Diplomat Among Warriors* (1964).

CHAPTER EIGHT: ESCAPE FROM PARIS

The amazing story of Etta Shiber and Kitty Bonnefous is told in Etta Shiber's *Paris Underground* (1943). Alan Riding's 2011 publication, *And the Show Went On: Cultural Life in Nazi-occupied Paris*, describes life under the occupation.

CHAPTER NINE: EAGLES AT DAWN

Art Donahue's account of the Battle of Britain is *Tally-Ho! Yankee in a Spitfire*, published in 1941. Space did not allow me to develop this theme in any more detail, but the 1943 account by Colonel James Childers of the Eagle Squadrons, *War Eagles: The Story of the Eagle Squadron*, is well worth reading. Alex Kershaw's 2006 *The Few: The American Knights of the Air Who Risked Everything to Fight in the Battle of Britain* is excellent, and David Johnson has more recently covered the subject well in his 2015 account, *Yanks in the R.A.F: The Story of Maverick Pilots and American Volunteers Who Joined Britain's Fight in WWII*. A rare but early account of American involvement in Britain's war effort is by Anthony Billingham, *America's First Two Years: The Story of American Volunteers in Britain 1939–1941*, published in 1942. A superb account of these early American flyers in the RAF is given by James Goodson in his 1983 account, *Tumult in the Clouds*. Charles Sweeny's autobiography is *Sweeny: The Autobiography of Charles Sweeny* (1990), written with Colonel James Goodson.

CHAPTER TEN: BLITZ

Raymond Lee's diaries were edited by James Leutze and published in 1971 under the title *The London Observer: The Journal of General Raymond E. Lee, 1940–1941*. Henry ("Chips") Channon's diaries were edited by Richard Rhodes James—*Chips: The Diaries of Sir Henry Channon* (1996). Negley Farson's *Bomber's Moon: London in the Blitzkrieg* (1970) is also a good personal account of an American living through the Blitz.

CHAPTERS ELEVEN AND TWELVE: OCCUPATION AND MESDAMES PIMPERNELS

There are several first-class accounts of Paris under the occupation. Charles Glass's *Americans in Paris: Life and Death Under Nazi Occupation 1940–44* (Harper Press, 2010) and Anne Sebba's *Les Parisiennes: How the Women of Paris Lived, Loved and Died in the 1940s* (2017) are excellent. A first-rate account of the Resistance in France more generally is given by Robert Gildea in *Fighters in the Shadows: A New History of the French Resistance* (2015). The English translation of Paul Palliole's memoirs is entitled *Fighting the Nazis: Memoirs of the Only French Officer in on the Secrets of D-Day*.

CHAPTER THIRTEEN: BERLIN

Leonard Kenworthy's accounts of his time in Berlin in 1940 and 1941 are *Autobiography of a Social Studies Teacher and Quaker* (1977) and *An American Quaker Inside Nazi Germany* (1982). His friend the Reverend Stewart W. Herman wrote *It's Your Souls We Want* in 1943 after returning to the United States from internment. I have not had space to explore the resistance movement in Germany and American involvement in this. One of the most significant stories is that of Mildred Harnack, the only American woman executed by the Nazis for spying, as told in Anne Nelson's excellent *Red Orchestra: The Story of the Berlin Underground and the Circle of Friends Who Resisted Hitler* (2009). For the story of Le Chambon-sur-Lignon, see Peter Grose's *A Good Place to Hide: How One French Community Saved Thousands of Lives During World War II* (Pegasus Books, 2015).

CHAPTER FOURTEEN: LONDON

Niall Barr tells the story of British-American military relationships extremely well in *Yanks and Limeys: Alliance Warfare in the Second World War* (2015).

John G. Winant's personal account of his time as US ambassador is brilliantly told in *Letter from Grosvenor Square* (1947), and Lynne Olson has told the extraordinary story of Winant, Harriman, Hopkins, and the Murrow Boys in *Citizens of London: The Americans Who Stood with Britain in Its Darkest, Finest Hour* (2010), which built on her early book with Stanley Cloud, *The Murrow Boys: Pioneers on the Front Lines of Broadcast Journalism* (1997). The work of the British Secret Intelligence Service in the United States is well told in Jennet Conant's *The Irregulars: Roald Dahl and the British Spy Ring in Wartime Washington* (2009), as is the story of Sir William Stephenson in *A Man Called Intrepid: The Secret War*, by William Stevenson (1976).

Index